An Introduction to Applied Sociology

by
PAUL F. LAZARSFELD
and JEFFREY G. REITZ
with the collaboration of Ann K. Pasanella

ELSEVIER
New York / Oxford / Amsterdam

ELSEVIER SCIENTIFIC PUBLISHING COMPANY, INC.
52 Vanderbilt Avenue, New York, N.Y. 10017

ELSEVIER SCIENTIFIC PUBLISHING COMPANY
335 Jan Van Galenstraat, P.O. Box 211
Amsterdam, The Netherlands

Library of Congress Cataloging in Publication Data

Lazarsfeld, Paul Felix
An introduction to applied sociology.

Includes index.
1. Sociological research—United States—Case studies. 2. Policy sciences—Case studies. 3. Social science research—United States—Case studies. I. Retiz, Jeffrey G., joint author. II. Pasanella, Ann K. III. Title.
HM48.L34 300 75-8274
ISBN 0-444-99006-2

Manufactured in the United States of America

Designed by Loretta Li

Contents

Acknowledgements

This publication was started with an initial grant from the Russell Sage Foundation. Its continuation over several years was made possible by a generous grant from the Office of Naval Research. The project officer, Dr. Bert King, gave patient and wise counsel without interfering with the evolving direction of our work. The whole text reflects the spirit of Columbia University's Bureau of Applied Social Research and the Applied Sociology Program of the University of Pittsburgh.

ONE

Historical Background

What is the relation between sociology and the world of practical affairs? This book is intended to contribute to an understanding of this topic.

THREE HISTORICAL PHASES

When sociology first came to the United States it was akin to a crusade for social improvement. The story has been repeatedly and ably told, especially by Luther and Jessie Bernard[1] and by Anthony Oberschall.[2] It usually starts with the creation of the American Social Science Association in 1865. Its purpose as told by Oberschall,[2] was

> to aid the development of Social Science, and to guide the public mind to the best practical means of promoting the Amendment of Laws, the Advancement of Education, the Prevention and Repression of Crime, the Reformation of Criminals, and the Progress of Public Morality, the adoption of sanitary regulations, and the diffusion of sound principles on the Questions of Economy, Trade, and Finance. It will give attention to Pauperism and the topics related thereto . . . (it will aim to obtain) by discussion the real elements of Truth; by which doubts are removed, conflicting opinions harmonized, and a common ground afforded for treating wisely the great social problems of the day.

So expansive a program could not easily be maintained. Soon subdivisions were formed, which gave rise to separate organizations such as the Economic Association and the Sociological Society. Early college sociology courses were likely to be taught by Protestant ministers interested in various reform movements. And even when the first graduate department in sociology was created at Columbia University, in 1894, the catalogue carried the following statement:

> It is becoming more and more apparent that industrial and social progress is bringing the modern community face to face with social questions of the greatest magnitude, the solution of which will demand the best scientific study and the most honest practical endeavor. . . . It is in the city that the problems of poverty, of meandering, of intemperance, of unsanitary surroundings, and

of debasing social influences are met in their most acute form. Hence, the city is the natural laboratory of social science.

Such an announcement is tantamount to an advertisement, and a cynical interpreter could find it amusing that intemperance and other, unmentionable practices were used to entice students to New York City.

The most visible result of this alliance between social reform and early sociology was the so-called social-survey movement. It has been described in great detail by Pauline Young,[3] whose competent review is still very much worth reading. She describes some of the major surveys in considerable detail, and one can see how the range of topics became more and more subtle. In the beginning, the emphasis was on wages and housing conditions. Soon, social relations in the family were added, subsequently supplemented by descriptive material on attitudes. In 1912, the Russell Sage Foundation created a department of surveys and information. By 1928, the director of this department, Shelby Harrison, was able to review more than two thousand social surveys—some national in scope, others local.[4]

By the end of World War I, a sizable number of sociologists were operating. Some had come out of the social-survey movement, others had acquired systematic training abroad or in the early graduate departments in the United States. Not surprisingly, these new sociologists wanted to win prestige and academic recognition for their work. This effort was characteristic of what we call the second phase.

For an Autonomous Sociology

This phase is much less well documented than the first one. Its beginning is best represented by the creation of the Social Science Research Council in 1923. Characteristically, its main activities were concentrated in a committee on methods. The purpose of that committee was to carve out the specific characteristics of the social sciences and the ways in which the various academic disciplines that founded the Council could be distinguished from and related to one another. To capture the flavor of this period, one should study the first major publication of the Council, published in 1931: Stuart Rices's *Methods in Social Science.*[5] In the introduction, Rice tells of the involved history of the book. In the end, the following formula was adopted: Major studies were to be discussed by competent analysts. Robert Park wrote on W. G. Sumner and W. I. Thomas; Floyd Allport discussed cultural change "illustrated" in studies by F. S. Chapin and A. L. Kroeber; Merle Curti discussed the methodological concepts of Frederick Jackson Turner; Lasswell described a specific case in which Malinowski tested a hypothesis in one tribe, and so on. Moreover, some of the authors discussed added to accounts of their work. Read today, the book has the flavor of *Who's Who* entries written by somewhat younger men about their slightly older colleagues. All 52 contributions emphasize the methods used by social scientists; as a matter of fact, the majority of the papers have the term "method" in their titles. The division into nine sections shows the same focus on methodology: temporal sequences with and without attempts at causal analysis; relations between measured and unmeasured factors; definition of objects; and establishment of scales, etc.

Stuart Rice was a major figure in the second period. In 1928, he had submitted a dissertation at Columbia on quantitative methods in politics; this paper virtually initiated the so-called behavioral movement in politics. During the New Deal he joined the Bureau of the Budget and became a kind of general adviser on the expanding research activities of the Federal government. He also wrote the introduction to Pauline Young's review of social surveys, which he obviously viewed as a special extension of his own SSRC publication. But the field had expanded so rapidly that the broad coverage of this first effort was insufficient. It seemed necessary to pursue some of the material in more depth.

In 1932, the SSRC asked the various component organizations to propose one major work each for special analysis. The Sociological Society nominated Thomas and Znaniecki's *The Polish Peasant,* and its review by Herbert Blumer set off a whole new wave of methodological concerns. His essay was followed by the transcript of an extensive discussion by well-known sociologists.[6] The main question was whether the diaries and letters on which *The Polish Peasant* was based adequately supported the main conclusions of the study. The qualitative-quantitative issue moved into the foreground of the efforts to establish sociology as a reputable science. Two further SSRC bulletins, delayed because of the war, were devoted to the value of using "Personal Documents"—a term designed to cover all qualitative material, including detailed open-ended interviews. Robert Angell's measured discussion of the sociological use of such sources can still be read with profit today.[7]

Concurrent with this somewhat defensive discussion of qualitative procedures, a new type of quantitative study began to proliferate. Many of the quantitative techniques had come from England. Thus, sampling procedures had been first used in England before World War I, when Booth's social survey was repeated in London and other cities. These procedures became widely known, and they were used in the United States in connection with market research. Large corporations marketing food or cars or household appliances wanted to know where they stood with consumers relative to their competitors, and the mass media, especially radio, wanted to demonstrate the size of their audiences to potential advertisers. Both corporations and media turned to consumer surveys. Questions on voter preferences and opinions on public issues were occasionally appended to these surveys and soon acquired a life of their own in terms of public opinion research. Parallel to sampling, techniques of "measurement" were refined wherever respondents had to be classified. Educators became increasingly immersed in tests and their theory. The introduction of tests by the Army during World War I stimulated new interest in general problems of classification. In the mid-thirties, the journal *Psychometrica* and Gallup's Institute of Public Opinion Research made their appearance almost simultaneously. The Social Science Research Council, in an extensive monograph by the psychologist Paul Horst[8] but supervised by the sociologist Samuel Stouffer, focused methodological interest on the problem of prediction.

While these developments had obvious practical implications, their technical sophistication enhanced the academic respectability of the social scientists and made it easier for them to separate their professional domain from those of the reformers.

Dividing any flow of events into phases can only be done with considerable hesitation. We are inclined to place this period of self-assertion in the period between the two world wars. The history of that period has not yet been written—no monograph exists comparable to the chapters of Pauline Young mentioned above. As a matter of fact, quite a number of elements are still not clear.

For example, it is not obvious why today some authors claim that in that period social science was able to emulate natural science, perhaps because the English word "science" has a restricted connotation; the Germans and the French talk about *Wissenschaft* and *science* in a broader sense. Without surrounding "scientific" with either a laudatory or a derogatory meaning, one might agree that the methods of the social and the natural sciences show differences as well as similarities. Actually, as far as we can tell, the term was rarely used at the time, except perhaps in the rather hilarious debates between Lundberg and Znaniecki, which, incidentally, also have not yet found their proper historical account.

We have no adequate record of the role sociologists played during the Depression. No major figure seems to have been included in Roosevelt's Brain Trust, a body composed mainly of economists and political scientists. But sociologists did play a role in the research activities of the various relief organizations, and a number of studies on the effects of the

Depression on the family and other aspects of social life were carried out. A detailed annotated bibliography of this material (112 items) was published at the time by the senior author and an assistant.[9] But its relation to the methodological trends of the period still remains unanalyzed. Most of these studies had a microsociological character, and this finally raises the question of what had happened during this phase to the broad historical sweep which characterized the origins of sociology. Only in regard to one author is some good documentation available.

W. F. Ogburn was originally connected with reform movements; after a while, however, he became perhaps the most prominent spokesman for the scientific emphasis in social research. He combined these two interests by concentrating on the study of social trends. In certain areas, empirical data extending over quite a long period were available: election returns, information on scientific developments, legislative acts, etc. Ogburn made the quantitative interrelations between these diverse social indicators the main theme of his work. This led to an episode which foreshadowed the transition to the period when the newly autonomous social science and the earlier concern with contemporary problems reconverged. This event, which occurred in the interval between the wars, has recently been analyzed in considerable detail by the historian Barry D. Karl.[10]

The starting point is a 1,500-page book which stands unread on the library shelves because it is regarded as a collection of outdated statistics —*Recent Social Trends* published in 1933. There is drama behind this publication. During his 1928 Presidential campaign, Herbert Hoover, who was both a trained engineer and an experienced administrator, advocated the use of social science data in conjunction with the problems of unemployment and old age, his platform issues. Once elected, he appointed a commission on social trends. The commission's executive director was William Ogburn. Disagreements soon developed between the President and the commission. In particular, Ogburn wanted to release only those reports whose every statement was based on solid data; but Hoover, faced with the Depression, was eager to procure any bit of information which would be helpful in legislative social planning.

Karl documents in detail the efforts of Hoover's staff assistant to reconcile the views of the President, the various members of the commission, and the several foundations that financed the enterprise. Ogburn was successful in his determination to delay a report, although some of the commissioners were, in varying degrees, interested in the possible utilization of the social sciences in social problems as Hoover visualized them. In

1932, when Hoover ran against Roosevelt, he still did not have the social data he wanted. The report was transmitted to him in January, 1933, after his electoral defeat but while he was still President. The authors in their introduction stated that "the clarification of given values . . . in terms of today's human life . . . is a major task of social thinking." As the historian puts it, "firm in their faith, they entered oblivion."

Actually, a resurrection of the report is desirable and can almost be predicted. After all, *Recent Social Trends* is practically the cradle of the modern social indicators movement as well as an outstanding example of another issue which commands increasing attention today: the relation between historiography and sociological data in the broadest sense—from cultural documents to demographic calculations. At the point where we shall discuss the training of "applied sociologists," let us remember that a paperback reissue of the report, together with Karl's historical account, would constitute a highly pertinent "case."

When World War II broke out, in 1939, it became increasingly clear that somehow the United States would become involved. By then, social research activities had become so ubiquitous that the government turned to social researchers almost as a matter of course. In one federal office, the Department of Agriculture, sociologists had played a major role for quite a while, particularly with respect to the land-grant colleges, whose specific task it was to improve the life and work of farmers.[11] But once the United States entered the war, new moves followed, at first slowly and then with almost explosive rapidity. In 1939, Roosevelt began cautious support of the Allied side through Lend-Lease and similar policies. The country was in no way united behind this effort, and apparently the President watched public opinion polls rather carefully. Hadley Cantril had left Princeton University to head a special opinion research agency, originally financed by Nelson Rockefeller. Before his death, Cantril published a book in which he tells of several instances of how he provided the Executive Office with information on public opinion here and abroad.[12] At the same time, the United States Army was greatly enlarged and took the unprecedented step of creating a division of research and information.

After Pearl Harbor, all government agencies inaugurated large-scale social research activities. The Office of War Information concerned itself with civilian morale; the armed services worried about training soldiers; the overseas operations of the Office of Strategic Services tried to anticipate enemy moves. These were among the many agencies that called upon the social sciences.[13] They used all the available techniques: content analysis, sampling surveys, detailed interviews, laboratory experiments, group dynamics, etc.*

When the war was over, it was clearly impossible to revert to the separation of sociology as an academic pursuit from the problems of governmental and private organizations. The convergence had become a fact, though a troublesome one. Neither the undisputed unity of the first phase nor the enthusiasm of the second could be recaptured. What we call the third phase is characterized by an ever-increasing flow of discussions of the utilization problem. We plan to describe the main issues as they evolved and to locate our book within the network of the various positions which have been taken.

Aspects of the Third Phase

Before World War II, one man, Kurt Lewin, had already called for a more systematic relation between academic research and the world of action. He coined the term "action research." It led to an important development, but it requires some clarification. Lewin was a prominent member of the Berlin group of Gestalt psychologists, but he had always held a more specialized interest of his own. In Germany, the notion of human action *(Handlung)* had been central to all of the social sciences. Lewin wanted psychology to make its special contribution by conducting experiments in realistic situations. Under the over-all title "Contributions to the Psychology of Action," he developed a series of now-famous concepts: level of aspiration, the dynamic pressure exercised by unfinished tasks, goal displacement, etc. In 1933, Lewin had to leave Germany; he finally settled in the United States. In a manner which is still controversial, Lewin merged his ideas with the work of Moreno, who had developed sociometric techniques for the study of small groups. What Lewin did was to add the role of small groups as an influence in the *Handlungen* of their members. The word "action" was still unpopular then with American behaviorist psychologists. Using the mathematical imagery which he had always favored, Lewin gave his work the title *Group Dynamics.* The details are well described in *The Practical Theorist,* a biography by one of Lewin's students, Alfred Marrow.[14]

---

*To the best of our knowledge, the full range of wartime social research has not yet been recorded. The monitoring of German radio broadcasts was substantiated by the fact that after the war, the judgments of the monitors could be compared with the records of the German Propaganda Ministry captured in Berlin. Alexander George, *Propaganda Analysis: A Study of Inferences Made from Nazi Propaganda in World War II* (Evanston, Ill.: Row, Peterson, 1959).

Marrow's family owned a factory which was plagued by morale problems. Persuaded that Lewin's psychological ideas might be of help, management allowed him to conduct experiments on individual attitude changes in small groups of workers.[15] He was successful, and other organizations asked for his help. At one point, Lewin decided to name the whole procedure "action research." The term was a felicitous combination of Lewin's basic interest in human action and his desire to apply his theories to a remediation of the work situation. It is, however, important to remember that during his lifetime (he died in 1947), Lewin gave the term "action research" a very specific meaning: the study of individual attitudes and decisions made under the influence of small groups, which in turn could be organizationally manipulated. Only later, and through a misunderstanding, was the term used by some authors in the broader sense of the use of social research in the pursuit of practical goals.[16] Lewin's best-known work in changing attitudes is probably his effort to revamp American eating habits during World War II. He found, for example, that group decisions were far superior to lectures or individual treatments in inducing housewives to switch to different cuts of meat.[17]

The official recognition of what was by then called applied sociology may be dated from a conference called in 1948 by the Social Science Research Council. We asked the Council what records on this conference were available in its file, and the archivist was kind enough to reply:

> The small conference to which you refer was held in the Council office on March 20, 1948, and the subject, according to our records was "The Expert and Applied Social Science" . . . Pendelton Herring served as its chairman. In a very brief report made at the meeting of the Council's Board of Directors in April, 1948, he noted that the conference was concerned with the possibility of clarifying the relations between the experts and those who use his knowledge in government and business. *Robert Merton, because of his interest in research on this problem, had been asked to prepare the agenda for the conference.* He had written and distributed to the participants a memorandum as well as a longer outline (dated November, 1947) of *a study he was then proposing to undertake.* Mr. Herring reported that the conference was much interested in the research aspects of the subject, and that there might be opportunity for aiding in the development of a project. However, *nothing further appears in our records.* [Emphasis ours.]

Actually, as a participant, the senior author remembers clearly that a review of the collective war experience was one of the reasons for the convocation.

The Social Science Research Council did not follow up Merton's research program; however, we shall come back to it presently. Most likely, this was a situation that was ahead of its time. For beginning about 1950, *three parallel trails can be traced.* The first leads through a rather bizarre landscape: the efforts of sociologists to invent new terms to match the new demands of the third phase. At the same time, the social scientists were scrutinizing their own operations vis-à-vis the natural sciences. (We shall look at *study groups* appointed on this topic and collections of examples in readers to describe applications in greater detail.) Slowly a series of signposts evolved along a third trail, directed toward a really productive analysis of the utilization process. The search for a new synthesis, which characterizes what we call the third phase, consists of the intertwining of these three parts.

It should be helpful to the reader if we were to insert at this point a schema which summarizes the remarks made so far and the material to be presented now.

Phase 1. The need for social improvement and the work of the sociologist are not distinguished.

Phase 2. Effort to establish sociology as a field of knowledge and understanding independent of any concrete social goal.

Phase 3. Current search for a new synthesis between practical work and sociological knowledge, now proceeding along three lines.

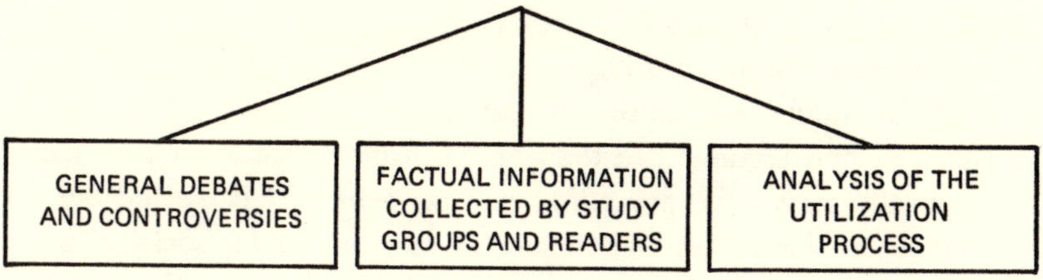

The purpose of the present book is of course to make a contribution along the third line of phase 3; our plan cannot be stated in a programmatic paragraph but will evolve in the sequence of our chapter. We hope, however, that looking at it in a comparative context will help to clarify our intention and to explain its tentative nature.

CONTROVERSIES OVER ROLE AND STATUS: TRAIL 1

Some of the participants of the 1948 SSRC conference chose to discuss whether "applied social research" was a worthy pursuit. Thus started a continuing debate about possible role conflicts and tensions.* One of the positions is clear, although in our opinion without justification. The argument goes that applied research is radically different from basic scientific work and therefore detracts talent and resources from true progress in the discipline. This implies a false comparison with the natural sciences. It is true that technical engineers could not succeed without the knowledge provided by abstract research in mathematics and the laboratory experiments of the "pure" sciences. But it is misleading to draw an analogy between the natural and social sciences. Nowhere in the social realm are there unconditional laws and basic theories already well established. Quite to the contrary, it is the study of concrete and circumscribed practical problem-areas that has contributed a good part of the present-day general sociological knowledge. Adapting a famous dictum by Lewin, one could say that nothing is more conducive to innovation in social theory than collaboration on a complex practical problem. Many examples come to mind. The notion of informal versus formal organization grew out of the Hawthorne studies, which were undertaken to improve the productivity of work groups. Surprising findings in the study of American soldiers led to the notion of relative deprivation and subsequently to a rich growth of work on reference groups. The present knowledge on attitude change is due in large measure to research on propaganda and advertising. The much-used distinction between a "cosmopolitan" and a "local" orientation evolved in a study of magazine readers.

In fact, these problem-oriented studies of concrete situations correspond to laboratory work in the natural sciences. However, this does not answer a second argument in the debate, namely that applied research automatically serves the prevailing system, even if it is carried out for foundations or for government agencies responsible for social change. This position, probably first articulated by C. Wright Mills, then, understandably so, became a tenet of the radical sociologists. Many young peo-

---

*We shall hereafter use the term "applied" without quotation marks and return to the question of terminology at the end of this chapter.

ple come to sociology feeling that contemporary society needs improvement or radical restructuring. Even at the professional level, academic sociologists are apt to lean toward the "left" both in comparison with their colleagues in other departments as well as with the American public at large. Despite the liberal attitudes of the sociologists, most social science research is funded and used by those existing institutions that can afford the rather large expenses involved. One of our colleagues, Paul Nyden, has written an analytical review of those opportunities for utilization that are lost because of lack of financial support; watchfulness of this issue is certainly needed.

Unfortunately, many of the discussions of the appropriate place for applied social research do not pose such clear-cut questions and are therefore either confusing or downright misleading. We shall exemplify this by three papers written about ten years apart, all of which introduce the notion of "social engineering" as a derogatory term.*

The three papers contain a large number of interesting ideas not reported in the following review. We use only small excerpts from them where the authors treat the same term in very different ways, in order to knock over a strawman who in our opinion does not really exist.

In the first paper, Hauser opposes the social engineer to the social scientist. We are offered a strange portrait of this engineer as one who makes "flat unconditional predictions of any course of events." He does so despite the fact that such events are "contingent upon conditions which he knows he cannot control either in a scientific or in an administrative event."[18] Somehow this certainty has to do with "values" which do not enter the work of the true social scientist. Things become somewhat ambiguous here. On the one hand the "specific values which may dominate the research are more apt to be those of the policy-maker or action agency for whom the research is being conducted." Here "value" is tantamount to "purpose," and the statement is of course correct. If the researcher does not like the agency he should not work for it; if he does, he implies that he is willing to help them. But in other places "values" seem to mean intellectual risks—making uncertain assumptions, guessing on probable future trends, which we just learned the social engineer is *not* aware of. The gap between knowledge and action must indeed be filled by a broad range of analyses in their own right. (Our Chapter 5 is an introduction

*The term was used as early as 1948 in a speech given by Lazarsfeld at the inauguration of an applied social research institute in Oslo, Norway. The term was employed to convey the reform role of the sociologist, just the opposite of the meaning the phrase took on later.

to this difficult task.) Hauser seems to be aware of this, because he complains that "social engineering tasks are today in the main performed by amateurs." But how does this lead him to state apodictically (p. 217): ". . . It would be well to recognize that the formation of social policy and social science action are not *scientific functions* and as a consequence should not be regarded as research functions" (emphasis ours). Our own text takes quite the opposite position.

Hauser's description of the social engineer sounds factual—but is, in our opinion, not true. Yet the concept has had a long life. More than twenty years later, Janowitz juxtaposed an "engineering model" to an "enlightenment model."[19] His picture of the social engineer is one who is

> . . . concerned with the research application of *existing* theoretical knowledge. [p. 3a].
>
> . . . holds the view that sociological knowledge produces definite answers on which policy and professional practice can be based [p. 4a].
>
> . . . makes a sharp distinction between basic research and applied research [p. 3a]

Again, the social engineer is one who fails to see the gap between knowledge and action. But no longer is the "social scientist" considered his more desirable counterpart. By 1971, Janowitz had lived through all the changes which occurred since World War II. He does not deny that "highly systematic work comes from men of the engineering orientation" (he refers to the work of Lazarsfeld). But that systematic work simply is not sufficient. There is another, preferable orientation: the enlightenment model. The sociologist who follows this beacon

> . . . is engaged in developing models or broad-scale studies of the most complex social system. The end results of such undertakings are bodies of data and new models, which may help society to clarify or even alter its social and political goals and objectives [p. 5a].

Here, then, the counterimage to the social engineer is not the "true" scientist, but the enlightener with his breadth of view and his high level of aspiration.

We admire his enlightenment model. As a matter of fact, we stand in awe of its difficulty and would be eager to have a concrete example. But again, we disagree with his characterization of a rigid, self-confident social engineer who thinks he has all the answers.

Let us not lose our theme that confusion characterizes this whole debate. Janowitz concludes his paper with the following remark.

The impact of sociology is basically indirect, but potentially pervasive. The impact is not to be measured and judged in terms of specific assignments and specific recommendations, but in the broader intellectual climate it seems to engender [p. 8a].

This might very well be true if we were concerned with broad cultural trends. But the title of Janowitz' essay as well as his initial statement—that he is concerned with "the links between sociological knowledge and social action"—has certainly become as vague as Hauser's discussion of "values," if read as a contribution to the understanding of the utilization process.

In between the two papers discussed so far, Gouldner's "Explorations in Applied Social Science"[20] had appeared. He was committed to a rather concrete approach to the problem of utilization, Hauser had been a student and assistant of Ogborn, one of the main exponents of the esoterically scientific second-phase described above. Janowitz had done work on underdeveloped countries and thus represented a broad macrosociological perspective. But Gouldner was an early member of the founding group of the Society for the Study of Social Problems which wanted to bridge the gap between sociological theory and social problems. So his paper begins with a sentence affirming his belief in intervention: "Not so long ago the words social engineer were a term of opprobrium." He attributes this negative attitude to the fact that academic sociology is basically conservative and recoils from the idea of change implied in the notion of applied sociology. (As a matter of fact, Gouldner later became the co-editor of *Applied Sociology*, a reader sponsored by the Society for the Study of Social Problems, which reprinted the paper from which we quote).

But despite the clear beginning, things quickly became more complicated.

According to Gouldner, there are two kinds of applied work, each of which follows its own model. One is clinical: here the sociologist tries to penetrate the motivation of his client, shows the client what his true interests are, and warns him of unanticipated consequences. These activities are characteristic of competent applied sociology, the kind of work we shall analyze in subsequent chapters of our text. But Gouldner tells us that there is also the incompetent applied sociologist, who is described as follows: "He has conceived and completed his assignment largely in terms formulated by his client."

He defines himself as the bearer of facts and figures. Why is this sociologist inept? Because he follows an "engineering model." So Gouldner's paper, which starts with the plan of giving the term "social engineer" some respectability, ends by using the same concept as a symbol of the poor performer. Yet, in principle, Gouldner approved of specific advice, while Janowitz prefers the social enlightener. If verbal contradictions occur within a single essay, there is obviously something wrong with the whole issue. In debates between various groups, any umpire would have to give up. Gouldner alludes to the staff of the Rand Corporation as typical social engineers, because they take on the language of their main sponsor, the United States Air Force: they use terms such as intelligence, mobilizing resources, etc. But we know (and shall elaborate presently) that Rand prides itself on all the virtues of the "clinical model": clarifying the client's goals and using complex analytical procedures.

Why the endless discussions as to the merits of applied social research and the role of the sociologist engaged in it? Perhaps when criteria for excellence are not clear, a term evolves which reflects the absence of high quality. Thus, there is no special word for an incompetent mathematician because there is no ambiguity about what constitutes a top-flight mathematician. But a person who does not live up to the day's standard of "culture" is a philistine—a term which has it equivalent in the German *banause* or the French *epicier*. Once such a term has acquired currency, it can be used to describe anyone whose activities in an unchartered field earn disapproval. It is characteristic that none of the three papers we have discussed emphasizes concrete studies in which social engineers have mismanaged problems.

We shall not pursue this review of the literature any further since we hope that we have made our main point: such general discussion does not clarify what utilization of social research means; in fact, it leads to stereotyping and to controversies which ultimately block such a clarification. We return to our historical review, taking up the second trail envisioned above: the push for self-scrutiny as typified by the emergence of public study groups on the social role of the social sciences and the appearance of the first collections of specific examples of applied social research.

THE STUDY GROUPS: TRAIL 2

The fifties saw the establishment of a National Science Foundation. Its purpose was twofold: to provide public funds for academic research and to link the research with the technical problems of American society, particularly national defense. The role of the social sciences in this new agency was not clear. At first, they were excluded, then tolerated, and finally officially accepted as a special division. At the top levels of government, particularly in the President's Science Advisory Committee, a similar controversy erupted. Finally, Jerome Wiesner, the President's special assistant for science and technology, appointed a sub-panel of his Life Sciences Panel, which issued a report on "Strengthening the Behavioral Sciences" (herein referred to as the Wiesner Report[21]) The aim of the report is clearly to convince the powerful natural scientists to accept the social sciences as a full-fledged partner. The first ten pages portray the development and present state of the behavioral sciences by selecting illustrative cases as close as possible to the tradition of the "hard" sciences: mathematical models in sociology, and the alliance of psychology and physiology are stressed. Having thus made the social sciences respectable, the recommendations advise public financial support along the lines of training, support of basic research, large-scale data collection, and the use of social sciences by "agencies with action-missions." Here also for the first time the idea appears that pilot experiments might be carried out *before* the enactment of social legislation (pp. 363 to 369).

The report was issued in 1962, and certainly made the National Science Foundation and the regular government agencies more receptive to the idea of funding social science projects. This in turn led to the expansion of empirical social research in universities and the organization of extramural research agencies eligible for public funding. A network of educational research and development centers and educational laboratories came into being. The emphasis on application mushroomed because the expenditure of public funds had to be justified by some demonstrable social utility. Also, the increasing complexity of contemporary social life undoubtedly made for a growing hope that the social sciences could help. The "War on Poverty" played a special role at that time.

But all of these developments were haphazard, and the need for some coordination—at least in terms of systematic review—grew urgent. Finally, in the mid-sixties, three study groups were formed. They rendered their reports almost simultaneously around 1968. The groups went in three distinct directions. One was appointed by the National Academy of Sciences and dealt specifically with the relation between the behavioral sciences and the federal government. (In honor of its executive secretary we shall refer to its findings as the Lyons Report.) The other was sponsored by the National Science Foundation and produced a book under the title *Knowledge into Action* which dealt mainly with utilization by nongovernmental institutions. (The report was written by its chairman, Orville Brim Jr. who was then president of the Russell Sage Foundation.)[22] The third report was sponsored jointly by both the National Academy of

Science and the Social Science Research Council. A very comprehensive review of "The Behavioral and Social Sciences" (usually referred to as the BASS Report), it was the collective effort of many social scientists.[23] The first two reports judged the situation from the point of the users: government and society at large. The BASS Report reversed the perspective: its main theme revolved around the implications of the utilization problem for the structure of the social sciences within and outside the university.

Let us look at some of the details of the three publications. The Lyons Report developed a detailed program for staffing government agencies at all levels with social scientists, thus carrying forward one of the mandates of the Wiesner Report regarding the desirability of mission-oriented social research. It starts with a review of the economist's role in government and asks that this policy be extended to "other fields of the behavioral sciences, especially sociology, social psychology, political science and anthropology." The future of these disciplines is predicted as being increasingly dependent on the policies of the National Science Foundation and the executive departments of the U.S. Government. The first three recommendations of the Lyons Report deserve to be quoted verbatim so that their implementation may be watched as time goes on:

1. That each major department and agency initiate a staffing study to *identify positions* for which substantial training and experience in the behavioral sciences should be an increasingly important criterion for appointment.
2. That each major department and agency initiate a series of continuing programs to *strengthen its staff competence* in the behavioral sciences.
3. That each major department and agency, with the assistance of an advisory panel of behavioral scientists, develop a *strategy for the use and support of the behavioral sciences* and maintain under continued review a long-range research program.

We have omitted the specifications related to these three points. They develop what the Wiesner Report calls mission-oriented research, and the third actually anticipates social experiments. It also stresses the keeping of historical and operating records. (We shall come back to this point when we discuss the need for case studies.) If, following point 1, more governmental jobs were to become available, university departments would have to decide what training their candidates need. If such training programs were developed, they would require internships which were recommended under Point 2.

Three further recommendations (4, 5, and 6) deal with international problems, clearly formulated under the influence of the Kennedy years. Three others are concerned with the need for social science advisers at top governmental levels. A final recommendation (10) proposes that the President and Congress create a "national institute for advanced research and public policy" which would provide a forum in the nation's capital for a full exploration of the "growth and new application of knowledge from all the sciences to the major issues of the society." It is quite likely that the creation of a special division within the National Science Foundation on Research Applied to National Needs is at least an indirect consequence of this idea. The report again stresses the importance of basic research, including qualitative methods (p. 99). But its main emphasis is on administrative proposals; they are explicitly related to the Programming, Planning, and Budgeting system which at that time was very popular in government circles (p. 55ff).

Unlike the Lyons Report, which deals solely with Federal policies, the Brim Report is organized along major sectors of present-day American life and society. The chapter divisions single out the following units: the professions, such as engineering, journalism, mental health, etc. (Chapter III); the activities of the federal government. (Chapter IV); business and labor (Chapter V); problems of community government (Chapter VI); education of the general public (Chapter VII).

On the surface, the recommendations only propose more research support and utilization in these areas. But the separate chapters do contain a large number of ideas as to what problems deserve special attention, and many helpful examples and references are supplied. There is no space here for the details, but anyone who offers a course on or directs work in applied sociology will find these one hundred pages a valuable source. The text exhibits an especially good understanding of utilization in the broadest sense—the need for spelling out the anticipated consequences of changes or modifications.

The possible functions of social scientists in various professional schools is discussed in Chapter III; instead of generalizations, it points to the differences between professions. (A comparative study of such curriculums could be a natural outgrowth of these preliminary hints.) Chapter IV is essentially a summary of the Lyons Report, which was obviously sent to the Brim group in advance of its publication.

Chapter V reiterates the observation that management utilizes the social sciences but labor unions do not, either to improve their internal organization or to strengthen their position in negotiations. Especially on this latter point, the report gives some imaginative suggestions and proposes that foundations give unions initial funding up to the point where they see the light and support it themselves. Incidentally, the text does not mention either recent studies on work satisfaction, a modern form of the old "surveys," or research on changes in the life-style of workers, which, under the slogan of embourgeoisement, is a topic of much concern to British sociologists.

Chapter VI really contains two different elements which the reader must somehow separate. Institutes for public administration have worried about and studied city governments for some time. The task now is (a) to relate such work to the rapidly growing studies of organizations, and (b) to upgrade police and health services by utilizing the specific findings of criminologists and medical sociologists. (Chapter VII urges the development and use of improved sociological materials for grade schools, high schools, and formal classes for adults.)

The Brim Report culminates in a plan for the creation of some twenty social problems research institutes, each devoted to a specific area such as addiction, juvenile delinquency, etc. Initially, the institutes would be funded by the Federal government. The operation of these institutes and their relation to potential sponsors as well as users is discussed in some detail, but their location, whether university-based or not, is left open. The relative advantages of the two forms are laid out for inspection, their administrative problems described with insight, and the special qualifications required by an institute director (we shall later describe him as a "managerial scholar") properly noted.

Lyons places the utilizer in the structure of the Federal government. Brim tells him what to worry about, wherever he may be. The BASS Report begins to ask where he will come from. It covers many other topics, however, because it sets out to give an over-all picture of the state of the field; it therefore necessarily overlaps with the two previous reports (known at least to the authors in draft). A brief general outline will be useful.

The first four chapters of the document circumscribe the social disciplines which the authors wish to cover, including research methods and examples of typical findings. From the detached view of a study group, some of the debates which still embroil the academic world seem pointless.

The distinctions between basic and applied social science are seldom sharp, and important scientific contributions have been made all along this line, with applied findings serving basic science just as basic science serves applications [p. 20].

In these first four chapters, recommendations are neither called for nor made. Chapters 6 and 7 single out issues connected with the desirability of developing social indicators. Increasingly more space is devoted to this issue (a topic not covered in our own text) as we move along from one study group to another. Understandably, the assembly of large-scale data banks about individuals leads to the ethical problems discussed in Chapter 8. The commission makes a strong effort to show that civil liberties will not be endangered. But eight recommendations, almost one-quarter of the total, are related to this problem in one way or another, a reflection of the commission's feeling that people will fear an overly successful social science. Incidentally, one recommendation urges historians to pay attention to data banks.

A block of 4 chapters (9–12) describes the present state of the social sciences in American universities. The section on professional schools is a good complement to Brim's Chapter III. While the former suggests topics of research, BASS gives factual data on how much social science is taught, and where. It also reports briefly on an inquiry made of deans of professional schools as to their future plans. A dilemma is noted: "Although the advantages of the professional schools as bases for applied and problem-oriented research are real, they are offset, to some extent, by the missionary-orientation of the various professions" (p. 191). The study group therefore refrains from making any recommendations and suggests further study. Chapters 14–27 deal with problems of financial support and international collaboration, extending the recommendations made by the Wiesner Report.

Three chapters are especially central to our topic. Chapter 5 deals with behavioral sciences and the problems of society. It begins with concrete examples: tax reduction as a remedy for recessions, studies at the service of population control, warnings against racial stereotypes. The relation between policy and social science knowledge is here for the first time raised as an intellectual problem and its study urged (especially pp. 96–97). In the same chapter, the participation of both social scientists and economists as members of high-level Federal advisory committees is recommended, echoing the Lyons Report at this point.

Chapter 12 contains the crucial recommendation and deserves to be scrutinized in detail.

> . . . The committees recommend that universities consider the establishment of broadly based training and research programs in the form of a *Graduate School* of Applied Behavioral Science (or some local equivalent) under administrative arrangements that lie outside the established disciplines. Such training and research should be *multidisciplinary* (going beyond the behavioral and social sciences as necessary), and the school should *accept responsibility* for contributing through its research both to a *basic understanding* of human relationships and behavior and to the *solution of persistent social problems.* [p. 201]. [emphasis ours.]

The proposal is preceded by a discussion of university institutes and their difficulties. It is followed by a rather detailed discussion of the curriculum and organization of such a graduate school.

The BASS Report stresses the solution of social problems and excludes the private sector as well as the operational problems of government agencies. This leads to an ambiguity in Chapter 13, which deals with research outside the university. It talks of "opportunities beyond academic boundaries." In the beginning, this refers to employment opportunities for researchers, and the information provided in pages 213 to 220 is helpful. But at the end, the discussion deviates imperceptibly to the question of whether nonuniversity social research institutes are a desirable development. Social problem institutes are considered an "opportunity" because they give the senior researcher a chance to work "without concern for such auxiliary tasks as the training of graduate students." This seems to us a strange way to end a chapter on the need for developing a new professional role, and we shall go further into this later in our book.

The three study groups provide a variety of examples, and we have indicated the places at which they can be found. Some are success stories, some tell of missed opportunities (e.g., BASS), and many suggest topics to be worked on. But they all have one feature in common: they tell of a problem and they talk of a solution—realized or not realized. But nowhere can one find a concrete description of what transpired in these situations. Probably reports of this kind cannot go into such detail. But they are needed, and some more or less satisfactory reports became available while the study groups worked on their assignments. We are thinking of the "readers" which appeared during the sixties and which we shall briefly review now.

THE WORLD OF THE "READERS": A CONTINUATION OF TRAIL 2

It is not known whether courses or seminars explicitly dealing with applied sociology were offered in the early sixties. But the study groups worked in contact with their academic colleagues and asked for advisory memorandums. Undoubtedly problems of utilization began to seep into the teaching programs of colleges and universities. But where would teachers and students find appropriate examples? No comprehensive textbook was yet available or even in sight. No wonder, then, that publishers and professors developed the idea of providing collections of reprints or commissioned articles to fill this new need.

The readers fall into two groups. One set is assembled by its editors to express a specific point of view or to contribute to a major debate. A second group draws on applications across all the fields in which material is available. Our selection is somewhat arbitrary. But we have examined a rather extensive bibliography and are confident it would not have made much difference if we had substituted other books.

Let us first draw attention to a reader with the somewhat restricted title *Social Scientists and International Affairs.*[24] In fact, the bulk of the papers in it are reprints dealing with general problems of the applied social researcher. The collection covers almost all the controversies to which we alluded earlier in our review and contains few concrete examples. We have already expressed strong doubts about the value of such general discussions,* but those who want to form their own opinion on this matter could not find a better source. The reader contains an excellent, well-selected, well-organized 40-page bibliographical appendix. The flavor of this reader can be judged by the four divisions into which the bibliographical appendix is divided: I. Social Roles of the Social Sciences; II. Social Science in Public Policy; III. Organization of Policy-oriented Social Sciences; IV. Decision-making Structures and the Use of Social Science Research.

A companion piece to this collection, a reader edited by Gideon Sjoberg, deals with a specific topic in this congery of discussion: the ethical and political difficulties and pitfalls in applied social research. The contributors give illustrations of client pressure to suppress information or of the sociologist's willingness to let objective research standards be lowered for the sake of the client. Other articles describe tensions growing out of the research-setting itself: an outsider doing research in South Africa; a woman investigating a military installation.[25]

Two other publications in this group bring us to more substantial though still specialized areas. It is not surprising that the students of Kurt Lewin were the first to produce a reader. They had done applied work

*We do, however, recommend Max Millikan's paper on "The Relation of Knowledge to Action" for closer study, largely because his position is generally in agreement with ours.

for more than twenty years and had developed a line of their own. In 1961, a collection appeared under the characteristic title *The Planning of Change: Readings in the Applied Behavioral Sciences.*[26] As one would expect, the collection concentrates on expositions of group dynamics principles and their possible applications to issues of leadership and changes in attitudes. The editors, obviously aware that they were engaged in a new type of enterprise, included many articles by non-Lewinians—prominent sociologists and social psychologists who, in one way or another, had written about social change. While some of this material has a macrosociological character, the real interest of the editors centered on small groups. This orientation was not changed when a second edition appeared in 1969. The editors stressed that nine-tenths of the material was new because so much progress had been made since the first edition. However, the progress they refer to consisted of the diffusion of the small-group tradition to large movements such as sensitivity training, contact groups, etc. The new edition is more concise, because almost all the macrosociological articles were dropped. The empirical examples have a standard plot in which the psychological doctrine is taken for granted, and the stories tell how sponsors were induced to use it and how satisfied they were once they did. The material provided is too brief to permit any further analysis, and the editors themselves are aware of these shortcomings. They promise the publication of a more detailed casebook, but as far as we know it has not yet appeared.

With some exaggeration we can say that the Lewinians tell their stories to justify their theoretical faith. The opposite position is taken by another reader, equally coherent, in which the contributors emphasize their goal, what they did to understand it better and how to reach it more successfully. Their collection, which grew out of a meeting held in 1968 by the Southwestern Sociological Association, is entitled *Planned Social Intervention.*[27] At that time, Daniel P. Moynihan had just published his attack on the role of the social scientist in the formation of social policy. The collection presents reports on various efforts made by sociologists to enlist the "maximum feasible participation" of the poor, as required by the poverty-program legislation. The contributors are well aware of the inherent paradox of the assignment, since a major ingredient of the poverty syndrome is withdrawal and inability to participate. Thus what the contributors really report are their attempts to overcome the handicaps. The accounts are evenly divided between success and failure. As a matter of fact, the whole volume is set up to balance proponents and opponents of social intervention. The collection starts with reprints from the leading spokesmen on both sides: Phillip Hauser reiterates his doubts about social engineers and C. Wright Mills states his well-known position that sociologists have a professional responsibility to advocate radical social change. In spite of the efforts to achieve a balanced selection, one can feel that the editors favor the interventionist role. This is made especially obvious in a rather unusual section called "Historical Perspectives on Planned Social Intervention." *Most of the essays in this book make good reading, but they fail to specify the exact nature of the sociologist's professional contribution. Certainly they all display thorough knowledge of the literature on the poverty syndrome, but this is not sufficient to answer the question: Why the sociologist?

What do these four readers contribute to our main theme: the application of social science to practical affairs? If we are asking exactly what theories or findings or tools were applied to what specific problems, we would have to say, "not enough." In contrast, a second group of readers are intentionally written for use in teaching. They appeared almost simultaneously, with very similar titles: *Sociology in Use,* by Valdes and Dean, and *Sociology in Action,* by Shostak. Valdes and Dean intended their reader for undergraduates. Their purpose is not to clarify the nature of utilization but to make sociology courses more attractive. They organize their cases around sociological concepts such as role, socialization, small groups, etc., the idea being that a teacher can make sociology lively by linking it to the interests of the students. At the end of the book they have a topical index, a list of about fifty sociological concepts with page references to the illustrative material in their 50 selections. They are well-chosen reprints from many sources, in line with the editors' purpose to cover a "wide range of human activity." This is the only reader with numerous examples from the world of business.[28] Some of the best-written contributions are explanations of problematic situations in sociological terms: the pressures on American soldiers captured by Chinese (Selection 21); the reasons for the average social worker's inability to understand the mental-health problems of low socioeconomic groups (Selection 24); the problems churches face as a result of recent social changes (Selection 35). Some of the papers propose or report solutions for concrete difficulties: in a labor

---

*No. 11 contains a description of the New Deal Resources Planning Board. Merriam, the originator of the Administrative Science movement, was one of the Board's leading members, as was Mitchell, the founder of the National Institute of Economic Research, the agency which originated the study of business cycles in the United States. (Arthur Burns had been its director before becoming the head of the Federal Research Board.) Both Merriam and Mitchell were among the four members of Hoover's Commission on Recent Social Trends; Merriam was its chairman.

negotiation (Selection 28); in improving the cooperation of flight crews (Selection 20); or in increasing the circulation of a newspaper (Selection 36). Quite a number of contributions are conventional evaluations of past treatments of propaganda efforts. Still, the reader is stimulating and typical of a middle-of-the-road effort: utilization is accepted as an interesting topic; it is, so to say, smuggled into the regular academic program but not yet seen as a problem in its own right.

The Shostak reader[29] also covers a large variety of topics, but explicitly moves "outside the classroom." Twenty-four of its 38 selections were solicited by the editor, who asked that the writer "recount real occurrences in the richness of the full experience." The contributions are classified by subject areas, not according to sociological concepts. In general, the editor has succeeded in his aim. The authors are explicit about their strategy for reforming a school system (Selection 3) or trying to rebuild a city after an earthquake (Selection 13). They give the criteria by which they help in locating a denominational center (Selection 7) or work on a desegregation brief (Selection 11). Three papers deal specifically with the role sociological ideas play in the war on poverty here and abroad (Selection 26–28). Many of these contributions are very detailed, and turned out to be helpful in the preparation of our own text. A future "theory of application" will certainly require a steady flow of such rich personal reports. But the interplay between narrative and systematization will have to be explicated. The story of such systematization has still to be followed up, and so once more we shall take up our historical review at the period after the last war.

ANALYZING THE UTILIZATION PROCESS: TRAIL 3

We have traced two developments in the postwar period. One is an ongoing and we think rather fruitless debate on the place of "applied sociology" in the total world of the social sciences. The second is an increasing interest in the substance of such work, as indicated by the efforts of the study groups and the appearance of readers, including some more or less concrete examples of efforts to utilize social science material or concepts. But these examples are essentially stories of successes or failures. They tell little about utilization as a process consisting of many interconnected phases, in which alternatives are discarded at every step, decisions must mix knowledge and intuition, and one decision locks into another. Nor do they take our position, that "intuition" deserves to be dissected and studied.

Fortunately, we can follow a third trail of work, where "application" itself is made a topic of research and analysis, in the hope that future practice can be improved and connections between past experiences understood. One might think that there was an ordered progression: first, general talk; then, planning and disparate examples; finally, a systematic approach. But this was not the case. Rather, it is as if sociologists had developed three styles of coping with the tensions created by the need to reestablish a balance between sociology as a system of knowledge and sociology as a contribution to practical decision-making. The three themes developed simultaneously, without much influence upon each other; each has to be traced historically if one wants to locate one's own position.

Our own text is part of the effort to establish the study of utilization as a field in its own right. We are not the only persons concerned with this problem today. A group in Ann Arbor, at the Center for Research on the Utilization of Scientific Knowledge, has for several years developed an elaborate model for knowledge utilization.[30] Northwestern University has a Center for Research on Research, and their periodic bibliographies are very useful. At Columbia University, the Bureau of Applied Social Research has always tried to be self-conscious about the meaning of applying research. The authors of the present text belong to this tradition, and feel they can document some of the events pertinent to the present context. They hope that similar accounts will become available from other centers, just as they try for continuity at their present academic locations.
demic locations.

Let us return once more to the 1948 SSRC conference. Merton was the obvious choice for the keynote address. In addition to his reputation as a leading theorist, his work as codirector of the Columbia Bureau and as one of its liaison men with Stouffer's Army research staff in Washington during the war had become well known. A brief analysis of his memorandum[31] brings out the main ideas of what we shall call the cognitive aspects of the utilization process.

Merton divided his presentation into two parts:

1. interpersonal and organizational problems stemming from the relations between the research worker and the "clientele" (operating agency, administrator, etc.),
2. scientific problems involving the difficulty of developing scientific research adequate to the practical demands of the situation.

For the moment we are concerned only with the second part. He began with a classification of problems, developed by the Bureau, indicating how unsatisfactory any such effort was bound to be. Altogether, he stressed that what is considered a practical problem requiring research is, because of that very fact, a sociological issue. He further stressed that, given the present stage of the art, it was important to find the right balance between what the policy-maker needs and what the social sciences can do.

> . . . with the *excessively large* problem only failure can presently be reported and with the *excessively limited* problem, the results are often trivial. It would be important to identify the *strategic, intermediate range of problems*, namely, those which have generalized theoretical and practical significance, but which are not too large in scope to be subjected to disciplined research. (175)

Once a problem is established, utilization becomes a sequence of steps that must be investigated separately. After a practical problem has been identified, it must be translated into a research design. This step of translation must avoid a number of dangers. Merton discusses what the sociologist can do if the policy-maker either overspecifies or overgeneralizes his problem. The topic of values is viewed differently, because it is related to the translation problem. There may be a tacit assumption on the part of the client that certain factors are unchangeable and, therefore, do not deserve to be studied; the sociologist, on the other hand, may have such strong preferences for certain research techniques that he overlooks others that might be more adequate to the policy problem on hand. After the translation into a research design, the utilization process faces what is probably the most difficult step of all—"the leap from research to practice." Any recommendation made by a sociologist explicitly or implicitly contains assumptions as to the future and must consider possible unanticipated consequences. Merton is aware of the reverse side of the coin: the policy-maker must accept the risks involved in some of these implications. But men of private and public affairs differ as to the size of the risks they are willing to take. This comes close to the mode of a formalized decision theory, where action is guided by a set of alternatives to which one attaches both subjective probabilities of future occurrences and cost-benefits should each materialize.

Merton proposed a program of research providing further analysis for these steps. He argued that four groups would be interested in such a review: the social scientist concerned with his professional role; foundations deliberating on the extent to which they should support work done for practical purposes; government and business who wish to know how much they can count on help from the social sciences; and finally, the intelligent layman who wants to know about this new controversy and who might influence it by his vote or other forms of political action.

And yet the SSRC did not follow up the idea of a comprehensive study. Perhaps one reason was the lack of material with which to work. There were no "readers" at the time, and no study groups had as yet collected telling examples. Certainly the Columbia group was aware of the need for case studies and their importance for describing the utilization process. The topic came up in connection with the task of training those sociology students who wanted to apply their professional knowledge to practical problems. In 1950, Lazarsfeld, with the cooperation of Merton, wrote a detailed plan for a "Professional School for Training in Social Research."[32] It subsequently influenced the corresponding section of the BASS Report mentioned above. One section, entitled "Case Materials Designed to Train Students in the Application of Social Research to Problems of Public and Private Policy," illuminates the idea of utilization studies from still another angle.

The point is made that "many problems and research situations have not yet found their way into books." On the other hand,

> Social research as written for publication seldom includes the varied details of the various rabbit-paths, culs-de-sac, and mistaken assumptions that ordinarily enter into the actual investigation. The student merely reading reports knows nothing of the mistakes that were made, and thus learns nothing about detecting and guarding against such mistakes.

In four pages, the memorandum then describes in detail how such cases should be prepared as to be useful for analytical purposes. We extract the main ideas in a running account. While the passage is couched in terms of training, the reader will find it a helpful counterpoint to Merton's memorandum. Together, the two documents set the tone for our present text.

The actual workaday experience of professional practitioners of social research in government, business, industry, labor and welfare organizations provides a storehouse of raw materials which can be drawn upon for the preparation of documents. Documentary records, successive drafts of research memoranda and reports, interviews with policy-makers and with researchers—these are some of the sources providing salient facts of each case. Through case materials of this kind, students can be trained to see more than the specific practical problems in hand. Are there types of applied research in social science that are particularly likely to fructify basic theory? At which points do there characteristically arise obstacles to the utilization of research in the formation of policy? For which kinds of practical problems is the use of applied social science presently pointless, and for which kinds is it extremely useful, if not indispensable? Does the role of research practitioner differ when he is part of a research staff attached to an operating organization and when he is in a research agency independent of the client organization? How does the researcher come to reformulate the practical problems of the policy-maker so that an investigation appropriate to the problem can be designed?

The fact is that we are only now beginning to learn something of the actual, rather than the supposed or ideal, relations between basic and applied social research. These would be clarified by training seminars centered on reports of actual cases of research applied to policy by practitioners who took part in the research. They would present a compact factual memorandum on the case including materials on the research organization, its formal and informal relations with the policy-makers in question, the form in which the policy problem was originally put, and the apparent expectations of the client regarding the nature of the research and the uses to which it might be put. The student members of the seminar, working as teams of two or three, prepare a research brief bearing on the case. The seminar meetings themselves represent a kind of clinical session, where the practitioner indicates, serially and piecemeal, what he did in fact do, comparing this with the suggestions set forth in the briefs of the students. Students come progressively to see that policy-oriented research involves a sequence of choices among alternative research decisions which might have been taken. They learn something of the way in which practice differs from theory, not in the ignorant sense of that phrase (which implies that theory is somehow inferior to practicality), but in the significant sense that considerations other than those expressed in an abstract theory need to be taken into account when research is oriented toward questions of policy.

The proposal from which these ideas are quoted has one other feature in common with Merton's program for the SSRC meeting. Neither of them was implemented. The same fate was destined for a third episode in this history, although the circumstances were somewhat more complex. The newly created Ford Foundation had a Division 5 (now defunct) which was dedicated to the behavioral sciences—a term created by the planning committee for that division. Its director, Bernard Berelson, was aware that the planning committee had urged the Foundation to sponsor "immediate studies of the current application of the knowledge of human behavior and of feasible means for extending such applications." He commissioned Wilbur Schramm to write an appropriate proposal. Schramm, one of the pioneers in communications research, was at the time directing a communications department at Stanford and had wide practical experience in public service and private consultation. He chose an advisory committee; among its members were a staff member of Rand, a representative of the Michigan Group Dynamics Center, and the president of a major advertising agency. One of the two sociologists in the committee was Donald Young, who, as the director of the Russell Sage Foundation, represented their traditional interest in application and who had also been chairman of the study group which had sponsored the Lyons Report. The other was Robert Merton, and his influence is very marked in Schramm's Proposal.[33] It was Schramm's intention to advise the Foundation about modes of advancing the complex activities of applying science to problems of human behavior. The term "utilization process" reappears throughout the memorandum. It contains a chapter on past accomplishments, but contrary to the usual cliché, Schramm stresses that a decreasing rate of success is to be expected as applications are made in fields of increasing complexity. An interesting section lists 21 rules that might help to advance utilization; rules 10 to 18 deal especially with the interplay between research and user. The document reports interviews with participants on both sides. Especially valuable are pages 19–27, which reproduce a speech by Samuel Stouffer not published elsewhere.

The final 25 pages contain the recommendations to the Ford Foundation. Cleverly, the author first discusses five reasons why they might not enter the field: the problem is not urgent; there is no solution in sight anyhow; other sources of financing are available; it is too expensive for the results obtainable; and finally, it could get the Foundation into public-relations problems.

After refuting these arguments, preliminary proposals are made, always stressing that only slow progress can be expected and that, therefore, no large expenditures are recommended. Two general objectives are envisioned:

1. More effective relationships between the custodians of behavioral science knowledge and the individuals and groups responsible for its application in society.
2. Better understanding of the social problem and process of applying scholarship to action—its mechanisms and methods, uses and needs, and conditions which limit its effectiveness.

A great variety of concrete tasks which deserve support are listed. Training is, of course, one, including analysis of "cases," the collection of which might be especially commissioned. Interestingly, very high priority is given to the "identification and classification of action problems in behavioral fields," the lack of which is felt by many authors, including ourselves. Schramm proposes machinery to attain this goal. It is imaginative but quite complicated, which might explain why no single author has yet succeeded (pp. 88–90). The culminating need is "research on utilization as a process in society." The mood of the Schramm report and its affinity to the war experience is best represented by this passage:

> The Foundation may be able in the future to specify and commission experimental research, but it is far more likely to have to wait for a promising situation and proposal, and then back a man. In time it should be possible to support a program of research on the utilization process as sophisticated as Hovland's program on persuasive communication at Yale, but there is now no Hovland interested in doing such a program. And it may well be that the time is not ripe. Preliminary case studies, statement of rough propositions, training of middlemen—all will help to prepare the way.

The Schramm document was never published in full. Parts of it are reproduced in Part III of the Reuss Committee report but without the recommendations to the Ford Foundation. It also does not contain the statements by experts, which is understandable, because this committee itself collected expert opinion. The reprinted parts, however, contain Schramm's 21 rules and are therefore still valuable.

Shortly after this memo was submitted, the Ford Foundation dissolved its behavioral science division. We hope that the files on this decision will some day be made available. Action on social problems was turned over to subject-matter divisions which undoubtedly commissioned studies relevant to their missions. But the chance to make "applications" a topic of research in its own right was once again lost. While an increasing number of writers expressed the need for such a move, it certainly was not the subject of popular demand among sociologists, as can be seen from the final episode in this historical account.

In 1960, Lazarsfeld was elected president of the American Sociological Association. The main task of the president is to organize the national meetings to be held, and to make developmental suggestions for the period after he leaves office. Both these tasks need approval by the Executive Council. If the president is not sure of such consent, delicate negotiations become necessary. This was obviously true in 1960, as can be seen from the opening of the memorandum which Lazarsfeld presented to the Council.

> I want to submit to you an idea for discussion. It obviously grows out of a strong personal interest of mine and and I am, therefore, prepared to accept your judgment if you consider my plan too one-sided. The main theme for the program I have in mind could have a variety of titles, like "Sociology in Action" or "Applied Sociology," or many others.

The Executive Council did indeed find the topic a bit undignified. Agreement was reached in a number of steps. First, the name of the theme was changed to "Uses of Sociology." Then, in the instructions to the chairman appointed for the 1962 meetings, Lazarsfeld had to insert a justification which could be used in soliciting papers:

> As many of us know, doubt is often raised as to the meaningfulness of the contribution made by the rapidly mounting stream of empirical studies and the increasing number of publications on applying theory to social planning. These doubts are broad in scope. At one extreme there are the doubters who ask whether we contribute anything useful to people active in government, social amelioration, labor, politics, business, etc. At the other extreme, there are voices raised to accuse us of attending to trivial problems only. And in between there are those who deny that we add anything to the general understanding of the educated citizen with a sense of social or professional responsibility which goes beyond either common sense or traditional literary essays.

Finally, the theme had to be given as broad an interpretation as possible.

> I hope that something like a spectrum of utility will develop that leads from the use of social theory in neighboring fields, such as history and economics, at the one end, to the utilization of particular empirical research by agencies wanting to pursue a concrete goal more effectively, at the other end.

After the convention, the ASA appointed a committee to prepare a book on the theme of "Uses." The prospective authors received a detailed guide which emphasized the need to avoid fruitless controversies and to balance intraprofessional biases. Papers were to stress the use of sociological themes and concepts as well as the use of actual studies, the use of research techniques, or the possible importance of the sociological mode of thought. Authors were urged to use specific examples of these applications.

The two central questions were:

1. What are the difficulties of translating practical issues into research problems?
2. What are the unavoidable intellectual gaps between findings and advice for action?

Each contributor was asked to cover one specific area: law, school administration, gerontology, etc. It took several years to get publishable papers, because the editors had not anticipated two difficulties. For one, even the best experts had never given much thought to utilization, and when they did search for information it was very difficult to come by. One of the contributors wrote to several hundred rural sociologists; only those who were connected with administrative enterprises were able to furnish concrete examples. Another polled the members of the ASA on medical sociology; the majority of the respondents had only a vague idea about what, if anything, happened, as a consequence of their own work.

> Clients seem to be more likely to know of uses than the sociologists themselves. But not only are clients difficult to sample; they are often corporations, in which the officers who may have acted on the basis of a report are not easily traced. A future theory of uses will require experimentation with various ways of gathering information [p. xxxi].

It should be remembered that only one of the readers discussed above was available at the time.

But a second handicap was much more portentous. In spite of the detailed guidelines the 41 authors had received, they shared no more than a general perspective and were not bound by a formal scheme for analysis. Although they provided a rich store of material, they inevitably produced chapters that were only loosely comparable. This made the editors aware that there was no whole picture. They wrote a 30-page introduction choosing an inductive path from the contributions to an underlying schema—a procedure sometimes called substruction. As the editors put it:

> In this introduction we draw on our authors' contributions to construct a paradigm for the understanding of the uses of sociology; we hope that it will help the reader select from the contributions those elements which are most appropriate for his purpose . . . either as a teacher, as a consulting sociologist, or as a critic of the chapters in this volume. On the one side is the person or the agency engaged in action, setting general policies, making day-to-day decisions. This person or agency can be designated as the "client." On the other side is the

sociologist. The collaboration or lack of collaboration between client and sociologist is the central focus of this volume.

The rest of the introduction elaborated the details of the schema and served as a guide for placing the various examples across fields.

In Chapter 2 of the present monograph we describe what we call this first "map" of the utilization phenomenon, discuss its function, and explain which aspects of it we intend to develop further. The remainder of our text is devoted to these new developments. Before entering upon this task, however, one more issue needs clarification.

THE PROBLEM OF TERMINOLOGY

We felt we were able to locate our conceptualization in a historical context and delineate it from related activities. But we were not quite able to escape the embarrassment of terminology. The ghost of the "social engineer" is still too much with us, and the term "applied social research" really contains a semantic contradiction: how can you decide by looking at a piece of research whether or not it will ever be applied? "Research done for application" is logically correct but terribly clumsy. Actually, this objection is really supplanted by tradition. We are accustomed to the term "natural sciences," although it is not the science but its object which is "natural." Other examples could be given where an adjective is used to substitute for a more accurate and complete phrase. Yet the distinction between basic and applied research is still troubling. It is like the little man who is not there and does not want to go away. The study groups usually say that the distinction makes no sense, but they use it nonetheless. Those authors who really want to describe the substance of the research have experimented with other pairs of terms. The editors of the *Uses* volume talk of field-induced versus autonomous research. They are clear-cut about the first element of the pair: it refers to work where the social scientist was commissioned to do a study. But the second term becomes a residual category. Autonomous research can range "from the desperation of the Ph.D. candidate seeking a dissertation topic to the unexpected insight of an ingenious social observer." The *Uses* editors add another dimension: whether or not the findings of a study make a contribution to the basic fund of knowledge. This leads to four types of research, and the implication is that the correlation between the origin of an inquiry and the significance of its findings is not as high as one might assume.

A few years later the National Academy of Education inaugurated a detailed plan entitled *Research for Tomorrow's Schools.*[34] The authors make a distinction very similar to that of *Uses,* but they employ the dichotomy of decision-oriented and conclusion-oriented research, terms borrowed from an article by a leading statistician, J. W. Tukey.[35] The idea is that the conclusions of the scientists always imply a ceteris paribus clause. A practical decision takes the conclusion and hazards the judgment that at *the present moment,* a certain action looks promising. In fact, decision-oriented and field-induced mean exactly the same thing and are fairly well-defined. But conclusion-oriented is closer to "true knowledge" than "autonomous," which simply meant everything that was not field-induced. As a result, Cronbach and Suppes are more worried about "puzzling" cases which are not covered by their distinction. What if a foundation commissions a composer to produce a symphony? We shall later find one other qualification useful:

> The conclusion-decision dichotomy has only a weak correspondence to the basic-applied distinction. Decision-oriented research no doubt is applied. Conclusion-oriented research, however, may also be used directly with educational institutions and instructional activities, and in that sense it too may be "applied research" [p. 22]

More generally, this raised the question of where to locate the urban planner who proposes a new form of mass transit, or the Marxist who proposes radical change.

Actually, Cronbach and Suppes are much more concerned with this issue than their conceptual introduction would lead one to expect. They fret about the role of the educational reformer who might be intuitively correct but neither possesses nor seeks enough evidence to back up his convictions. The authors then adopt a highly successful editorial strategy. Before they present their program of research needed for education, they insert 40 pages of historical material on "American Scholars and Educational Progress: 1855 and 1958." This story is in itself interesting. But most of all, it makes the two orientations and their interplay much more lively. It would be fine if their approach were followed in other fields where the historical sources are easily available, say in poverty or mass-communications research.

We now turn to another verbal distinction introduced by James Coleman.[36] At first his introductory statement is rather puzzling. After mentioning the Cronbach-Suppes dichotomy he writes:

> Here I will not use these terms, nor will I use the roughly parallel but often misused pair of terms "basic research" and "applied research." Rather, I will call the research that is designed to advance knowledge in a scientific discipline "*discipline research*" and will call the research designed as a guide to social action "*policy research.*"

The author gives no explanation of why he uses different terms for the same distinction made by his predecessors. But one can infer his motives if one remembers that Coleman is a sociologist, while Cronbach and Suppes are psychologists. Emphasis is not on the minutia of the utilization process but on the meaning it has for the participant actors. In discipline research

> results are not intended to serve as a guide to action in specific policies; its *audience* is an audience not of political actors but of political scientists. In policy research, the *audience* is a set of political actors, ranging from a single client to a whole populace, and the research is designed as a guide to action.

We shall presently come back to Coleman's ideas and to the policy research movement to which his terminology alludes. At the moment one point has to be anticipated. Coleman says:

> Making *policy recommendations* based on the research results should be governed by the investigator's personal values and appropriately include advocacy. *Those stages that lie within the disciplinary world,* execution of the research and statement of the research results, should be governed by disciplinary values and *do not appropriately include advocacy.*

Equating recommendations with advocacy seems to us logically wrong. It bars the inclusion of recommending as a legitimate step in the utilization process and thus loses it as an important object of discipline research and training.

We have reviewed three publications dedicated to the task of putting social sciences to use. And even these three share in the intradisciplinary ambivalence which characterizes this trend today. No wonder that we enter this arena with trepidation. We certainly do not wish to add further definitions. If we are forced to be very precise we have prepared our defense. We do not claim that we shall deal with one rather than another type of research. Our topic—to state it one last time—is to study the process of utilization itself. If we phrase this in paradoxical terms, we can say we propose to do basic research on application. We want to reach conclusions about work done in a decision-orientation; we feel that the discipline of sociology should include the scrutiny of policy research.

On the last point we shall have more to say, for this is the one term which still requires examination. Janowitz identifies his "enlightenment model" with Lasswell's notion of policy research, an endeavor focused upon the "fundamental problem of man and society rather than upon the topical issues of the moment." This is certainly different from Coleman's orientation, which includes both the school-busing issue and the sale of new antibiotics as matters requiring policy research as a "guide to action." But even in the broadest definition of social action there comes a moment when the gap between knowledge and decision has to be faced and bridged.

One more remark before we leave this terminological digression. Not only will we use whatever terms seem appropriate as we proceed, but we shall even shift somewhat arbitrarily between the terms sociology and social science. Parts of social psychology and social anthropology are practically undistinguishable from sociology as defined in various university departments. So why not use such words interchangeably if we can make language less pedantic without confusing the reader?

THE PURPOSE OF THIS TEXT

We can now pick up our historical sketch where we left off before this detour. We showed how slowly a cognitive approach to the process of utilization developed. We want to advance it along the following lines:

a. We are very specific about the steps in the utilization process as we see it. Thereby we can coordinate a variety of examples by locating them at points in this process even when they are not full-blown cases. At the same time, our analysis should provide a scheme for the collection of better cases. The cumulative scrutiny of concrete situations will certainly turn up observations which do not fit into the structure we have developed thus far. If so, new components must be added in the future.

b. We have chosen as the core of our presentation the role—if any—which sociological knowledge plays in the conduct of practical affairs. Or to put it in terms of our imagery: we are studying the road the social scientist travels in making a recommendation, and the fate of his advice in the hands of a man of action. We call this an imagery because in fact the process is extremely complex, full of interactions and feedbacks and embedded in a diversity of organizational contexts. But by starting with "advice" as a schematic construct, we hope to achieve an important goal: the relation between basic and applied sociology (using these two terms as place-holders for all the other distinctions) is not discussed in generalities. We inspect the realistic junctions at which the two meet and intertwine.

To analyze intuition is notoriously difficult. And thus we are very much aware that we are at the bare beginning of such an effort. No generalizations are yet possible. The best one can hope for is a first classification of the ingredients that have to be added if one wants to move from knowledge to action, even when such knowledge has been deliberately assembled for the sake of intervention. In this sense our Chapter 5 is the most important but the least advanced one in our volume. It will serve well if it brings a neglected issue to the attention of our colleagues and elicits further work.

c. At the end of our book we make specific suggestions for the education of young sociologists who want to prepare themselves for roles within the utilization process. But in fact the whole volume is permeated by the idea that education in application is vitally needed and sadly lacking. For example, we list appropriate parts of readers; we discuss the problems of serving on governmental commissions; and we also discuss many stressful points in the contact between sociologist and client.

We advocate research on utilization as a special pursuit, but we know that progress in research and innovations in teaching are intimately linked. We shall find that traditionally-trained sociologists do not perform well in public service; we shall see that the commercialization of social research deprives academic programs of opportunities for experiment and of sources of data. It would be absurb to think that the existence of a textbook would make a crucial difference. Maybe it is only a symptom that no such textbook yet exists. But in our opinion it really is a necessity if one wants to see a better coordination of the various forces pointing in the direction of more and better utilization of sociology. Unashamedly we state that it is such a textbook we are offering here.

NOTES

1 Luther L. Bernard and Jessie Bernard, *Origins of American Sociology* (New York: Crowell, 1943).

2 Anthony Oberschall, *The Establishment of Empirical Sociology: Studies in Continuity, Discontinuity, and Institutionalization* (New York: Harper and Row, 1973).

3 Pauline Young, *Scientific Social Surveys and Research,* Part I (Englewood Cliffs, N.J.: Prentice-Hall, 1946).

4 A. Eaton and S. M. Harrison, *A Bibliography of Social Surveys (New York: Russell Sage Foundation, 1930).*
5 Stuart Rice, *Methods in Social Science* (Chicago: University of Chicago Press, 1931).
6 "Critique of Research in the Social Sciences I," *Bulletin, XLIV* (New York: Social Science Research Council, 1939).
7 Robert Angell, "The Use of Personal Documents in History, Anthropology, and Sociology," *Bulletin, LIII* (New York: Social Science Research Council, 1945).
8 "The Prediction of Personal Adjustment" (New York: Social Science Research Council, 1941).
9 P. Eisenberg and P. F. Lazarsfeld, "The Psychological Effects of Unemployment," *Psychological Bulletin, XXXV* (1938), pp. 358–90.
10 Barry D. Karl, "Mr. Hoover's Experts," in D. Fleming and B. Bailyn (eds.), *Perspectives in American History,* Vol. III (Cambridge, Mass.: Charles Warren Center for American Studies, 1969).
11 This part of the story is well documented; *see* E. de Brunner and J. Kolb, *Rural Society* (3d ed.; Boston: Houghton Mifflin, 1946).
12 Hadley Cantril, *The Human Dimension: Experiences in Policy Research* (New Brunswick, N.J.: Rutgers University Press, 1967).
13 The history of the Army Research Branch is sketched in the first chapter of Samuel A. Stouffer *et. al., American Soldier: Adjustment during Army Life,* Vol. I *Studies in Social Psychology in World War II* (Princeton, N.J.: Princeton University Press, 1949).
14 Alfred Marrow, *The Practical Theorist* (New York: Basic Books, 1969).
15 These experiments are well described in Chapter 14 of Marrow's biography.
16 Nevitt Sanford, "Whatever Happened to Action Research?" *Journal of Social Issues, XXVI* (1970), 3–23.
17 Guy Swanson, Theodore Newcomb, and Eugene Hartley (eds.), *Readings in Social Psychology* (New York: Henry Holt, 1952).
18 *Journal of Philosophy of Science,* 1949, pp. 214, 215.
19 *Sociological Models and Social Policy* (Morristown, N.J.: General Learning Press, 1971). This is one of the "modules" printed in two large columns per page; in our references we indicate the left and right columns by "a" and "b," respectively.
20 *Social Problems,* 1961. The paper was reprinted in A. Gouldner and S. M. Miller (eds.), *Applied Sociology* (New York: The Free Press, 1965).
21 The report is reprinted as Appendix III to Gene Lyons, *The Uneasy Partnership: Social Science and the Government in the Twentieth Century* (New York: Russell Sage Foundation, 1969). This is an important source book for our topic.
22 These two reports are government publications. Lyons himself wrote an informative article, "The Social Science Study Groups," for I. L. Horowitz (ed.), *The Use and Abuse of Social Science* (New Brunswick, N.J.: Transaction Books, 1971).
23 The BASS Report was also published commercially by Prentice-Hall, in 1969.
24 Its subtitle is *A Case for a Sociology of Social Science* Elisabeth T. Crawford and Albert D. Biderman, eds., (New York: Wiley, 1969).
25 Gideon Sjoberg (ed.), *Ethics, Politics, and Social Research* (Cambridge, Mass.: Schenkman Publishing, 1967).
26 Warren G. Bennis *et. al.* (eds.), *The Planning of Change: Readings in the Applied Social Sciences* (New York: Holt, Rinehart and Winston, 1964, 1969).
27 Louis A. Zurcher and Charles M. Bonjean (eds.), *Planned Social Intervention* (New York: Chandler Publishing, 1970).
28 D. Valdes and D. Dean (eds.), *Sociology in Use* (New York: Macmillan, 1965).
29 Arthur B. Shostak (ed.), *Sociology in Action: Case Studies in Social Problems and Directed Social Change* (Homewood, Ill.: Dorsey, 1966). As this goes to press, a new reader edited by Shostak has appeared. It could be considered a new edition of his first

reader, but now has a different title: *Putting Sociology to Work* (New York: McKay, 1974). It is again organized according to subject matter, but all contributions are new, and the appeal is clearly to a larger public.

30 See, for example, Ronald Havelock, *Planning for Innovation through Dissemination and Utilization of Knowledge*, 1973.

31 "The Role of Applied Social Science in the Formation of Policy." *Philosophy of Science* XVI (1949), 161–181.

32 Reprinted in P. F. Lazarsfeld, *Qualitative Analysis* (Boston: Allyn and Bacon, 1972).

33 *The Use of Social Research in Federal Domestic Programs.* (Washington, D.C.: Committee on Government Operations, 1967).

34 Lee J. Cronbach and Patrick Suppes, eds., (New York: Macmillan, 1969).

35 "Conclusions vs. Decisions" *Technometrics* II (1960), 423–433.

36 Policy Research in the Social Sciences (Morristown, N.J.: General Learning Press, 1972).

TWO

Mapping the Utilization Process

In the first chapter we argued that the literature on applied sociology has remained rather vague, never really describing what utilization entails. The present book is based on many published examples of situations in which a sociologist embarked on a study to help solve a practical problem or in which a policymaker called upon a sociologist to help him make a decision. But what is missing in this literature is a systematic analysis of what is meant by utilization as a sociological phenomenon.

Often a simple-sounding word embraces a complex reality. An election, for instance, certainly adds up to more than the number of votes obtained by the contesting parties. It encompasses the campaign efforts of the political organizations, the way the voters actually arrived at decisions, the historical circumstances under which the election was held, etc. In studying an event of this kind, definitions are of little or no help; the investigator must decide what material he wishes to cover and how he intends to organize it.

We propose a special term for this cognitive approach: mapping the area under discussion. Instead of verbal definition, we shall talk of maps which are intended to lay out the subject matter to be dealt with and the interconnections of its parts.

Our main map, A, is taken from *The Uses of Sociology*[1] and has as its core the interaction between a practical decision-maker (whether an individual or an agency) and a professional sociologist who supposedly provides knowledge to improve the chances for a sound decision. In shorthand form, we speak of the client and the professional, but these terms apply only to this specific transaction. The "client" might be a lawyer, and the "professional" a university teacher.

We have made several important refinements in our thinking about the map since the earlier book. Altogether, the fundamental transaction between client and professional turned out to be a much more complex cycle than was anticipated; in Chapter 3, we shall describe this develop-

MAP A. The Terrain of the Utilization Problem

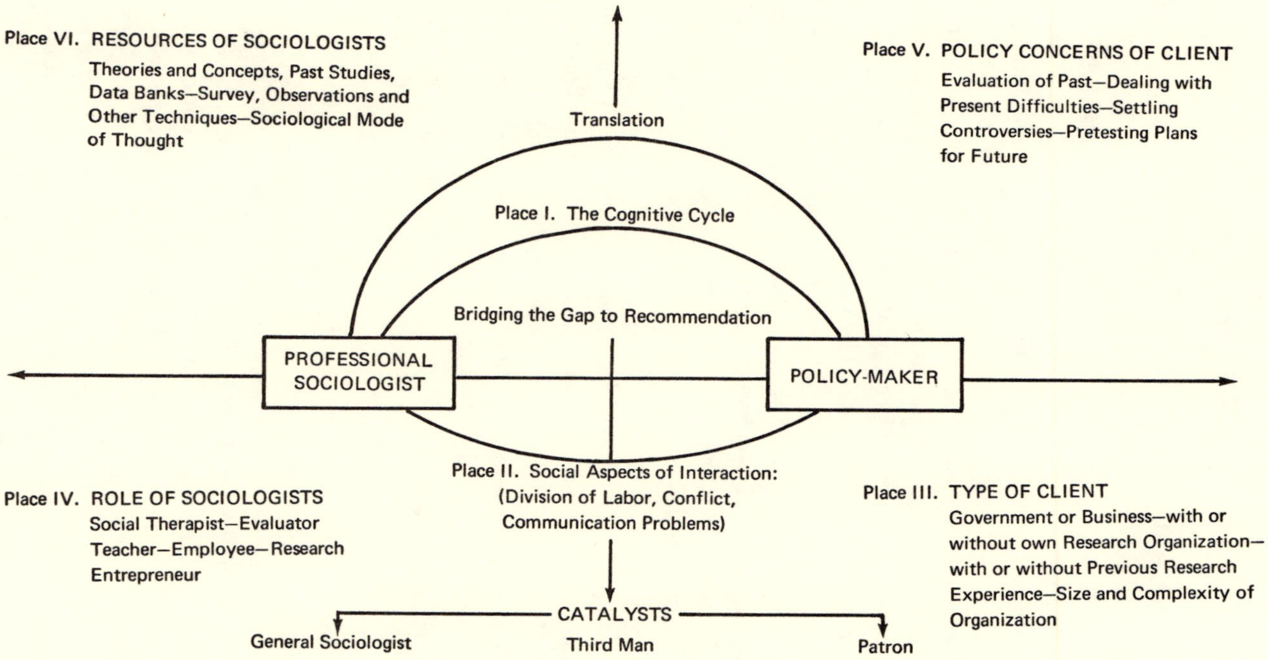

ment. More specifically, we decided to analyze the step from knowledge to recommendations for action as conceptually distinct from the execution of recommendations. We shall say a good deal more about this in Chapter 5.

As we look at Map A, let us imagine a client who has a practical decision to make but, not being sure about what kind of research would be appropriate, he turns to a sociologist for help. This sociologist must translate the client's concerns into a piece of research. Then, once existing data have been compiled or a new study has been made, he must bridge the gap between knowledge and action. The truth will not make the client free if he does not know what to do with it. We think of this cycle from translation to recommendation as the cognitive aspect of the interaction, and it properly occupies Place I in Map A.

Before delving into this, it will be helpful to look at the other elements in this map. First of all, it is obvious that the cognitive cycle does not occur in a social vacuum. The client and the sociologist enter into social interaction. All the conventional sociological concepts are bound to apply: conflicts; misunderstandings; compromise; and above all, division of labor. We believe that these social actions belong at the core of the map and are thus located in Place II.

The simple notion of "sociologist" and "clients" needs elaboration. For purposes of our discussion they are not individuals but "roles" or types. Places III and IV identify these. There are different *types of clients* (Place III): business corporations or government agencies either complex or simple in mission and structure, just as there are variations in the *sociologist's role* (Place IV). Is he a professor who conducts an occasional consultation, the representative of an independent consulting institute, or a member of the policymaker's research staff? Places III and IV are clearly linked: some types of client organizations call in consultants, others have sociologists employed on their own staffs, etc.

But roles and types are in a way formal categories; they have to be supplemented by content. In Map A, this is taken care of by Places V and VI. The *client* has a variety of *problems* (Place V): he may want to know whether a past action was wise; he might want to cope with a current dilemma or lay the ground for future action. The *sociologist* can draw upon a variety of *resources* (Place VI): he knows the import of basic sociological concepts; he has available the empirical findings of his field; and he may be technically equipped to provide new data. At first this sounds like a strange kind of exchange, in which the client reaps all the benefits, but the transaction is balanced by the fact that applied research for a client often pays off in new knowledge for the academician—a topic we discussed in Chapter 1.

Map A has an additional feature: a double symmetry. From left to right it separates the professional and the client; from north to south it separates respectively the substantive and cognitive aspects of the whole topic from its more social and formal elements.

Unfortunately, this is not enough to cover the whole territory we want to encompass. So at the bottom of the map three new parties not mentioned before are introduced. On the left side is the *general sociologist.* He and the professional sociologist are alike in skill and overlap in interest; very often they might be one and the same person. The professional sociologist is the focus of our interest because of his relation with the policy-maker. The general sociologist might be equally interested in the nature of industrial supervision or the rules of mass persuasion, but he happens to be conducting university seminars or writing books about these topics rather than conferring with policy-makers. In an extreme case the generalist appears as critical sociologist. He tells us how bad the situation is, but does not necessarily offer suggestions for improvement.

The main self-definition of the general sociologist is that of a social scientist who does autonomous research, who selects his problems for himself. But certainly he often works with the help of grants; this introduces the new man on the right side of the map. For the moment we might call him the *patron.* On the American scene he is most clearly typified by the foundation, but there are other kinds of patrons. For example, many industrial organizations have divisions called basic research. When they do, the parent organization plays a double role: it is partly client and partly patron. With governmental agencies the matter is even more complex. The National Science Foundation gives unrestricted grants, and most government departments support what they call mission-oriented basic research; but in addition, these agencies have "in-house" research staffs. We have studied the files of one government agency where a series of drafts for budget requests reflect the ambivalence between pride in the purely scientific direction of their work and defensive assertion of its utility (Chapter 7).

The patron and the general sociologist are not the only co-actors in our play. In the middle of the last line of the map a "third man" appears. In the introduction to *The Uses of Sociology,* the following comment was made:

> As the role of the social sciences expands, a new profession might develop: a third force, a middleman, who mediates between the sociologist and the client. He would be able to understand the social scientist and be well acquainted with the practical problems of the sponsors [p. xxviii].

At one time we thought that a new occupational position was needed, a person who ideally would have both the talent and training to take the knowledge which was delivered to him and extract more implications from it than either of the two basic partners could. But now we think of it tentatively in different terms: as the intellectual problems of field-induced research are progressively studied and clarified, some sociologists might choose to include "utilization" as part of their training and equipment as scholars. This would broaden the role of the sociologist rather than requiring the entry of a "third man."

A map such as ours can serve at least four purposes. For one it serves as a definition of a topic whose meaning is still evolving. This is true in the elementary sense that it lists the elements to be included, and excludes those considered irrelevant.

The second merit of a systematic map is that it provides a framework for planning and integrating case studies of utilization. The most ubiquitous complaint in the literature is the lack of detailed descriptions. Where case studies are incomplete, we can at least note which aspects are included, so that this information can be collated. Even if each single paper is meager, in the aggregate a picture may emerge. Around one unit in the map, one locates material in some available publications. Selecting a different topic, another subset of reports yields some pertinent information. The map permits the synthesis of whatever concrete experiences are reported in the literature and provides the framework for comparison and exploratory classification.

The third and perhaps most important service of a map is its use in the development and organization of conjectures about the ways the parts of the maps are related to each other. Thus, for instance, the mode by which practical problems are translated into research designs will affect the range of recommendations which can be developed later on.

Finally, maps permit us to channel progress within a given subject area. In a new field no one can cover all its branches. But a specific study or publication is better understood if it is located within the frame of a broader program. As a matter of fact, the map itself, always somewhat arbitrary, can indicate what its proponent considers central and in what sequence new work is feasible or desirable.

This last function applies especially to the organization of the present volume. We strongly feel that the cognitive utilization process is most in need of elaboration. Thus, the next three chapters are devoted to a refinement of the factor given Place I in Map A. First, Chapter 3 provides an overview of what we consider the six main cognitive phases of the cycle. The two key phases of translation and recommendation are then singled out for more detailed treatment in Chapters 4 and 5. The latter phase seems particularly crucial. Knowledge never dictates which policy will be most effective in solving even very specific problems; and yet knowledge is relevant to decision-making. This forces the question of what it means to say that knowledge is useful. Chapter 5 responds to this query by analyzing the bridges needed to fill the gap between knowledge and recommendation, and we consider it the most innovative of our efforts vis-à-vis the existing literature.

The utilization cycle is not, of course, solely a cognitive process. At every phase it requires and is affected by the social interaction between client and sociologist. But the focus on the cognitive dimension raises key issues when we come to consider the social aspect. For example, what difference does it make *who* identifies a practical problem, *who* conceives a research procedure, *who* formulates recommendations? The concept of possible divisions of labor is clearly relevant. How does the cognitive cycle affect the acceptance of recommendations, by whomever formulated? What is the relation between the cognitive content and social aspects of communication between social scientists and policy-makers? When we explained Place II in our Map A, these interconnections were stressed, and Chapter 6 discusses them in detail.

From there on, our text becomes more selective; we leave certain parts of Map A undiscussed and combine other elements. It is simply not possible to do everything at once, and it seemed a mistake to delay publication for the sake of an ideal completeness which, if at all, could only be achieved step by step. Thus, classification of practical problems requiring aid from social research (Place V) seems at the moment impossible. The number of such situations is too vast, and no reasonable sampling procedure is in sight. Also, so many principles of classification can be thought of that a general effort would be nothing more than a logical exercise. But in every chapter we tried to take our examples from many subject areas, so that the reader should get a cumulative impression of the present state of things.

The types of clients (Place III) are also quite diversified. But they provide the organizational context of the utilization process and therefore could not be neglected. We made one major organizational distinction: between action agencies—private or governmental—on the one side and universities on the other. The action agencies are by and large the consumers, and the universities the providers, of personnel, information, and skills. Our stress shifted to the role of social-research departments and research centers within these organizations. This necessarily directed our attention to research units outside this broader organizational context, the profit- and non-profit-making independent research corporations. This general organizational approach led to the selection of a few major topics in Chapter 7. The various roles the applied sociologist can play and the resources he brings to bear on these tasks (Places IV and VI of Map A) are discussed at a number of points in our text.

Still, the organizational aspect of our topic is less carefully handled than the cognitive; but we hope this is only temporary. In the fall of 1973, the Columbia–ONR project held a conference at the Greyston Center at which the organization of research was systematically discussed by two participants, Professors J. Coleman and J. Nehnevajsa. We intend to make the proceedings of this conference available.

NOTE

1 P. F. Lazarsfeld, W. Sewell, and H. Wilensky (eds.), *The Uses of Sociology* (New York: Basic Books, 1967). p. xii.

THREE

The Cognitive Aspects of the Utilization Cycle

We now begin to fill in the center piece of our general map. Place I, it will be remembered, represents a cycle which begins with the practical problem and ends with an effort at solution with the help of sociological knowledge acquired along the way. This, as it develops is continuous, without sharp demarcations. But for the sake of discussion it is necessary to divide it into a number of steps.* In teaching courses on applied sociology and in reviewing the literature, we have found a division into the following steps useful:

Step 1: How is the existence of a problem established?
Step 2 What machinery is set up to collect pertinent social-science information?
Step 3: How is the practical problem translated into a research design?
Step 4: How is the knowledge so collected converted into recommendations for action?
Step 5: How are these recommendations actually implemented?
Step 6: How is the whole cycle assessed with the possibility that shortcomings discovered in retrospect might make it necessary to reenter the cycle with new problems?

The following pages will describe the six steps (Map A) in some detail. But as mentioned before, steps 3 and 4 respectively, dealing with the translation and the recommendation problems, will be discussed more extensively in the next two chapters and therefore will be sketched only briefly here. Let the reader also remember that in this chapter we deal with the cognitive aspects of the utilization process: those phases which have entailed the collection of social-science information or the ex-

*The difficulty of constructing steps and phases is well known to historians and to students of child development.

MAP B. The Cognitive Steps in the Utilization Process

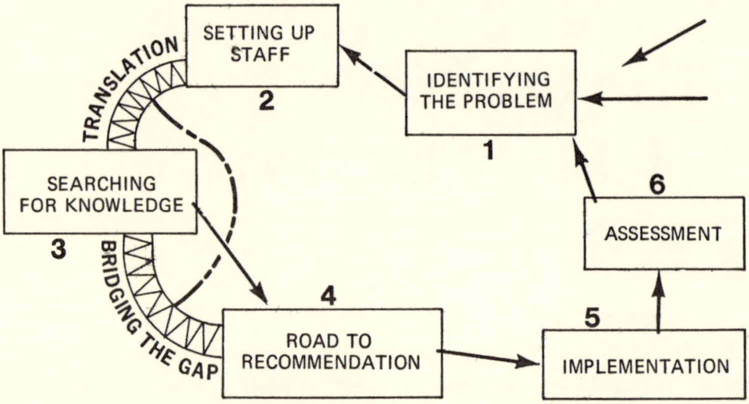

traction of conclusions (always tentative) for practical ends. Topics related to the concrete interaction between the client and the sociologist will be included in Chapter 6.

STEP 1. IDENTIFYING THE PROBLEM

"Problems" are not as clear-cut as at first it may appear. People have to become aware of them in some way, and before a problem can be translated into a research design, an extended dialogue between the sociologist and the man of action will be necessary.

How does an organization become aware that it has a problem? One possibility is a catastrophic event, such as a breakdown of operations or an exposé by a newspaper. It is puzzling that often such events seem to occur before a problem is even recognized from within, but a more detailed analysis will show how difficult it is for top management of an organization to be familiar with every operative detail. As a result, a kind of *half-knowledge* develops. Managers are sufficiently aware of uneasy aspects of their operations, so that they can swiftly mobilize for action. If everything goes well or if danger signals are sent, this half-knowledge has great economic advantages. But if it is used as a screen to block out potentially unpleasant situations, it can become dysfunctional. For example, executives of American television networks were greatly disturbed by the quiz program scandals, although they must have had half-knowledge of the deceptions. The U.S. Space Administration was certainly embarrassed when it became known that long before the Apollo tragedy, the chief contractor's work had been criticized, but the project leadership did not take full cognizance of it. Doubtless the auto industry knew of cars "unsafe at any speed"; by blocking out such knowledge, it saved money in the short run, though it risked much more stringent control of the industry in the long run.

Aside from the disastrous event, there are three more orderly ways of discovering problems. One is continued formal monitoring of activities. Certain indicators emerge easily from organizational records as, for example, profit or sales records. Other data may require special collection—surveys of employee morale or of customer response. In the area of public policy, the demand for "social indicators" has been voiced from many sides. In social and government service organizations, the systematic and periodic sampling of complaints is conceivable though rarely executed. For politicians, the public-opinion polls provide a way of focusing attention on problems.

A second source of problem-awareness can be designated by the old-fashioned term "correspondent," and it has existed throughout history on various levels. The prerevolutionary regime in France requested that the regional intendants report periodically on the problems of their regions. They in turn based their reports to the central government on information solicited from local police chiefs and justices of peace. Today, union officials keep abreast of problems through contact with the heads of local chapters. During World War II, the American government organized periodic content analyses of local newspapers.

A third and increasingly important aspect of problem-awareness is directed toward the anticipation of future difficulties. The significance of professional "futurists" is not that they can really predict the future, but that they are skilled in providing managers and society at large with systematic lists of problems that might arise. The trouble is there has not yet been much attention paid to such efforts—neither the public nor the government was prepared to listen to individual voices warning of air pollution or energy shortages. In Canada, the government has established an Institute for Research on Public Policy which is specifically mandated to search for unsuspected problems.[1] They explicitly exclude the study of previously identified concerns, such as ethnic conflict. The whole *problem* of *problem-awareness* has led to a line of activity which is sometimes called quality control. Students of the "managerial revolution" know that the first drastic change in modern private industry occurred when corporation management became so complex it had to be separated from ownership and handled by managerial experts. In turn, their task became so difficult and absorbing that a "third arm" had to be developed, independent of managerial control: experts charged with discovering malfunctions, identifying neglected opportunities, and watching new developments. In public affairs, posts like the ombudsman or the Council of Economic Advisors play this role.

Most writings on applied sociology begin with the stage where a problem is already articulated. Case studies on problem solutions should include detailed descriptions of how problem-awareness developed. From such material one would be able to judge whether the themes of problem-awareness or quality control can be developed in cognitive or institutional terms.[2]

STEP 2. SETTING UP STAFF

Once a problem is perceived, machinery is set up to conduct the search for a solution. Inside experts and/or outside consultants are mobilized. Committees may be organized. If there is a research department, it may be called upon to assemble the required help. (It may also have sounded the original alarm.) The procedures actually followed will depend mainly upon budgetary and administrative practices. There are however two general problems which are likely to come up at this phase: (a) the substantive merits of interdisciplinarity, and (b) the differences in the traditions of the various groups of experts involved in the utilization process.

a. Strangely enough, there is scarcely any literature on how interdisciplinary collaboration works out in the subsequent phases of the utilization cycle. Within the social sciences much has been written about their theoretical relations and benefits.[3] But again, for their actual operation in a concrete utilization we can refer only to specific examples.

An interesting combination of psychological and sociological variables was attempted by a major life-insurance company. The success of an insurance company depends upon the efficiency of individual salesmen who work independently, using personal contacts and occasional door-to-door selling. Conventional research was directed toward finding the right criteria for the selection of these salesmen; demographic data and personality tests were correlated with sales success. The company appointed an advisory group to review this research. Its sociologist member noticed that salesmen gathered once or twice a week in an office to write their reports and receive informational instructions from a regional supervisor. A study was thereupon inaugurated by Milavsky to determine how these institutional contacts in the regional offices affected the work of the salesmen.[4] "Work" was not defined as the sales record, because this depended too much upon characteristics of the agent's territory. Instead, Milavsky characterized work as intensity of activity—number of visits and revisits, resourcefulness in opening up new channels. He found that these variables were related to the combination of supervisory style and degree of unionization within a local office. Agent activities were strongest in those offices with strong unions and democratic leadership *OR* in those with weak unions and decisive management.

Joint use of sociological and economic data can be found in the activities of a trading-stamp company, analyzed by Pasanella.* The company promoting trading stamps faced two problems. Merchants had to be convinced that stamps were a sufficiently strong promotional device to offset the extra costs and time involved; housewives had to be persuaded that saving stamps made shopping at stores offering stamps worthwhile, despite the competition from food discounters. These needs required a balancing of market analyses with attitude studies. Thus, while retailing experts were helping individual stores to locate their weak points and streamline their operations, sociologists were conceptualizing steps in a stamp-saving process, with leads from interviews with housewives. For example, comments from housewives revealed that one of the danger points in stamp-saving came immediately after the stamp books had been filled and redeemed for merchandise. A kind of "let-down" feeling ensued. The company then directed some of its advertising efforts toward recapturing these savers.

In the above example, it was the user who combined two kinds of data. An actual collaboration of political scientists and sociologists was exemplified by a study done to monitor a change in the governmental structure of New York City.[5] A mayoral directive provided for administrative decentralization of municipal service agencies, and a study was inaugurated to watch the course of the innovation in several experimental districts. Periodical opinion surveys were conducted to gauge the needs, complaints, and satisfactions of the neighborhood population. At the same time, political scientists studied the services rendered by the district agencies and their relation with the central administration. The purpose of the study was to establish the feasibility and priorities of an administrative decentralization program. The difference in research approach between representatives of the two disciplines led to different kinds of findings, which some-

---

*Our Chapter 4 gives more details on this study.

times reinforced one another and sometimes called for additional clarification. Although the qualitative findings of the political scientists or the sociologists' survey results by themselves might have been misleading, taken together they helped to construct a more accurate picture. In one case, the political scientists' interviews found that most community leaders in experimental districts knew about the Administrative Decentralization Program and felt that it facilitated delivery of services in the neighborhood. The sociologists' survey, on the other hand, discovered that few community residents had even heard of the Administrative Decentralization Program, and that the public rating of many neighborhood municipal services actually declined during the two years of the program's operation. In other instances the findings of the sociologists confirmed those of the political scientists. For example, political scientists found that the character and visibility of the experimental program varied from one district to another and was largely contingent upon the personality and style of the program's district manager. These findings were confirmed by survey results comparing districts with different types of district managers.

The interface of architecture and sociology seemed successful in the design of mass housing for a public-housing agency. In a Puerto Rican section of Manhattan, a sociologist observed that the residents used their living space in distinctive ways. Kitchens were social centers for eating, as well as locations for parties and informal social activities. Living rooms were "sacred space," reserved for more formal activities, and contained all the best furniture, pictures of saints, and family memorabilia. It was suggested that kitchens be made larger than specified in the standard plan and that access to the apartment bypass the living room. Because windows were so widely used to observe street activity and to communicate with passersby they should be located appropriately both in living rooms and in kitchens. At the same time, the architects and planners assessed the technical problems raised by specific housing sites, selected a location, proposed particular building materials to meet both social and budgetary requirements. The housing agency accepted the plan and the units were built accordingly.

Interest in interdisciplinary work seems to come and go in waves. At the moment it seems on the upswing, for two reasons. One is intrinsic to scientific work itself. Social scientists have observed how in the natural sciences whole new areas have opened up by combining elements of older disciplines—biochemistry, nuclear astronomy, etc. The hope, not universally shared, is that progress in the social sciences may also come from similar combinations. In a stimulating analysis Norman Storer argued that from an academic point of view, departments, as they have historically developed, perform their functions very well.[7] As a matter of fact, he says that "interdisciplinary research turns out to be useful primarily when a *problem* has been first identified and *then* scientists . . . are brought together to work on it. . . . Even successful collaborations . . . are rarely viable beyond the concrete research problems that initially gave them their start" (emphasis by Storer). The extreme opposite position is represented by a detailed report on a symposium organized by an organization attached to NATO and published under the title *Interdisciplinarity.*[8]

Storer's observation points to a second source of pressure for combination of disciplines which is extrinsic but whose importance should not be underrated: the dissatisfaction of clients and sponsors with the seemingly low utility of the social sciences. Somehow the idea has developed that if one were to use all kinds of social scientists simultaneously, the chances of producing utilizable knowledge would be multiplied.

b. Combining different skills in building a research team to work for a client is not only a matter of content but of the types of resources involved. This becomes especially evident when it comes to combining the traditions of social scientists with those of other groups. The two topics which are most often discussed are the relation to expert laymen and to lawyers.

By "expert laymen" we mean men and women who have had vast experience in a concrete field of action, without necessarily having devoted systematic study to it: police commissioners, managers of foreign assistance, bankers, organizers of unions or social movements, etc. How should their expertise be combined with the more systematic but also more distant knowledge of the sociologist? The most elaborate discussion of this problem can be found in an article on "The Epistemology of the Inexact Sciences," by Helmer and Rescher.[9] For them

> the expert has at his ready disposal a large store of mostly inarticulated background knowledge and a refined sensitivity to its relevance, through the intuitive application of which he is often able to produce *trustworthy personal* probabilities regarding *hypotheses* in his area of experience.

Notice that the contributions of these experts are more than observations. They provide knowledge of regularities and hypotheses about future events which are vague but trustworthy under the circumstances. The article, as the title indicates, links the notion of the expert with rather abstract concepts such as subjective probability and degree of confirmation. Unfortunately no concrete examples are available which would permit us to probe problems like these: When is the opinion of such experts so convincing that no further research seems needed? Does it ever happen that systematic data and reported experience contradict each other, and if so, how is the matter resolved? Can practitioners help interpret surprising statistical findings? Do disagreements among experienced laymen lead to new research ideas?

Several other authors have reflected on this issue. Orlans has stressed that the sociologist should not assume that the client is an empty vessel into which social-science wisdom has to be poured; the combination of "abstract and concrete knowledge" seems to Orlans an important problem.[10] Brewer states that "policy-makers are visceral theorists.[11]"

A concrete example is furnished in a study which Carol Weiss did for our Columbia project.[12] The U.S. Congress had to decide whether or not to extend its college-student-loan program and asked the Office of Education for a study of past experiences. The latter contracted with the College Entrance Examination Board, and the inquiry was finally conducted under the direction of its main financial expert, Mr. John Kirkpatrick. He decided to proceed along two parallel lines. He commissioned a large questionnaire study, mainly directed to financial-aid officers in a large sample of colleges. But he also set up a network of agents in each state who interviewed "lay experts," such as bankers, members of state departments of education, etc. How Kirkpatrick reconciled these two sources of information is analyzed in Carol Weiss's technical report. She concluded that the opinions of the lay experts tended to carry more weight, and that the quantitative survey data on financial-aid officers was used mainly when it reinforced conclusions arrived at in the more informal conversations with bankers and education officials. Incidentally, staff members involved in the survey research were greatly disturbed by the finding; they felt it showed how unscientific the decision-makers were.

The relation between sociologists and lawyers is of great interest because the two groups face each other increasingly in temporary commissions set up by public authorities. As a characteristic example we chose a report of James Short, one of the research directors on the Presidential Commission on Violence.[13] A number of task forces were set up, and each was to be jointly directed by a lawyer and a social scientist. In fact, only three task forces had such dual directors. Two were headed solely by academics and two by lawyers. According to Short, the units with one lawyer as director were "the most smoothly functioning Task Forces." He attributed this to the very different work styles of lawyers and social scientists. The lawyers "were accustomed to the quick gathering and assimilation of concrete facts and their use in advocacy, in contrast to the more deliberative style of research and preference for abstract theoretical formulations of academics." With joint directors, these differences gave rise to conflicts over the selection of topics for investigation and the kind of data sought. Lawyers tended to focus upon topics that lent themselves to fairly immediate recommendations: thus there was no Task Force on War. The lawyers preferred hearings and sworn depositions as data sources, while social scientists worried more about the possible intimidation of antigovernment witnesses and the self-selection of political exhibitionists. The sociologists wanted to include such topics as the community context for violence or the effects of different urban administrative structures, even if it became necessary to rely on less concrete evidence or to undertake new research. A further difficulty was occasioned by the fact that the commissioners to whom the task forces reported often were themselves lawyers and tended to work more easily with those task-force members who were their professional colleagues.

Short's observations would be easily duplicated in many other instances. For one who is concerned with the public-service function of sociology, this raises an important question: Should the graduate education of at least a sector of future sociologists better prepare them to act as agents of utilization?

STEPS 3 AND 4. THE SEARCH FOR KNOWLEDGE AND THE ROAD TO RECOMMENDATION

If one wanted to reduce the cognitive utilization cycle to a bare minimum, one would compress it in the following two arcs:

1. How is a practical problem *translated* into a search for pertinent knowledge?
2. How is the unavoidable gap between knowledge and action *bridged* by additional considerations so that recommendations can be produced to help with the solution to the problem on hand?

Because the "translation" and the "gap" problems are at the core of our discussion, we have reserved a more detailed discussion for the next two chapters.

The present remarks are preparatory to Chapters 4 and 5, and only point up briefly the relation between the two phases. When it comes to deciding what kind of research may be needed, the sociologist will be looking ahead to the time when a decision is needed. Research is planned to minimize the problematic aspect of the subsequent policy decision; translation is made with potential gaps in mind.

But this cannot be the only consideration. In planning a study, the sociologist will be well advised to look around carefully to see what material is already available. There is a general tendency to begin afresh, to conduct a new survey or field study. But with the advent of data banks, it will prove useful to ask first whether a data-retrieval system exists. Experiments are sometimes called for, but they are costly and time-consuming. It is worthwhile to explore substitute methods which might be less exact but sufficient for the immediate purpose. Thus in evaluating the effectiveness of a specific campaign, it might be sufficient to do sophisticated interviews on the reasons why consumers have bought a product under study.[14] Often casual information obtainable in a company can, if properly used, yield important information. Roethlisberger and Dickson's famous study is known mainly for the discovery of the Hawthorne effect. That it contains an important chapter on how to analyze and utilize worker's complaints is generally overlooked.[15] (More of this in Chapter 4.)

Inversely, a study might have been carefully planned without leading to any useful recommendation. Then it will be necessary to draw upon what is sometimes called "personal knowledge" to pinch-hit for information not collected in the translation phase. Ackoff and Rivett give characteristic although possibly apocryphal examples. Tenants in an office building complained that they lost much time in waiting for elevators. Three solutions were considered: adding elevators, installing faster ones, or "banking"—having the existing elevators stop at different floors. The first two were rejected as too expensive; the third did not markedly reduce the waiting time in the lobby. A consulting psychologist turned the problem around. Why did white color workers who were known to waste time in their offices object to waiting a short time? He analyzed the problem in his own mind and ended up with "analysis and advice":

> While tenants were wasting time in their offices they were doing something else which, though unproductive, was pleasant. But while waiting for an elevator they were much like the proverbial bump on a log. He suggested that large mirrors be put on the walls in all elevator lobbies. The mirrors obviously gave the women who were waiting something to do, and the men were occupied by staring at the women without appearing to do so.[16]

No one at the earlier phase thought of studying why people grew impatient.

The closeness of the link between a research plan and the anticipated decision process may be affected by the policy-maker's own situation or outlook. A conservative or defensive client who needs an airtight decision will be inclined to commission research very differently from that commissioned by a client willing or able to take greater risk. But in any case, the recommendation phase will always go beyond the knowledge acquired in the translation phase. These "additional ingredients" are probably the next serious challenges for the cognitive analysis of the utilization process, and Chapter 5 is devoted to a review of what can be said about it at the present moment.

STEP 5. IMPLEMENTATION

Even when a recommendation has been accepted, many difficulties still remain, especially if the "client" is a complex organization. Then it can easily happen that something agreed upon at the center has to be carried out at the periphery—in local government agencies or in factories remote from the business headquarters. The latter case has been studied by economists in terms of information theory and cost analysis. But we have few detailed descriptions of the implementation process as a network between people who are far removed from each other in terms of geography and hierarchal levels. One of the few exceptions is a book by Walter Williams, a former senior social research analyst for several Federal agencies.[17] Williams feels that the implementation process has gotten too little attention from social scientists and discusses in great detail the complexity of converting fairly abstract social-policy concepts into meaningful field-operational terms. According to Williams, five difficulties must be overcome:

1. Recommendations are made to the top-level decision-makers; the language used for this purpose is quite different from the implementation prose suitable for use in the program offices.
2. The central agency is often not aware that an action recommended might require considerable changes in the local agencies.
3. This difficulty becomes especially acute if the action required from the local agency calls for "the flexibility to change or replace local personnel."
4. Most implementation requires traveling staff which mediate between the central agency and the people on the operating level.

The training of this traveling staff for downward communication and upward feedback is often quite inadequate.

5. A field agency can be under local political pressures of which the headquarters is not aware. After having gained acceptance of a recommendation by central political powers, political blockages at the local level could defy ultimate action.

Rather than repeat his example, we can illustrate the problems with a large-scale educational program—the so-called "Follow Through" project. It consists of 22 models for elementary instruction, each of which were developed at an educational research center and then tried out in a number of local schools. Helen Maccoby has given an overview of all the programs.[18] We are fairly well acquainted with the one emanating from the Pittsburgh Learning Research and Development Center (LRDC) and will illustrate Williams's points from their experiences.

1. The LRDC instructional program is very much influenced by the theory of behavior conditioning. It was funded on the basis of important theoretical work by its director, Robert Glaser. Obviously, the original terminology had to be translated to make the program operational for teachers. Workshops in Pittsburgh and at the seven application sites were held, but at this moment it is not clear how successful they were. The participation of the local schoolboards might be partly reinforced by collateral advantages of available federal funds.
2. Clearly the program requires considerable changes in local teaching practices. On this point careful classroom observations have been made. The practices vary and their effect on the progress of pupils is known.
3. In the local communities a new position, that of the educational specialist, was created. Many are teachers who have studied the new program carefully and now act as advisers to their former colleagues. From preliminary detailed interviews with this new type of personnel it is not yet clear whether they really live up to their new task and have avoided friction with fellow teachers.
4. LRDC has indeed a special consultant for each of the seven sites who commutes between the center and his district. The job is strenuous and requires relatively frequent changes in personnel; there is probably not enough regular interchange of experience between the seven consultants. Nor is the feedback function fully worked

out. They report back to the administrator of the whole Follow Through project, but it would be equally important for them to inform the psychologists back at the Center who work on the development of new teaching techniques. It appears that the group of developers think of themselves as basic scientists and are not too interested in listening to field reports.

5. There are some problems which might be called political. The local board of education has decided to participate in the program for reasons which are not convincing to the school principal. The relations between teachers who teach the new way and those who teach along the old line can lead to stress. Part of the follow-through money goes to the organization of parent support—they can act as teachers' helpers and take special instructions of how to support the homework of their children. Such parent organizations can take an unexpected turn in their activities.

The files of the Pittsburgh LRDC office as well as of the local sites are full of interesting material which would permit us to elucidate the history of this implementation phase. A study of these documents, supplemented by detailed interviews with as many participants as possible, is now in preparation.

The LRDC case is relatively simple; the articulation between the parts of the implementation process is provided by the organization of the personnel involved. In other cases implementation studies have to begin on an even more fundamental level. What are the crucial turning points to which research should pay special attention? This turning-point problem can be examplified by still another project now being carried out by the Vera Institute for Criminal Justice.[19] The Institute has started an elaborate demonstration project intended to relieve the overcrowding of jails. The specific problem is that within a few hours after being arrested, the defendant comes before a judge who can make one of three decisions: he can put him in jail to await trial; he can release him on his own recognizance (ROR) until trial; or he can set bail. The Vera Institute realized that the overcrowding of detention facilities could be reduced by increasing the number of RORs. An experimental project was set up which boiled down to a group of Vera agents taking the responsibility for seeing that released defendants appeared at the final trial. The project's criterion of success is whether the proportion of "missing" defendants diminishes.

To implement this plan it was important to investigate the various steps between arrest and final court appearance. Directly after the arrest, Vera interviewers obtain background information on the defendant on which they base their recommendation to the judge who makes the first decision. The recommendation is derived from a point system based on the personal history—whether the defendant has a permanent address, the nature of his job, etc. What is the correlation between this point system and the final appearance? What confidence have the judges in accepting the Vera recommendations? What accounts for this confidence, and how could it be improved?

When a man is released under the responsibility of the Vera Institute, he is informed that he has to stay in periodic contact with their office. How well does a defendant understand these instructions? How difficult is it for him to stay in touch? In some cases a local philanthropic organization is asked to act as an intermediary. Does this increase the number of contacts?

If a defendant does not maintain communication with the Vera group, one of their regional representatives makes a visit to his address. How often is the address fictitious? How often can a defendant not be located? If the local representative finds the defendant, what is the explanation for his failure to keep contact: misunderstanding; negligence; the hope of being forgotten? How often and under what circumstances is contact reestablished by the visit of the neighborhood representative?

The Vera project today covers only one borough of New York City. The general plan is for the city to take it over and extend it to the other four boroughs if it turns out to be successful. But success is not just a matter of final outcomes. If one wants to improve a procedure, one has to know and understand the crucial points along the way at which upgrading is both necessary and possible. To this end, a mixed staff is needed; computer experts who provide rapid statistical information; observers and interviewers attached to the cycle through which the released defendants move; and sophisticated contact persons who can talk with the judges and relay suggestions to the project staff.

In the two previous examples, the central organization was equipped to study and improve the implementation phase. The whole problem becomes even more acute when there is no provision for implementation. The best example again comes from Presidential commissions whose work ends with a report to the President or to Congress. The report of the Commission on Student Unrest contains recommendations to only vaguely defined "policy-makers": "the police," "university administrators," even "the public." The complaints of social scientists who have worked hard on a commission's research, have even won its acceptance for their ideas, and then seen their work go for naught because nothing happened as a result of their report are endless. One rare exception is represented by the Crime Commission.[20]

The Commission was aware that the most of its recommendations would have to be implemented by state and local governments. To lay the groundwork for this, it made three major efforts. First, it funded state planning committees to review local crime and delinquency problems to consider the relevance of its recommendations for local application. Representatives of these and other state organizations met at a Commission-sponsored national conference to stimulate plans for the reform of state criminal systems. Second, the Commission's reports were mailed to all members of Congress and the state legislatures, to police, correctional agencies, and courts throughout the country, as well as to members of related professional and academic groups. And finally, staff members participated in the development of the "Safe Streets Act of 1968," which created a new agency in the Department of Justice charged with funding and monitoring needed Federal, state, and local innovations in law-enforcement and criminal-justice programs. The Commission's success in fostering implementation should serve to stimulate similar efforts in parallel situations.

STEP 6. ASSESSMENT

Once a recommendation has been made and accepted, and after it has been implemented administratively, the question arises whether the whole process of utilization worked well.

Step 1: In retrospect it might turn out that the problem was conceived too simply. Suppose the problem were how a campaign budget should be divided between television and newspapers. Subsequently one might have suspected that what really affects people most in their voting intentions are personal influences. The problem would then have shifted to who influences whom and how can the individuals be reached. (It is probably now well known that this crudely summarizes a real episode in the history of research on political campaigns.[21])

Step 2: In setting up a research machinery it might turn out that certain skills were overlooked. The problem of rate-setting in public utilities has traditionally been handled by economists and accountants. At one point AT&T wondered whether sociological problems were not also involved and called a meeting of sociologists to discuss this matter. While it was financially not possible to set up a suggested internal council of social advisers, the meeting itself brought up new ideas which are available in mimeographed form from the Bureau of Applied Social Research.

Step 3: We have already mentioned that the translation of a practical into a research problem can take very many forms. While the participants might be aware of substantive alternative possibilities, they are more likely to overlook hidden prejudices.

Step 4: The rational reconstruction of the bases for recommendations is undoubtedly the most difficult task for one who tries to analyze the utilization process. This is also the point where in the assessment phase we are most likely to find oversight or mistakes in judgment. No single example can do justice to the complexity of the problems involved; the reader might do very well to scrutinize all the cases reported in Chapter 5 and ask himself whether he would have made different recommendations.

Step 5: We have mentioned that the typical issue in the implementation phase is the relation between center and periphery. In turn the problem of feedback is crucial, but probably more complicated than it sounds. It is not always quite clear to whom in an organization local difficulties are most profitably reported. Thus in the Follow-Through example discussed before, there were two possible addressees: the director of the field staff and the educational developers who worked on new instructional material. Only during the assessment phase was it noticed that the communication between these two separate divisions had shortcomings which the over-all direction had failed to notice.

It is often said that hindsight is easy, but we think not. We believe that assessment must be built into the process at each phase.

There is one general rule which can make this assessment function more productive: it cannot be done if no machinery is devised to make all the phases of the utilization process available for retrospective review.

This is a hortative rule, and therefore the testimony of experienced researchers is very pertinent. Rosenfeld, who has reviewed the utilization of research in the drug field, stresses the importance of keeping records of everything that happened.

> Specifically in the field of social action, failures point to the need for re-examining the premises of action more carefully and often *pinpoint an important but overlooked condition in the situation.* It is clearly our duty to explain this to heads of agencies and their financial backers and convince them that by *keeping adequate records and periodically analyzing their mistakes and failures,* they will provide a most enlightened and forward-looking attitude which will reflect most favorably on their management of their agencies.[22]

Miller, in a paper on urban reform, makes the same point, but refines it in one respect. There is a tendency to overlook alternative possibilities which were considered during the utilization process but discarded. It would be very important to keep rather detailed information on these stillborn ideas, and the reasons why they were not acted upon.[23]

The relation between conventional evaluation studies and what we here call assessment deserves some further comment. In recent years the techniques of evaluation have been discussed partly because it is increasingly required by law and partly because an increasing number of the necessary studies are being done by commercial agencies. Assessment is a much broader concept than conventional evaluation, but there exist at least two relations between them. If simple statistical evaluation study shows the lack of consistent success of a planned action, then assessment as conceived here is needed to find out at what point of the utilization process it went wrong; even if an evaluation study shows positive effects, a more detailed assessment would be productive if it clarifies the reasons for the success.

But minor formal evaluation might well have a place within a broader assessment effort. Take as an example the pretrial experiment mentioned above. On the one hand, it tries to provide a better prediction system to single out good release risks; on the other hand, the continuing contact between the agency and the released defendants is monitored in order to improve its operation.

This second part is more extensive than the first because it requires the evaluation of the relative contribution of each step to the final appearance of the released man in court. An outstanding effort of what he called "formative evaluation" has been made by Sam Sieber.[24] The Office of Education experimented with the idea of educational county agents, similar to the regional agents of the Department of Agriculture. Sieber and his colleagues organized the staff which concurrently recorded the activities of these agents. But while these observations went on, the researchers extracted from the field agents' reports suggestions for improvements which they transmitted to the county agents. In Appendix J to their extensive study, the researchers discuss the advantages and disadvantages of this procedure.

The steps described in the present chapter are very much related to each other. The way a practical problem is translated into research will obviously affect the kind of recommendations made; a study of the implementation process can show that the original problem was not well perceived. Finally, one should keep in mind that the whole cycle described here could be entered at various points. The problem might be so clearcut that only the kind of skills needed and discussed in Step 2 would require review. Inversely, the whole cycle might well have been taken for granted, but in the assessment phase new topics could become visible. This would require starting the whole cycle again, with a more refined problem in mind.

NOTES

1 R. Ritchie, *An Institute for Public Policy Research* (Ottawa: Queens Printer, 1970).

2 Armand Feigenbaum, *Total Quality Control* (New York: McGraw Hill, 1961).

3 Neil J. Smelser, "Sociology and the Other Social Sciences," in *The Uses of Sociology,* P. F. Lazarsfeld, W. Sewell, and H. Wilensky (eds.), (New York: Basic Books, 1967).

4 Ronald Milavsky (Ph.D. dissertation, Columbia University, 1967).

5 N. Friedman and T. F. Rogers "Administrative Decentralization and the Public" (New York: Bureau of Applied Social Research, December, 1974; mimeographed).

6 John Zeisel, "Symbolic Meaning of Space and Physical Dimension of Social Relationships," in J. Walton and D. Cairns (eds.), *Cities in Change: Studies on the Urban Condition* (Boston: Allyn and Bacon, 1973), pp. 252–63.

7 Norman W. Storer, "Relations Among Scientific Disciplines," in S. Z. Nagi and R. Corwin (eds.), *The Social Context of Research* (New York: Wiley-Interscience, 1972).

8 *Interdisciplinarity—Problems of Teaching and Research in Universities* (Paris: Centre for Educational Research and Innovation, 1972).

9 Olaf Helmer and Nicholas Rescher, "The Epistemology of the Inexact Sciences," *Management Science,* VI (October, 1959), 25–52.

10 Harold Orlans, *Contracting for Knowledge* (San Francisco: Jossey-Bass, 1973), pp. 192–204.

11 Garry D. Brewer, *Politicians, Bureaucrats and the Consultant* (New York: Basic Books, 1973), p. 235.

12 Carol Weiss, *The Consequences of the Study of Federal Student Loan Programs* (New York: Bureau of Applied Social Research, 1970).

13 Report by James Short to the ASA Convention, 1973.
14 Charles Kadushin, "Reason Analysis" in D. Sills (ed.), *International Encyclopedia of the Social Sciences.* New York: Crowell-Collier and Macmillan, 1968).
15 F. J. Roethlisberger and William J. Dickson, "Management and the Worker" (Cambridge, Mass.: Harvard University Press, 1943, chapt. 12).
16 Russell Ackoff and Patrick Rivett, *A Manager's Guide to Open Research* (New York: John Wiley and Sons, 1963), pp. 20–21.
17 Walter Williams, *Social Policy Research and Analysis* (New York: Elsevier Publishing Company, 1971.)
18 Helen Maccoby and M. Zillner, *Experiments in Primary Education* (New York: Harcourt, Brace & World, 1970).
19 Paul F. Lazarsfeld, "An Evaluation of the Pretrial Services Agency of the Vera Institute for Criminal Justice," 1974; mimeographed.
20 Report by Lloyd E. Ohlin to the ASA Convention, 1973.
21 E. Katz and Paul F. Lazarsfeld, *Personal Influence* (New York: The Free Press, 1954).
22 E. Rosenfeld, "Social Research and Social Action in Prevention of Juvenile Delinquency," in A. Gouldner and S. M. Miller (eds.), *Applied Sociology* (New York: The Free Press, 1965).
23 Miller, "Research on the Inner City," *ibid,* pp. 460–68.
24 Sam Sieber, Karen Louis, and Loya Metzger, *The Use of Educational Knowledge,* Vol. 2, Appendix J. "Formative Evaluation" (New York: Bureau of Applied Social Research, 1972).

FOUR

Translating a Practical Problem into Research (Step 3)

We have spoken of the "professional" and the "client"; this implies that not only are distinct types of problems brought to this professional, but that he has the special knowledge and techniques to cope with them. Perhaps our terminology is overly positive. Doctors, lawyers, and social workers attend professional schools and are thus recognized as professionals; but where are the schools of applied social science? What in fact are the particular problems that the social scientist is equipped to handle?

If we do not want to write a textbook of sociology, we must begin with an examination of the sorts of practical problems the sociologist is asked to solve. Immediately, one is overwhelmed by the variety of locus, specific content, temporal orientation, audience, and duration. The problem may be inside the client organization (employee dissatisfaction, retirement policy) or outside of it (marketing, planning for organizational expansion); it may have to do with past performance (evaluation of a community action program), current troubles (a threatened strike), or planning for the future (state educational needs); it may involve the interest of the client (a public utility), the interests of a "constituency" (patient-care in a hospital) or some combination of the two (juvenile delinquency); it may be a matter of encouraging activities (use of health facilities) or forestalling them (racial conflict); it may be a problem requiring almost immediate attention (preparation of a legal brief), or one involving long-term goals (general review of the criminal-justice system); there may be a great deal of relevant research already available (employee morale) or there may be little or none (school-bond-issue support).

We are dealing in this text with a middle-range of practical problems where the translation into social research is neither completely trivial nor so complex that the idea of translation loses its meaning. Thus, at one extreme, we have the search for precise factual information. If the surgeon general wants to know how many high-school graduates began smoking in 1974, we know pretty well what the task is. Although we must still solve the technical problems of sampling or of defining what "smoking" is, or of ascertaining the accuracy of the data, there is no real debate about how to "translate" the practical problem into a research design.

At the other extreme, the same health officer might want help in attacking the drug problem among juveniles. It would be meaningless to talk here of translating a practical problem into one research design. We have to move into greater specificity before we embark upon any translating. Would stricter legislation reduce drug use? What kind of rehabilitation programs have proved successful? Different "translations" would be required for each of the subissues identified.

Even with such a restriction in the range of practical problems to be covered, we still have little material with which to work. The reason is that although available publications tell about the policy problem to be dealt with and the study actually done, alternative considerations and discarded possibilities are rarely reported. Consequently, we must give this chapter a rather tentative character. We shall begin with a detailed discussion of three specific examples. Then we shall turn to some general topics which are likely to come up wherever a "translation" in our sense is needed.

Our examples were selected to cover three very different situations. For the first, we decided to describe the main features of a research program serving a single organization. We had access to the files of a business organization—a company marketing trading stamps. They had done about 150 studies, and one of our associates (Ann Pasanella) reviewed the kind of work done.[1] This case will afford a brief overview of the research activities of a frankly commercial agency. The content of these reports has been studied in considerable detail, and the analysis has contributed to our next chapter, which deals with recommendations. The file review led to some categories which should prove useful as similar collections are complied.

Our second illustration describes the decision-processes of an individual scholar charged with a major study of great social significance. James Coleman was the director of the study on Equality of Educational Opportunity requested by the U.S. Congress. In one paper[2] he describes in detail how a rather vague mandate was converted into a concrete study (which, incidentally, later became the object of very intensive discussion[3]). He thinks, as we do, of utilization as a process in which a crucial phase is "translation," and most of the time he uses the term in the same sense as we do.

In the middle, between these two cases, stands the third. Here we have neither an outsider reviewing a research file nor an author explaining his own experience. Levinson has consolidated the work of a specific group of applied sociologists—we might call them organizational therapists—into a guide on how to proceed with organizational consulting. This book, entitled *Organizational Diagnosis*,[4] comes nearest to our own idea of a textbook, although it takes some effort to relate the idea of "diagnosis" to our own imagery of utilization process.

THREE EXAMPLES

Example 1. A Documentary Analysis of a Research Program

The site of our documentary analysis was a trading stamp company. This company provides trading stamps to retailers, issues a catalog of items offered for redemption, and runs the redemption centers. The trading stamps are used as promotional devices by the stores that offer them. One of their purposes is to attract new customers; another, to win the loyalty of a store's old customers; and a third, to increase the actual size of each purchase. Over the years, stamps have proved to be very effective in these respects, and stamps can now be found at supermarkets, drug stores, gas stations, and hardware stores though supermarkets remain the heaviest users of all. The retailer usually issues one stamp for every ten cents spent, the customer collects the stamps in savings books, which can then be exchanged for the merchandise of his choice. The catalog of merchandise offered to the stamp-saver specifies the number of books required for each listed item.

The trading stamp business was a profitable one until the sixties, when food prices began to rise. Whatever the "true" reasons, the public attributed the soaring prices to inordinate profits by the supermarkets. Given this increasing sensitivity to price, stamps became a target of consumer opposition. Although many women were convinced that stamps raised prices, they still thought them worth it. Now they grew less certain. Some of the supermarkets lowered prices; others announced that they were dropping stamps or games or other promotions in order to save the housewife money. As the consumer movement gained momentum, the stamp industry had to come to its own defense. Not only were consumer boycotts a threat to stamps, but there were efforts to end stamps through legal action.

The research office of the company under our scrutiny actually was set up during the stormy days of the stamp hearings. A research director appointed at that time appeared at many of these hearings. It was the company executives' feeling that the scholarly bearing of the director, a former professor, lent credibility and authority to the company lawyers' claims about the stamp operation. Indeed, as the judicial onslaughts subsided the director extended the research program into many social science areas. By the early seventies, a sizable collection of studies had become available for review.

One way of classifying the research assignments was in terms of the intended targets. There were three of them: the housewife; the retailer; and the legislator. From the housewife came detailed information about reasons for stamp-saving, and stamp-dropping; attitudes toward this company and its competitors; responses to various advertising themes; reactions to such new forms of shopping as food discount houses. From the retailer came parallel information about shopper reactions as well as retailing methods—how merchandise was arranged, how the stamps were made visible in the store, how a store operated in regard to its competitors, etc. In fact, much of this information was eventually fed back to the retailers with suggestions for improved functioning, for economies in operations, for exploiting the features of stamps, for pricing policies, etc. The housewife, however, did not receive the research results; rather, it was the company's aim to use this data in order to attract new stamp-savers and retain its following among existing ones in the light of competition from other stamp companies.

The third audience was the legislator, the watchdog, or the consumer group. Here, research on pricing policies, on the dynamics of competition, on comparisons between stamps and advertising and games, all were meant to argue that stamps were a promotional device like any other. As we have noted previously, the research director testified at national hearings on food retailing and at special hearings before state legislatures. For the most part, he built his own case around the inevitable consequences of a competitive marketplace—the variety of ways by which stores sought to outreach their competitors. He frequently alluded to research findings in his testimony.

Of the 150 studies in the file, 43 reported on housewives' attitudes and stamp-saving, 92 dealt with retailing problems, and 7 were specifically prepared for legislative hearings. The remaining 8 were mixtures of two or more approaches. These numbers can be misleading were one to make a direct analogy to the perceived intensity of company problems. For example, most of the studies with the legislator as target built upon the accumulated knowledge of previous research into the effects of stamps on shopping patterns or on prices,* and the absolute number does not adequately reflect the amount of organizational energy behind the work.

Still another way of looking at the research assignments is in terms of its time orientation. One choice is to look *backward*, to evaluate the outcomes of particular policies or experiments in marketing techniques. For example, did a mail order system for delivering merchandise to the stamp-redeemer prove popular? (No.) Did customers like stamps directly affixed to products? (Yes.) Such evaluations were not in strict cost-benefit terms. Rather, they sought to assess the ease of entry to a new market or the tone of housewives' reactions to new marketing methods.

Studies of the *present* dealt largely with consumer attitudes toward stamps and with ongoing analyses of the company's position in the marketplace as contrasted with its competitors. Here the idea is to take soundings with two aims in mind: Is everything functioning normally, stably? (Do shoppers still regard stamps as a worthwhile attraction?) Or, are there signs of impending danger, of malfunctions? (Do consumers have less favorable attitudes toward stamps than they did a year earlier?) The real problem with such research is how to decide when a dangerous situation threatens —in other words, how to identify a problem as it is crystallizing. How much of a drop in favorable attitudes is a meaningful loss? How many boycotts make a consumer movement? It takes great skill and experience to judge.

Studies of the *future* are even more perplexing in this regard. A few of the studies at this company have a distinctly futuristic aspect. They seek to conceptualize broad changes in retailing methods, in the distribution of population, in American values themselves. But for the most part, these are reports on what would happen *if* the company entered the credit-card field or tried to interest the farm-supplies industry in stamps, etc. Some of these studies were based on field tryouts with an extrapolation to a wider or different market, such as another part of the country, a different age group, etc. Others were more in the nature of speculative papers integrating some investigations already carried out. How can one counter the growing practice of food discounting? Would it be preferable to invest in better training for salesmen *or* in more intensive advertising

---

*That the effects of stamps on retail prices is not easy to disentangle can be seen from an in-house review of 22 studies in the public domain. Five identified increases in prices due to stamps; four found decreases; two found short-lived decreases after stamps were dropped; the other ten studied generally found no differences between stores distributing stamps and those that did not.

of stamps themselves? All of these were questions about future activities to which research was expected to provide some answers.

When the 150 reports are arranged as to time focus, they take the following shape: 35 studies review past performance, 25 refer to the more distant future, and the rest (59 percent) deal with current problems. Though the *present* appears to receive greatest emphasis, the real function of all these studies is to improve the operations of the company in terms of future policies and programs. Unlike many evaluation programs for large-scale research, timetables and methods are geared to specific needs. They look at some innovation in marketing and are expected to contribute to a decision. (Whether they in fact do, and exactly *how* they do, would have to be the subject of detailed study.)

A classification of research output by target or temporal orientation (or other possible aspects) reflects the outcome of the translation process, a process that may be examined at more than one level. In a sense, each individual study grew out of a dialogue between researcher and company executive and was designed to address some specific problem as it had been delineated. This interchange, which took place 150 times, would have to be carefully reconstructed to assess properly the translation phase of the cognitive cycle. Such a reconstruction could also clarify a second aspect. To what extent does each study respond only to a specific problem, in isolation from other related problems? How should a research program be coordinated? We have described the stamp company's research program as a response to an antistamp movement. Each study may be viewed in terms of how it fits into this broader context. It has been mentioned that studies of housewives bear upon retailing strategies, that studies of both housewives and retailers are useful in dealing with legislators, and that studies of past performance are used to plan for the future. Research programs, as exemplified as well by the specialized applied research institutes and by government agencies and commissions of inquiry, are usually analyzed in terms of their administrative aspect, and the cognitive integration of such programs deserves more attention than it has received.

Example 2. The Report of a Research Director

The 1964 Civil Rights Act passed by Congress mandated a study of the availability of equal educational opportunity, to be conducted by the Commissioner of Education. The Act called for a survey

> concerning the lack of availability of equal educational opportunities for individuals by reason of race, color, religion, or national origin in public educational

institutions at all levels in the United States, its territories and possessions, and the District of Columbia.

The study was finally entrusted to a group of researchers headed by James Coleman, then Professor of Social Relations at Johns Hopkins University. The publication of the results in 1966 evoked a large body of literature consisting of debates and re-analyses of the original data. Only *The American Soldier* has occupied a similar place in the history of American empirical research.

In 1972, Coleman himself reviewed his experience under the aspect of utilization. He begins by drawing the distinction between policy research and discipline research which we discussed in Chapter 1, and he ends with the question of whether universities are equipped to do policy research. His development of ten "principles governing policy research" forms the core of his paper. Some of his principles are of a technical nature: the importance of timing in policy research; the desirability of making partial research results available to the client at various points of the work; and so on (principles 1, 2, 4, 6). Two other principles urge the researcher to keep in mind that the client must ultimately accept his recommendations (principles 8 and 9). It is in principle 5 (p. 6) that he brings up that which he and our own text call "translation." Here is his wording: "For policy research, the research problem enters from outside any academic discipline and *must be carefully translated* from the real world of policy or the conceptual world of a client without loss of meaning" (Emphasis ours.)

Before discussing the wording of this principle, let us see what is covered by the six large columns devoted to it.* Coleman first distinguishes two types of situations: those in which the policy issue does point directly to the research problem and those in which it does not. As an example of the latter, he brings forth the school-voucher experiment organized by the Office of Economic Opportunity, where parents receive money which they can use for the education of their children in any way they choose. It would of course be absurd to judge this plan simply on the basis of a possible improvement in the reading ability of pupils because their parents feel more involved in their scholastic achievement. The voucher scheme can have far-reaching implications for the structure of the whole school system, for the supply of teachers, for the degree of segregation. (In a later part of his paper, pp. 16 and 17, Coleman takes this point up

*The essay is a "module" printed on large pages in two columns.

again and discusses in detail 14 possible consequences of the voucher plan.) Obviously one study cannot cover all these contingencies, and so it becomes important to estimate which aspects would be most important to the sponsor.

It is at this point that Coleman turns to his own work on the equal-opportunity assignment. He tells how he tried to discover the intent of Congress and the interests of various groups suffering from inequality. A review of the statements by members of Congress indicated that different Congressmen meant very different things by equal educational opportunity. Consultation with members of interest groups (civil rights, religious and ethnic interest groups, as, for example, Puerto Ricans) "gave no narrowing of the range of items that were meant by the term."

Coleman finally extracted five ways in which the notion of "equal opportunity" could be understood and therefore studied. Three of these translations were rather conventional variations on a theme which the author called "input." One can compare schools attended by students of different racial, ethnic and religious groups according to certain criteria which supposedly affect their educational efficacy. Moving from the more tangible to the more complex, these criteria were as follows:

> Resources provided by the community (per pupil expenditure, school plans, libraries, equality of teachers, etc.).
>
> Degree of racial integration in the schools (following the 1954 Supreme Court decision that racial segregation in the schools is inherently unequal).
>
> Social climates in the school (teacher morale, teachers' expectations of students, level of interest of the student body in learning, and so on).

Each could be measured to provide guidelines for efforts to reduce inequalities between disadvantaged groups, and Coleman actually covered them by his study. But he extended the notion of inequality far beyond these. Instead of asking only whether different groups are given the same setting in which to learn, he raised the question of *whether as a result of their schooling they had the same opportunity to succeed in life.* This latter variable was measured by the pupils' test scores, which Coleman called the "output" criterion of equal opportunity.* The main and much-de-

---

*If one thinks of life as a sequence of phases, then in general the "outcome" of a previous one contributes positively or negatively to the "opportunities" of the next phase. Actually, Coleman used two output criteria; but the distinction is difficult to explain and not important for the present discussion.

bated finding of the study was that black children ended up with much poorer test scores than white children even when working under comparable school conditions; the "input," surprisingly enough, made little difference.

We are not concerned with the interpretation of this finding. The essential point is this: translation in the sense of our Step 3 is not simply an intellectual problem. It requires knowledge of the sponsor's intent, and this is in itself a research problem for at least two reasons. For one, the sponsor might be a set of organizations or institutions with differing attitudes among its components; and secondly, the study might have unexpected effects on outside groups who might in the long run create severe difficulties for the sponsor. (We shall come back to this point in the next chapter.) Coleman did not simply try to average out a variety of instructions and viewpoints. Quite to the contrary, it was he who finally decided that output measures were the best translation of the "real" inequality problem. Both inquiry with the client *and* decision by the researcher are equally necessary. And sometimes the best result may be to "raise questions where none had been before" by "shifting policy attention from its traditional focus on comparison of input to a focus on output"—a focus which, according to the author, would affect all future work surrounding the notion of opportunity.

There is one marked omission in Coleman's story: He does not say what consideration made him choose his main criterion. A punster might say that Coleman omits the input of his decision. But more seriously, we notice that the cognitive aspect of the translation step is not really discussed. By briefly reviewing the rest of his paper, this will turn out to be a deliberate omission.

We start by going back to the wording of principle 5 quoted above. Research done with utilization in mind "enters from outside"; this is of course tantamount to "field-induced" research as defined in the introduction to the *Uses of Sociology*. But the term "world" of policy or of a client is not casually added. It plays a major role in the essay and deserves some discussion.

Coleman evokes the imagery of two worlds: the world of action and the world of academic disciplines. Each has its own norms and its own conceptualization. The problem of utilization of social research consists of moving from the first world into the second and then back again into the first. These worlds are characterized by their values and norms. As a result, the "principles of policy research" turn out to be rules for how these values could be coordinated without the academic world losing its integrity. The best example is principle 7, which deals with "transmission"—

a very good term for what in our schema we call the road to recommendation.* Here is the author's wording:

> The canons of scientific method and the values implied by these canons govern the *execution* of policy research. Values from the world of action govern the *formulation* of policy research problems. The transmission of policy research results back into the world of action may be governed by either set of values, depending on conditions.

The term value or its equivalents appers five times in this one statement, and many more times in the remaining principles. There seem to be two reasons for this emphasis. One is strategy: Coleman wants to make "policy research" interesting and acceptable to his colleagues, and he feels that above all, irrational resistance and misunderstandings have to be overcome. But he probably also is convinced that "norms" are the proper topics for a sociologist. We have of course no quarrel with his fine contribution, but our emphasis is different: we are concerned with the *cognitive* reconstruction of translation and transmission processes.

It is precisely this cognitive task which our book considers the core of a future theory of utilization and which has been badly neglected by the large majority of early authors. This chapter and the next one will try to clarify the meaning of this cognitive component.

Example 3: A Textbook on Organizational Therapy

Applied organizational analysis has become a major enterprise, and a great many commercial firms now are engaged in this activity. So far, there is little consensus on how to go about solving an organization's problems; each research firm may have a different strategy, depending upon the intellectual or ideological background of its researchers. In this context, a recent major effort by Levinson to spell out his own approach in the form of a textbook, entitled *Organizational Diagnosis,* is of considerable interest.

In its preface, Levinson describes his own background and how he arrived at his research strategy. He began in 1954 with a survey of mental health problems in industry, and then organized a Division of Industrial Mental Health at the Menninger Foundation in Topeka, Kansas, a major American center for psychoanalytic training. His initial fields of interest

---

*The paper consistently uses the term "transmission" in the sense of a counterpart to "translation;" only twice does Coleman talk of two "translations back and forth," which we assume to be a verbal lapse.

were industrial accidents, alcoholism, and absenteeism as symptoms of psychological problems. But in time he decided that to solve these problems, one had to understand the organizational context in which they occurred. In the setting in which he worked at the Menninger Foundation, this was certainly a novel idea, but Levinson says he found little help from others there or from financial analysts or market consultants in deciding how to analyze organizations to solve their problems. And in line with our own thinking, he felt that organizational theory did not readily lead to an applied strategy (p. 5). He therefore decided that the general strategy (though of course not the content) of the psychiatric examination could be used to "diagnose" organizational problems. A detailed outline of the psychiatric examination was available in Karl Menninger's *A Manual for Psychiatric Case Study*. Levinson simply borrowed it and adaptated it to the analysis of organizations, developing its use over many years of teaching in the business schools at M.I.T., Harvard, and the University of Kansas.

There are four major sections to Levinson's schema. The first two cover what Levinson calls factual data:

1. Genetic Data (organizational background and history)
2. Description and Analysis of Current Organization as a Whole (organizational structure and operation)
3. Interpretative Data
4. Analyses and Conclusions

The psychiatric tradition is evident here in at least one formal aspect: the client's statement of the problem is entered under the heading "IB, Historical Data." Problems as described by all key persons in the organization are recorded, but they have little impact on the cognitive structure of the subsequent inquiry. They are treated as symptoms and are not to be taken at face value. It is traditional in psychiatry to view the patient as not understanding his "real" problem, otherwise he would not be seeking help. We have already seen that this view of the client is also becoming traditional in the literature on applied sociology: the problem as stated by the client always should be regarded as tentative.

Section III is really the core of the outline. In effect, it is a checklist of organizational woes or problem areas that the researcher should try to assess. This section of the outline contains 169 subheadings. Each item is illustrated with quotations from case studies and business periodicals. Obviously there is not enough space here to mention them all, but the following sector gives the general idea:

IIIA. *Current Organizational Functioning*

1. *Organizational Perceptions*
   Example: "The consultant will have to judge how accurately and with what understanding management is listening to its personnel" (p. 174).
2. *Organizational Knowledge*
   Example: "What body of information does the organization possess upon which and with which it can act? Such a body of information is usually transmissible in the form of techniques, history, experience, specialized competence, research data, and project reports. How an organization acquires and makes use of knowledge is an indication of its adaptability (p. 195)."
3. *Organizational Language*
   Example: "The consultant will want to be alert to elucidating, enunciating, and clarifying advertising themes sufficiently to be able to differentiate between illusion and reality because the greater the gap, the more the intraorganizational difficulty (p. 226)."
4. *Emotional Atmosphere of the Organization*
   Example: "What is the level of intensity of emotion the organization? . . . How strongly, how much, in what direction, under what circumstances, and for what duration, can the people within the organization express the range of their feelings? These factors may be difficult to judge. Perhaps the best subjective yardstick for the consultant is the question, "How appropriate is this expression of feeling?" (p. 234).
5. *Organizational Action*
   Example: "What is the pace of the organization? With what degree of enthusiasm or lethargy does it pursue new products, different markets, innovative technology? How aggressive is it in its competitive efforts? In speaking of the degree of 'vigor' of an organization, the consultant will be making a value judgment. Implicitly or overtly he will be comparing this organization to another, in the same or in a different field (pp. 240–241)."

We give only one quotation taken from Levinson's discussion for each subheading, just to convey the flavor of the topics: Does management understand the point of view of its employees? Does management keep up with new ideas in its field?, and so on.

Whether Levinson's list of organizational disorders is truly exhaustive need not concern us here; we are interested in exploring the logic of the basic approach. Clearly Levinson has made a real effort to cover all possible sources of organizational malfunctioning. Such a list is useful as a reference point for the applied researcher (and indispensable for the student, to whom Levinson's text is directed). It serves to dramatize the translation problem, because it shows how hopeless would be the task of investigating all possible problems. Levinson emphasizes the exercise of "judgment" by the social scientist in selecting items from the list.

Levinson suggests specific procedures for preparing a comprehensive case study of the total organization. The case description will involve six steps:

1. A breakdown of the organization to be studied into its component parts.
2. The planning of a sample of interviews to be representative of those parts of the organization as a whole, including careful attention to leadership.
3. A supplementary sample of people to be questioned by printed form.
4. Observation of people at work.
5. An examination of already available records and relevant data (such as financial reports, annual reports, personnel statistics, and previous consultants' reports).
6. Interviews with important persons outside the organization (such as competitors, suppliers, cooperating organizations, professional associations).

As these steps are carried out, the researcher must decide what should be the focus of the investigation. One operating principle does emerge: by following Levinson's general advice for the initial stages of the case analysis, one is supposed to acquire information needed for wise judgment about which subsequent steps to take. Every Levinson-type study begins in roughly the same way: with get-acquainted discussions with clients, a tour of the organization, and with an examination of organizational charts and other relevant documents. There is advice on what to heed in these early phases. In his first contacts with members of the organization who find out that a study is going to be made, the researcher should note their reaction: Do they doubt that a study can really produce anything useful? Are they concerned about confidentiality? Do they express doubts that the study will be used? Do they ask to be allowed to do their own study? In addition, the researcher should note whether he has to ask to inspect the organization or is invited to so do. At some point early in the investigation, the researcher should be able to put together a "preliminary mapping" and "early overview" of the organization. He should then draw together his first "general impressions." As examples, he mentions observations on "current preoccupations" of members of the organization, their "favorite expressions," and the key people or favored work groups in the organization. These observations then become working hypotheses, the basis for making decisions about what to investigate.

> These observations become orientation points. They are guides to what might be learned in the study and a consolidation of early experience which permits acceleration of the acquaintance of the consultant with as broad a group of people and situations in the organization as possible [p. 31].
>
> The consultant is his own instrument. He should ask himself: What does this place feel like? How effective and efficient does it seem to be? How would it feel to work here? . . .
>
> The consultant must attempt to recognize his first feelings about the organization, some of which may be fleeting. He must be alert to momentary negative feelings because he will tend to disregard them, particularly if the atmosphere is subsequently cordial. Such feelings should not be disregarded. . . . [p. 73].

In other words, to make translation decisions, Levinson advises the researcher to examine his own emotional response to the organization. The main example furnished in the text is a 130-page case study of a furniture and appliance retail outlet employing 920 people in two locations: Atlanta and Macon, Georgia. Sales had been climbing steadily and the management had plans for expansion. However, at the same time, profits had fallen off, and management expressed concern about its capacity to expand successfully. The case study conforms exactly to Levinson's outline for such studies. Under the heading "first overall impressions," the author (Andrew G. Spohn) describes his tour of the stores. A number of very specific events are related, followed by this concluding remark:

> The mood in both stores was similar. People were courteous, polite, but somewhat sullen. They seemed without vitality, except for the department managers. The sameness of the personnel, sameness of merchandise, and sameness of the facilities was somewhat depressing to the task force [p. 383].

These impressions may well have influenced the subsequent study, but it is impossible to know exactly how strongly. Certainly the themes reappear. Employees were given a questionnaire designed to see whether their expectations for their jobs and for management were being met (they were not); management reactions to employee grievances were probed to see if the grievances were taken seriously (they were not); management was studied to find out whether they were sophisticated in planning new merchandising campaigns based on current consumer preferences (they were not).

We have included a discussion of this book because it helps to explicate what we call the translation problem. The author illuminates it by going, so to say, halfway. He shows the interplay between systematic thinking and the judicious collection of essential information. The points at which the investigator's judgment come into play are clearly marked. But the nature of this judgment is not further explored. This, of course, was not Levinson's purpose, and he cannot be criticized for this omission. But we want to raise the question whether one cannot go a step further. Certainly we do not hope that anyone can translate intuition into a rational deductive procedure. But some progress might be made by thinking out more specifically what elements enter into the decision to collect information relevant to a specific practical problem. In the second part of this chapter we shall at least classify some of the alternatives encountered in Step 3. Then it will be seen that subjective judgment is still involved in these decisions. But by being more specific as to what sort of judgments are needed and how they might be supported, we hope to clarify still further the cognitive aspects of the utilization process. Our three examples were taken from quite different substantive fields. From here on we shall draw upon a broad range of subject matters but refer to them in much less detail.

SOME TRANSLATION PROBLEMS

Lacking a large inventory of concrete studies, we can cull only a few central topics which are necessarily common to all translation problems. First, every study done to help in a practical situation will have certain groups in mind: those who are to be influenced or helped; and those who might carry weight in whatever decision is finally made. We shall refer to all of these as "target groups". Secondly, a number of "variables" are available, and their choice is part of the translation problem. Thirdly, some problems deal with the future. But no practical problem is completely new; to use previous research experience and to transfer its results into a new situation will be a fourth topic for discussion in this chapter. Finally, we produce two examples of misdirected translations.

The Choice of Target Groups

Returning now to cases where new inquiries are needed, an obvious question arises which has been alluded to previously: Who should be studied? Sometimes the practical problem on hand suggests the answer. Early in 1944, when Hadley Cantril was a research adviser to Franklin Delano Roosevelt, the President was concerned that further bombing in Rome might upset American Catholics. The research group decided to ask a previously selected sample group this question: "If our military leaders believe it will be necessary to bomb Rome, but take every precaution to avoid damage to its religious shrines, would you approve or disapprove this decision?" Although Catholics disapproved more often than Protestants, two-thirds of them nonetheless did approve. Cantril reports that two days later, railroad yards and airports in Rome were heavily bombed.[5]

Here, when we talk about target groups, we do not, of course, mean the Romans, but rather those interested sectors of the American public who would feel intensely affected by the decision. In other cases some preliminary exploration is needed before one can decide on the most promising target group. A concrete case is reported in a study done by the New York City Milk Research Council[6] involving young people who did not drink milk. Two such groups were identified. One showed an intense dislike of milk, traceable to an early childhood experience (for example, as a child the subject might have been given contaminated milk). It seemed unlikely that this group could be easily converted. Instead, the Council was advised to concentrate its resources on a second group, in which milk consumption had declined dramatically in the early teens because milk was considered "childish." Here, some leeway for persuasion seemed possible. An extensive campaign was launched, with sports heroes stressing the energy potential of milk.

Sometimes it is necessary to study not only one target group, but also to inquire into collateral groups which play a role. James Short provides an example from the Walker Report on the violence involving police and demonstrators outside the 1968 Democratic Convention Hall in Chicago. Investigation focused on obtaining sworn depositions from eyewitnesses to the violence. This, he says, resulted in neglecting the part played by city officials not actually participating in the violence.[7]

In comparision to the demonstrators and the police on the street, here the collateral group—incompletely studied—was an "elite." The reverse problem was faced by the Canadian government in deciding how to respond to the demands of leaders of ethnic service organizations for assistance in preserving traditional cultures and languages. Leaders representing Ukrainian, Polish, Italian, and other ethnic groups wanted the government to subsidize ethnic schools, newspapers, radio, television, cultural centers, and other facilities as part of its announced policy of "multiculturalism." The ethnic minorities were certainly part of the target group, and studies of them could have been useful if they led to recommendations for preventing the gradual decline of traditional ethnic cultures and languages. However, these minorities constituted only one-third of the entire population, and the necessary programs would not only be expensive but would affect the character of the entire society. Thus, the acceptance of any such measures by the majority groups (French or English, depending upon the part of Canada involved) might also be seen as part of the problem, and studies of the prevalent attitudes toward ethnic minorities might be essential for deciding how various plans could be introduced. Interestingly, the government decided to commission the study of the ethnic groups themselves, partly because they wanted to know to what extent the ethnic leadership was representative of grass-roots opinion. It was felt that measurement of these opinions could be combined with a study of the conditions fostering the retention of ethnic languages and cultures. The ethnic-group studies did find considerable support for the retention of ethnic cultures, and the government has decided to study majority-group attitudes next.[8]

Having distinguished between primary and collateral target groups, we have to add one more possibility: substitute target groups. The American Jewish Committee wanted to know whether a long-range advertising campaign would reduce anti-Semitic attitudes. Such an investigation would of course extend over a considerable period of time. As a substitute, they put cards into subways and then interviewed riders. The idea was that people subjected to a daily dose of persuasion over a short period of time would be representative of the general population exposed to less frequent propaganda over a longer period of time. The possible pitfalls in such an assumption are numerous, but the results were nevertheless quite suggestive. The riders aware of the cards did not change their ethnic attitudes, but those hostile to Jews were more willing to restrain the expression of their feelings. In the long run, less overt anti-Semitism might help in the general reduction of anti-Semitic attitudes.[9]

Another good example is provided by Lawrence Podell.[10] Establishing eligibility for public welfare has involved very expensive field investigations of the applicant and all legally responsible relatives. The usefulness of these investigations has been in some doubt. They may serve to prevent fraud, but they may also deter eligible older people who do not want to drag their adult children into confrontations with the authorities. Investigations may force negligent fathers to support their children, but they may also break up families irreversibly. Researchers for New York City welfare agencies sought to study these effects and proposed a set of criteria to decide eligibility without the field investigation. They also proposed that a sample of applicants be fully investigated both to check the criteria and to continue to deter fraud. However, it would still have been difficult to know all the effects of stopping the field investigations altogether. Coincidentally, at a crucial stage, most of the city's social service staff went on strike. Field investigations had to be suspended, and applicants were interviewed in the local offices for temporary certification. After the strike, all applicants were to be subject to the full investigation. Podell argued that, to some extent, this provided an opportunity to see whether a suspension of field investigations for all applicants would have any negative effects. At the time of this writing, no more is known about the final outcome of using an unusual situation to create a substitute group for the study of a general problem.

Most of our examples revolved around problems of organizations with the outside world. But as we mentioned at the beginning of this chapter, a public agency frequently will be concerned with its own efficiency, a factory manager will worry about the productivity of his workers, or a white-collar union with the degree of satisfaction its members derive from their work. Such "inside" problems of course have their own target groups within the organization.

It is not always easy to distinguish the two types of issues. If an organization wants to improve its marketing division to get better results with its customers, is that an inside or an outside problem? In such a case, the target groups might be both—say, the sales force and the shoppers. For these reasons we have decided not to add further examples from a field one might call organizational therapy. For one, much literature exists which is explicit on this area. Secondly, the Levinson example given earlier provides a very good idea of the translation problems implied in this tradition.

Choice of "Variables": Some Suggestions

Once the essential target groups have been decided upon, the question arises of how they should be characterized. Some authors warn that one should not collect information on variables which cannot be controlled by the policy-maker. For example, H. W. Riecken says that:

> By fixing attention upon variables . . . such as early childhood experience, the structure of the nuclear family, father's occupation, age and sex, ordinal position in the family, and similar fixed characteristics . . . most sociologists provide theoretical and explanatory structures that have neither interest nor promise for the social problem solver because he cannot use them as handles or levers.[11]

Certainly one research strategy is to try to identify variables representing conditions the policy-maker can manipulate to achieve his goals. Our previous examples show that no positive guidelines yet exist, but we might offer a few suggestions. One involves "deviant case analysis." Instead of comparing people who present a problem with those who do not, one might perhaps study a group that has managed to overcome the problem without any assistance by the policy-maker. For example, Harold Watts suggests that poverty studies focusing on people who escaped from poverty are likely to produce useful information.[12] That is, one should study the factors leading to upward mobility, rather than the causes of poverty per se. The underlying principle is that people who overcome a problem against great odds may have used resources that the policy-maker, too, might employ. Of course, this is not necessarily a foolproof assumption. The "deviant cases" might depend more upon idiosyncratic skills than common resources. Nevertheless, the suggestion should be kept in mind, for it could prove useful. Delinquency researchers have studied adolescents who live in gang territories but do not join such groups themselves. How do they resist? These deviant cases are significant.

A second suggestion is that there are times when critical situations need to be studied or dissected so that they can later be modified. Zeisel[13] reports an analysis of phases of the judicial process with the purpose of finding out at what point the "delay in court" could be alleviated. Merton and Devereux[14] describe a study of the setting in which telephone calls were made to determine how calls to "Information" could be reduced. For example, it was found that in some locations, printed directories were not available. Supplying more directories would presumably lessen the load on information services.

But suppose the variables are not so easily incorporated into modifications? Our third suggestion deals with the use of variables that at first may seem inflexible; still, simply taking account of them may prove informative. Thus it is known from long experience that certain social categories such as age, sex, or socioeconomic status will be important classifying variables in designing survey research. Obviously, age cannot be manipulated by the policy maker, but age differences in observed behavior can lead to useful conclusions.

Take as an example a study done for a department store. The problem was this: Most of the stores in the city had begun to stay open one evening a week. Should the client follow this trend? One way to translate this problem into a research design was to determine what differences, if any, existed between the customers of the client store and some of its competitors. Brief interviews with shoppers corroborated one assumption of the client: his customers were indeed of higher socioeconomic status. But routine tabulations showed that their average age was also higher, even within individual economic strata. It seemed likely that younger housewives were more likely to work during the day and to take advantage of the evening shopping hours at the other stores. The client store was in danger of losing out among the younger strata of the population. As usual, other considerations had to enter into the final decision: the attitudes of the employee unions, the nature of the neighborhood, the available transportation. But the client did decide to keep the store open one evening a week; probably the most persuasive factor in this decision was the fear that its customers would become increasingly overage.

Another example of using the seemingly immovable variable comes from a study by Suchman.[15] He wanted to find out why some groups were reluctant to use free medical facilities. He found that certain ethnic subgroups, those with less "scientific" attitudes toward health problems, were especially resistant. This information is very relevant, even though one would not try to manipulate the ethnic composition of the community. Instead, the findings could easily be linked with available knowledge about the ways social networks can be tapped to reach specific subgroups. For example, one might use ethnic clubs and societies as a communication medium. Or, medical personnel with appropriate ethnic backgrounds might be particularly effective persuaders.

Sometimes it requires a great deal of imagination to see how variables can be manipulated. "If a person feels alienated from his community because his job is relatively meaningless, one can hardly change the nature of industrialization in America," says one author.[16] But as a matter of fact, this is exactly what is happening now in the effort to restructure or humanize jobs. It has been found that worker satisfaction arises largely from the accomplishments, recognition, and responsibility of the work itself, whereas dissatisfaction is related to wages, working conditions, and supervision. Ford's research[17] at the American Telephone and Telegraph Company sought to test this idea in a series of experiments. In one Minneapolis office, 14 keypunch operators issued the payroll. Each was responsible for some small part of the work required to put out each paycheck. Turnover was high. Ford changed their jobs, giving each girl complete responsibility for preparing checks for specific individuals. This meant that each operator had a large group of "customers," carrying out a complete transaction for each individual one. Ford reports that both turnover and absenteeism declined.

Our suggestions about the choice of variables in the translation phase have given some hints as to how the seemingly "nonmanipulable variable" can be subsumed within a utilization plan. This is one area where further codification would be welcome.

Research for Planning

Translating a problem into research always involves some attention to outcomes or possible ramifications. But in undertaking research for planning purposes, the translation phase has a distinctly futuristic cast. The policy-maker is himself looking into the future; he wants advice about introducing something new: a product, a service, a technique, a law. In general, he wants to be able to predict whether the innovation will win acceptance.

Sometimes the researcher thinks that an opinion survey would be useful in designing the innovation. Thus, after German defeat in World War II, the return of large numbers of troops to the United States posed a logistics problem. The soldiers could not be brought back simultaneously. Who then should have to wait behind? The Army made a survey[18] to see what the troops themselves would consider fair. Should the wounded men precede those who had children waiting at home? Which should count more heavily, total length of service or actual combat experience? From the answers to such questions, the analysts developed a sophisticated point system which gave each soldier a potential score from 1 to 80. The higher the score, the sooner the man could leave. At the time of demobilization, the point system was explained to each member of the armed forces stationed in Germany. There seems to be general agreement that the procedure ultimately avoided a great deal of potential friction, and it has recently been applied by the Navy in assigning personnel to ships.

Sometimes the researcher hopes to use institutional records of some sort for planning purposes and does not choose to design an opinion survey, even though public opinion will ultimately be important to the policy-maker. The attempt to improve patron safety in urban mass-transit systems is a good example.[19] Police records were ingeniously mined to reveal time, location, and type of subway crimes as well as the kinds of victims and offenders most frequently involved. The studies were intended to give some leads for the redesign of subway stations. What were the most dangerous situations? (Waiting alone on subway platforms.) When do the majority of crimes occur? (In the evening.) What do criminals do directly afterward? (Flee through nearest station exit.) Translating the security issue into these terms made it possible to draw up some suggestions about spatial aspects: stations should have as few corners as possible; activities on the platform should be visible from without through strong glass walls or barriers wherever possible; movable barriers should be provided to compress waiting space during hours of sparse use, etc.

There is quite a distance between planning a transit system and planning a whole new community. Probably the earliest such study was the plan of rural sociologists for the Columbia River Basin development project in the forties. As described by C.C. Taylor,[20] the sociologists decided to study the prior experiences of potential community members. Research on their standards of living, patterns of social life, and use of community facilities was meant to help the planners structure the new community to resemble the previous communities as closely as possible.

More recent research for new community-building has dealt less with the prior experiences of the inhabitants and more with the meaning of the transition itself.[21] It was found that the apartment renter who wants to move to a house in a new community expects a radical change in his whole life style. The man who once walked to work but must now commute by car anticipates a whole new set of pressures. How does the planner build these expectations into the structure of the new community, and how successful is he? Current research on such questions at Twin Rivers, the first planned unit development in New Jersey, is still in progress and is frankly exploratory. The sociologist in charge of the research stated from the outset that not much was known about the relation of spatial features to human behavior. Thus the research was designed to entail a combination of techniques (depth interviews with inhabitants; content analysis of community publications; observations of shopping patterns) as well as a wide range of indicators (tenant complaints; mobility rates; photographs of fields and play spaces; defacements and building vandalism) in order to provide an opening wedge.

On Borrowed Experience

Clues to the solution of a policy problem often may be gleaned in prior instances in which similar problems have been faced. If such instances can be located and sufficient data are available for their study, the main difficulty lies in the transferability of the findings from one setting to another—the famous problem of the use of "historical analogy." Everyone wants to learn from history, but the question is always which historical parallels are appropriate. This problem should be considered in advance of the detailed study of possible parallel instances, so that evidence bearing upon transferability can be gathered systematically.

An example of borrowed experience can be found in some research done by the NAACP for the Supreme Court in 1954, described by Kenneth Clark.[22] When considering the question of segregation in the public schools, the Supreme Court posed the question whether desegregation should be carried out immediately or whether a gradual change might be less disruptive and, therefore, more effective. The social scientists turned to an examination of previous experiences with desegregation in the United States, using information from professional journals, general periodicals and newspapers, unpublished research manuscripts, and from actual participants. The thinking of the Court was focused on the problem of segregation in Southern schools. However, little information was available on previous instances of desegregation in that particular context, so it was necessary to consider evidence from other areas. But not all such evidence was considered relevant. Desegregation experience in most Northern states was considered a doubtful indication of difficulties to be expected in Southern schools, because of (supposedly) greater racial tolerance in the North. Attention then turned to experience in two particular contexts thought to be more relevant. In the border-state areas, where attitudes were more like those in the South, some desegregation experience was available from which one could derive significant indicators of what would generally be expected from southern states if they were required to undergo similar changes in pattern. In addition, some relevant experience also could be borrowed from the South itself, though in the context of institutions other than public schools.

> Some direct examples in southern states of changes from segregation to nonsegregation in Army camps, in schools run by the Army, Navy shore installations, churches, industrial plants, and labor unions were found and indicate in general that these *states do not differ significantly from northern border states in their ability to accommodate to a specific change in social situations.* [Emphasis added.]

In this last instance, the problem of transferability is not avoided; it merely takes a different form. The relevant experience in the South comes from settings other than public schools, and the issue is the applicability of this experience to the desegregation of the Southern public schools. The combination of similar experience borrowed from more than one setting reinforced the conclusion in favor of rapid, as opposed to gradual, desegregation.

The problem of transferability is only somewhat different when one has to consider the relevance of one's own past experience in dealing with a specific problem. Conditions may change, and the question arises whether previous research is still pertinent or whether new research is needed. For example, the Educational Testing Service had to decide whether research on racial bias in aptitude tests, which was done at a time when relatively few black children applied to college, could be interpreted in the same way when open admission was coming into view. In the judicial field, research in the early sixties by the Vera Foundation on the problem of bail had to be repeated in the early seventies, because many judges doubted its relevance after the dramatic increase in the crime rate in the late sixties. As a matter of fact, one may legitimately ask how research for the 1954 Supreme Court decision had to be supplemented before new decisions on desegregation strategy could be made.

Sometimes transferability may be very difficult to decide, but the relevance of borrowed experience may be considered anyway if the problem is very acute and simple remedies seem futile. The attempt to evaluate the different narcotics policies in Britain and America is a classic case in point. E. Schur[23] did an extensive study of the administration of the British narcotics policy providing for the legal distribution of drugs to drug addicts through medical channels. The policy is intriguing, because of the relatively few addicts in Britain and the large number in America, which presumably would adversely affect the success of such a policy in America. Collecting information to counter invalid suppositions about the comparability of the two cases is a formidable task.

It should be emphasized that borrowed experience includes not only the use of historical analogy, but also the transfer of general sociological findings and theories from one context to another. On the one hand, the policy problem may be seen as parallel; on the other, the historical tone or experience may be perceived as relevant. This problem of transferability is common to both situations.

Amitai Etzioni[24] has discussed the transfer of sociological findings and generalizations. His examples indicate the varying degrees of "intellectual distance" involved in such transfers. There is relatively little distance between the statement that consumer decisions are only faintly affected by advertising when consumers are uninterested in the product and the statement that information campaigns to increase public support for the United Nations will only affect those already interested in the U.N. (They tend to be those who already support it.) There is much greater distance between the idea that people choose friends similar to themselves and the conclusion that international communities can be formed among nations that share significant characteristics. Etzioni cites examples which do not support such a conclusion—e.g., the failure of Arab countries to form a viable union or the recurrent armed conflicts in Europe.

Existing knowledge developed in some context other than the immediate concern may become useful if it can be transferred. The well-known leadership studies sponsored by the Office of Naval Research did lead to transfer-application, though not in the manner originally anticipated. The emphasis at the outset of the research program was on the development of a personality test which would aid in the selection of potential leaders. But it soon became apparent that leadership characteristics varied with the task situation. One set of studies, for example, specified the situations in which authoritarian as opposed to democratic leadership qualities were needed. Other studies probed a variety of aspects. For example, information from such disparate student groups as radical antiwar demonstrators, conservative John Birch Society members, and middle of the roaders pointed up some of the difficulties in leading ideologically heterogeneous groups. The degree to which leaders discriminate between the most effective and least effective workers was another variable for study. Overall, the research would seem to indicate that there is no single personality type which makes for effective leadership in all circumstances, and that leaders must be able to handle a variety of situations. From the point of view of application, the emphasis shifted from developing a test to identify leaders to setting up a program for training leaders. Recently, the Navy's Group Psychology Branch sponsored a textbook on principles of leadership for use at the Naval Academy and probably in the NROTC programs as well.

Most ONR-sponsored research at non-Navy sites is in some way deemed relevant to the Navy context. One broad research program concerns the behavior of isolated and confined groups. The Navy is, of course, concerned with isolation aboard ocean vessels, but the research has been conducted in remote communities in Kansas and Nevada. Another type of study investigates panic behavior under laboratory conditions, though the Navy would hope the results might contribute to the management of panic under battle conditions. Problems chosen for study outside the Navy context have to be made with that context in mind. The problem of planning for transferability is always present. It is not sufficient merely to require that the research concern some general topic such as "leadership." Brooke[25] cites the example that in the leadership studies program it would probably not be useful to study the selection of group leaders by democratic process, since this never occurs in the Naval organization.

Part of the problem of transfer simply is locating the most pertinent information. A. M. Rose gives a good illustration in his discussion of the social scientist as an expert witness in court cases.[26] One court case concerned a pregnant black single woman whom a Minnesota welfare agency wanted to send back to Florida, her home state. The woman had applied for welfare assistance. The agency wanted her deported on the grounds that she was "mentally incompetent" and likely to require public support. According to the agency, the evidence for this finding was her pregnancy and a very low intelligence test score. The social scientist testified for the defense. He presented two arguments to rebut the prosecution and utilized a variety of studies in support of those arguments. First, he argued that behavior cannot be evidence of mental incompetence if it is part of a "subcultural pattern." Illegitimacy, he claimed, was a subcultural pattern among blacks in Florida. He cited statistics showing a 20 percent illegitimacy rate there, and he also described sociological studies of sexual behavior of lower-class Southern blacks. Second, he argued that low intelligence test scores do not necessarily imply the inability to support oneself. He mentioned research showing how social and cultural factors can cause low test scores and that many jobs do not require a high I. Q. On the basis of this testimony, the woman was not deported. Thus the sociologist proved to be useful by locating specific studies in the literature and suggesting how they were relevant to the problem at hand.

In the end, one could say that the use of social theory is essentially the use of earlier experiences ordered systematically. One example here will suffice to give the general idea. H. Zetterberg[27] asserts that there are "principles of theoretical sociology" which can be of assistance in dealing with at least some types of problems. His main example concerns a museum in a moderately large city. The museum's problem was low attendance. Zetterberg notes that "the published literature of sociology contains no studies of museum audiences," so that he was forced to borrow ideas from other research on parallel problems. He identified the following "principles of theoretical sociology" which deal with markets:

1. The larger the population reached by the market call of an offering, the greater the market response.
2. The greater the number of opportunities available to a population to heed a market call, the greater its market response.
3. The greater the variety of offerings in a market call, the greater the response.

On the basis of these principles, the following solutions are formulated:

> If the Museum expanded its mailing list, it would increase attendance. Since the upper class and the upper middle class is already "reached," the advice is to increase coverage of the lower middle class and working class.
> If Museum functions were scheduled at times giving people greater opportunity to attend, attendance would increase.
> If the programs of the Museum were more diversified, attendance would increase.

Zetterberg gives other, less formalized examples of advice, based on knowledge from other research. For instance, he observed that the aversion of local artists to the museum might be damaging, since they were influential "opinion leaders" in matters of art. The suggestion was to win over the artists by providing them with exhibition space, even if their work is less than excellent.

A more intuitive approach is recommended by Cyril Sofer, a prominent figure at the Tavistock Institute of Human Relations, where management consultation has been developed over many years. In his book, *The Organization from Within,* Sofer describes three major consulting episodes. Although he maintains that the insights he gained in his academic studies of sociology and other social sciences were vital to his performance, he candidly admits that it is difficult to identify precisely the source of the knowledge he himself used in specific instances. On this point, he is not apologetic; the consultant

> first immerses himself in the situation. He is able to come back to the basic disciplines only when later mulling over the material. It is fatal to be thinking:

What principle is there in sociology or psychology that could be applicable here?[28]

One should be sure not to confuse two situations. When the social scientist is in the middle of a utilization episode, this "immersion" might be creatively positive. But after the event, he should try to give the best account of the event he can. Wordsworth once said that a good poem is emotion relived in tranquility; somehow a similar retrival of a utilization experience for the purpose of communication with others is of greatest importance for advance of the whole field. But there may be another misunderstanding involved in Sofer's emphasis on intuition which cannot be analyzed. He is after all an organizational therapist, exemplified by our summary of Levinson's book. We had considerable difficulty in his discussion to distinguish between problems of "translation" (our Phase III) and Phase IV, when recommendations are called for. It should not be so difficult to keep records—as we urged in Chapter 3—on how a research strategy was decided upon, which alternatives were discarded, and why. The subsequent phase—how to convert whatever knowledge was acquired into guidance for action—is indeed much more difficult to reconstruct. We turn to this topic in the next chapter.

Misdirected Translations

Before we do go on, we wish to give two examples of what might be called misdirected translation. In each case, the design of the study did not match the purpose for which it was undertaken.

The state of California promulgated a law directed toward the unification of elementary-school districts. The idea was to combine the elementary schools of each county and to relate them to a single high school. Since the state would be divided into large school districts, individual communities with jurisdiction over a single elementary school would relinquish control to the county. The law provided for two kinds of exceptions. One would be of a geographical nature: If a county were naturally subdivided by a mountain or a river, it would be designated as two high school districts. Secondly, and more interesting from our point of view, the law stated that if a community had a very strong "community identification," it could retain its independence from a larger high-school–dominated district. In each county of California, a citizen's committee was appointed to hear objections to the unification proposals. In the case under discussion, one high-school district was supposed to take over eleven elementary schools. Some of the eleven communities with jurisdictions over the elementary schools protested on the grounds of "community identification."

Researchers[29] had developed a clever questionnaire. They inquired into such matters as place of employment, verbal expression of community identification, location of community services used, membership in social organizations, knowledge of community leadership, church attendance, informal acquaintance and interaction, and satisfaction of recreational needs. From such information a scale of community identification was formed.

Interviewed on a double-level sampling were a total of 303 respondents; first, towns were sampled, and then, a few people within each town. The research indicated that "not even a moderate level of community identification existed." Some influential members of the county committee insisted that the results did not apply to their own communities and continued to oppose unification. Obviously, the study could not meet this objection to its findings.

A more effective research design might have been as follows: first, ascertain which town representatives were clearly against unification; then use more intensive sampling in these towns to find out whether these communities showed especially high community consciousness. (In general, teachers and middle-class parents favored unification.) The final decision was, of course, a political issue, and it went back and forth as the case moved to ever higher decision-making bodies. Finally, the result of the study was accepted and unification ordered.

Our second case originated during the period of Senator McCarthy's attack on the State Department, the Army, and American colleges for harboring Communists. Writing in a magazine, Robert Hutchins, President of the Fund for the Republic, stated that teachers were so intimidated by these attacks that they did not dare express their own opinions in the classrooms and eliminated references to "leftist" literature lest they become suspect. Hutchins was challenged as to the source of his information. He commissioned Columbia's Bureau of Applied Social Research to do a study, and gave them complete independence as to its design and content. After some discussions among a group of highly qualified advisers, it was decided to concentrate on the teaching of social science in colleges, because there the damage wrought by McCarthy would be most visible. The study showed that Hutchins was basically right. He clearly had in mind the kind of quality institutions he was acquainted with, such as Chicago, Harvard, or Columbia. There, a carefully developed "apprehension" test showed that the teaching of the social sciences had indeed been affected by the red-hunting spirit of the times.

But Paul Lazarsfeld, the director of the study,[30] had not selected only elite colleges. Instead, he was partly guided by methodological considerations. In his study, he sampled all of the 1200 existing colleges and then sampled professors within each of these. Inadvertently, this deflected the Fund for the Republic's basic goal. It was never made explicit, either by client or investigator, that Hutchins was really concerned with a small group of top-ranking colleges. The sampling procedure necessarily led to a heterogeneous group of institutions, including Catholic women's colleges or Christian missionary academies, in which "subversive teaching" was highly unlikely. Almost half of the primary list of institutions were of this type; therefore, the over-all proportion of "apprehensive" professors was relatively small. The final publication did, of course, report findings separately for the various types of colleges. But a large part of the budget had been spent on studying colleges where attacks on potential Communists were unlikely in the first place.

In retrospect, one can see that the study design had another shortcoming. What Hutchins was basically concerned about was the protection of academic freedom. It was almost an accident that he voiced his concern in terms of teachers' apprehension. These attitudes were transitory and probably irrelevant once McCarthy was gone. It probably would have been a better translation of Hutchins' concern to concentrate the study on a different topic: i.e., to what extent did college administrations protect their faculty members against attacks from the outside? *The Academic Mind* provided some information on this problem, but the budget allotted to studying inappropriate respondents was so large that it was not possible to conduct a systematic inquiry into the conduct of the college administrators. In a sense, then, the findings of the study were too limited to be applicable in a different setting.

NOTES

1 Ann Pasanella and Janice Weinman, *The Road to Recommendation*, ONR Technical Report No. 3 (New York: Bureau of Applied Social Research, 1973).

2 James S. Coleman, *Policy Research in the Social Sciences* (Morristown, N.J.: General Learning Press, 1972).

3 F. Mosteller and D. P. Moynihan (eds.), *On Equality of Educational Opportunity* (New York: Vintage Books, 1972).

4 H. Levinson, *Organizational Diagnosis* (Cambridge, Mass.: Harvard University Press, 1972).

5 Hadley Cantril, *The Human Dimension: Experiences in Policy Research* (New Brunswick, N.J.: Rutgers University Press, 1967), pp. 53–54.

6 W. McPhee and L. Brown. *Some Useful Roles of Social Research* (New York: Bureau of Applied Social Research, 1960), pp. 55–56; mimeographed.

7 J. Short. "The National Commission on the Causes and Prevention of Violence: Reflections on the Contributions of Sociology and Sociologists," paper presented at the 1973 meetings of the American Sociological Association, New York, pp. 23–24.

8 K. G. O'Bryan, J. G. Reitz, and O. Kuplowsky, *Non-official Languages: A Study in Canadian Multiculturalism* (Ottawa: The Queen's Printer, forthcoming). The follow-up study of majority-group attitudes is being directed by John Berry of Queen's University, Kingston, Ontario.

9 McPhee and Brown, *op. cit.*, pp. 23–24; see also L. Srole and B. Kass, *Impact of Public Service Advertising,* BASR Report B0394. (New York: Bureau of Applied Social Research, 1951; mimeographed).

10 Lawrence Podell, "The Uses of Sociology in Public Welfare" (unpublished manuscript), p. 15.

11 H. W. Riecken, "Social Sciences and Social Problems," *Social Science Information,* VIII (1969), 110.

12 U.S. House Committee on Government Operations, *The Use of Social Research in Federal Domestic Programs,* II (Washington, D.C.: U.S. Government Printing Office, 1967), p. 26.

13 H. Zeisel, "The Law," in Paul F. Lazarsfeld, *et al.* (eds.), *The Uses of Sociology* (New York: Basic Books, 1967), pp. 82–88.

14 R. K. Merton and E. Devereux, *Use of Social Research in the Solution of Business Problems* (New York: Bureau of Applied Social Research, 1956).

15 E. A. Suchman, "Socio-medical Variations among Ethnic Groups," *American Journal of Sociology,* LXX (1964), 319–31; Suchman, "Social Patterns of Illness and Medical Care," *Journal of Health and Human Behavior,* VI (1965), 2–16.

16 S. Kegeles, "Some Unanswered Questions and Action Implications of Social Research in Fluoridation," *Journal of Social Issues,* XVII (1961), p. 77.

17 R. Ford, "The Obstinate Employee," *Public Opinion Quarterly,* XXXIII (1969), and also Ford, *Motivation Through the Work Itself* (New York: American Management Association, 1969), pp. 66–68.

18 R. Bowers, "The Military Establishment," in Paul F. Lazarsfeld *et al.* (eds.), *op. cit.*, p. 252.

19 R. Shellow (ed.), *Patron Security in Urban Mass Transit* (Workshop on Transit Security, Carnegie Mellon University, February 24–25, 1975; mimeographed).

20 C. C. Taylor, "The Sociologists' Part in Planning the Columbia Basin," *American Sociological Review,* XI (1946), pp. 321–30.

21 Suzanne Keller, "Planning for Life in a New Community," paper presented at the Sociological Research Association, August 28, 1973.

22 K. B. Clark, "Desegregation Background: The Role of Social Scientists," in D. Valdes and D. Dean (eds.), *Sociology in Use* (New York: Macmillan, 1965), pp. 302–5.

23 E. Schur, *Narcotic Addiction in Britain and America: The Impact of Public Policy* (Bloomington, Ind.: Indiana University Press, 1962).

24 Amitai Etzioni, "Nonconventional Uses of Sociology as Illustrated by Peace Research," in Paul F. Lazarsfeld *et al.* (eds.), *op. cit.*, pp. 814–19.

25 Joel Brooke, *The Utilization of Basic Social Research: A Case Study* (New York: Bureau of Applied Social Research, 1972).

26 A. M. Rose, "The Social Scientist as an Expert Witness in Court Cases," in Paul F. Lazarsfeld *et al.* (eds.) *op. cit.*, pp. 106–8.

27 H. Zetterberg, *Social Theory and Social Practice* (Totowa, N.J.: The Bedminster Press, 1962), p. 141.

28 Cyril Sofer, *The Organization from Within* (Chicago: Quadrangle Books, 1962), p. 136.

29 T. L. Gillette *et al.*, "Sociology and Education Policy," in A. Shostak (ed.), *Sociology in Action* (Homewood, Ill.: Dorsey Press, 1963), pp. 39–44.

30 P. F. Lazarsfeld and W. Thielens, Jr., *The Academic Mind* (Glencoe, Ill.: The Free Press, 1958).

FIVE

The Gap between Knowledge and Recommendation (Step 4)

After all the necessary research findings on a policy problem have been gathered and all the facts are in, a decision based on this material must be formulated. It is clearly the critical stage in the whole process of research utilization. One view of decision-making assumes that once goals, interests, and normative considerations are spelled out and all the facts analyzed, decisions inexorably emerge. This is as mistaken as the opposite view that rational analysis invariably impedes the "art" of decision-making. A more balanced approach suggests that, although systematic knowledge can contribute to decisions, there is always a gap between knowledge and recommendation. This gap can be filled only by creative thinking which responds with guesses of varying degrees of risk.

That a particular decision depends on the interests and values of the policy-maker is obvious to everyone. If a study should show that more coffee breaks increase worker satisfaction but decrease productivity, then business executives will oppose more coffee breaks and union leaders will favor them. This is not the type of situation to which we want to call attention. In the introduction to *The Uses of Sociology,* the authors put the matter this way:

> In a general way it is easy to see why no unique road leads from knowledge to action. Unpredictable events might occur; countermoves of competitors cannot be known in advance; reasonable moves in social policy might have quite unanticipated consequences. The client as decision-maker will have to make guesses and take risks beyond any contributions the sociologist can provide.[1]

We agree with the general idea, but we think the term "road from knowledge to action" covers too large a step and must be divided into two phases. First we have to investigate how specific research or other intellectual resources lead to recommendations for action. Secondly, we can probe the additional factors that affect the implementation of recommendations. It is the *gap between knowledge and recommendation* which concerns us in this chapter. No plan for action ever derives directly from confirmed information, however subtly it is interpreted. Many other elements have to be added before a recommendation can be drawn up. By using examples from our own experience and from the published literature, we attempt to describe the elements that enter at this phase of the utilization process. The various ways in which the client and the social scientist may share in this task will be discussed in the next chapter.

THE IMPORTANCE OF STUDYING GAPS BETWEEN KNOWLEDGE AND RECOMMENDATION

There are good reasons for suggesting that "gap-filling," as sociointellectual behavior, should become the subject of systematic study. Familiarity with the type of thinking to be expected after an applied study has been completed can help prepare both policy-makers and sociologists for their interaction. In general, two possible dangers exist. On the one hand, social scientists sometimes overstate the policy implications of research findings (or, in our terms, fail to specify and justify their "gap assumptions"). M. Tumin's summary of what he called "major research findings" in the area of race relations furnishes a striking example. Among his list of "findings" is the following statement: "Desegregation and integration of Negoes and Whites in *all* social contexts are *indispensable* to the achievement of equal opportunity and training for Negroes and *for the achievement of stable political order for the society.*"[2] This is obviously not a research finding at all, but rather something like a policy-statement. Sociological research is not likely to provide any complete, definitive statement about the consequences of a policy designed to bring about "desegregation and integration of Negroes and Whites in all social contexts." Tumin's summary makes us wonder what assumptions he used to bridge the gap between actual research findings and his conclusion. Applied sociologists must be ready to bring to light these assumptions.

On the other hand, there is the real problem of failing to suggest the policy ramifications of research. In the extreme case, there may be a denial of any policy implications at all, on the grounds that the research results are tentative. The difficulty with this position is that all research results are to varying degrees tentative. A study is not useless because it does not answer all questions; research never does. Neither is "further research" always an appropriate recommendation; often policy must be made without it. The study of gaps between knowledge and advice should help establish this and should indicate what degree of risk is typical in the use of social research.

Systematic study of these gaps may also teach us more about how to translate policy problems into relevant research designs. Generalizations about the gap between knowledge and decision are already being used to formulate certain rules. For example, D. P. Moynihan concluded from his overview of poverty programs of the late sixties that the only type of study social scientists should contribute to the policy process is the evaluation of past policy. "What institutional role may the social sciences expect to play in public affairs? The answer seems clear enough. *The role of social sciences lies not in the formulation of social policy, but in the measurement of its results.*"[3] Moynihan bases his generalization primarily on the detailed discussion of a single case—the application of the well-known Cloward-Ohlin "opportunity theory" to Mobilization for Youth, an antidelinquency program which became embroiled in controversy and was eventually canceled. In this case, Moynihan's diagnosis of the difficulties suggests that they arose when program emphasis shifted away from opportunities and toward community organizing, where immediate and effective opposition was expressed. It is difficult to see community organizing as an application of the original opportunity theory in any direct sense. In principle, Moynihan is undoubtedly right to criticize social scientists who become too self-assured about the implications of their knowledge in terms of policy-making. In his words, "A big bet was being made. No responsible persons had any business acting as if it were a sure thing" (p. 171). Restricting social science inputs to evaluation studies will not, however, eradicate political folly. Rossi suggests it would tend to have conservative consequences.[4] In any case, since applied sociologists do not restrict themselves a priori to studies that evaluate existing policy, more should be known about what kinds of gaps between knowledge and decision arise and how they are bridged.

A PRELIMINARY CLASSIFICATION

Two basic elements go unquestioned. First, we assume that the policy problem, including the goals of the policy-maker, his general resources, and relevant ethical considerations, is sufficiently defined to permit analysis. Second, we accept the sociologist's empirical findings and conclusions as given, without touching on the topic of research methodology. Our focus will be the policy recommendations. Since decisions rarely (if ever) can be made with complete confidence, even on the basis of extensive knowledge, what typical assumptions are made and how are they justified?

In filling the gap between knowledge and action, we feel intuitively that there will be guesses about current trends and speculations about future developments. But can we be more precise than this? Only a large collection of detailed case studies would provide us with a systematic inventory of all the elements involved. But at this point we want to clarify the notion of the gap by using brief examples from published literature and organizing a few basic ideas around them.

We are provisionally inclined to distinguish two types of "gap situations." In one, research has provided material which seems relevant to a policy problem, but where the available knowledge is still too general. Rather than suggesting alternatives for action, the research manages to amplify the difficulties the decision-maker faces by showing the complexity of the situation. Nothing in the findings points clearly to a solution. What is still needed is an "invention"—a specific course of action designed to change the situation. Invention is a creative act, though, and proverbially difficult to analyze. Sometimes it seems close to the research analysis; at other times it is much more remote. Some examples of these varying distances are given below.

When we have managed—by whatever route—to boil our analysis down to the choice between a few possible courses of action, we have the second type of gap. Once again, though, analytical reflection must intervene. For this type of gap, inventions of alternative strategies are not problematic. What is required is a kind of qualitative cost-benefit analysis: How do the alternatives compare as to ease of implementation and relative promise?

Of course, the two gap situations outlined above are not sharply distinct. A choice will often have to deal with aspects that have not been studied through research; here imaginative analysis will be needed, comparable to the producing of the alternatives themselves. But our conceptual distinction should become clearer as we turn to our examples.

INVENTION OF EFFECTIVE STRATEGIES

Inventions may range from simple technical modifications to complex institutional innovations. There are three general types of inventions: new services for existing needs; new roles; and new services for newly identified needs. We shall give some examples of each type.

New Services for Existing Needs

When research finds the cause of a problem to be a simple technical snag, a new service must usually be designed. Again, turning to AT&T research, when it was found that commerical users did not bother to consult their directories but turned directly to information service, the new service invented was to provide commercial switchboard operators with a list of the most frequently called numbers.[5] This was a way of improving directory facilities. (It might have been decided to try to induce callers to use their regular directories; this is a situation we shall discuss later under the heading of "Changing People.")

Even when a study shows the cause of a problem to be a simple technical difficulty, the proposed remedy may not work without "debugging." For example, during World War II, the Department of Agriculture wanted to improve milk production. Local officials were inclined to favor improvements in production facilities, but a study showed that while facilities were adequate, many farmers feared a price collapse after the war. Being unaware of government programs and price guarantees, they did not want to increase productive capacity. The government finally decided on an information campaign with two components: radio announcements and meetings between individual farmers and Agricultural Adjustment Administration staff members. The latter technique did not work immediately, but fortunately, a concurrent evaluation showed why it was ineffective. The AAA staffers were not sufficiently well informed about agricultural programs. A training course for these men had to be conducted before the program could be continued.[6]

New Roles

Finding a way to eliminate snags is not always the task; the invention can take the form of a new role, often linked to an institutional modification. For example, the Kodak Company was concerned with the fact that although home movie fans bought expensive equipment and used it enthusiastically for a while, they tended to stop taking pictures after a while. Since the company's income was derived mainly from the steady sale of film, it became important to find the reason for this decline. A study showed that the camera owners wanted to show their films, but before long they would run out of willing viewers. Without this social stimulus, interest in picture-taking vanished. To remedy this, it was proposed that new audiences be created by organizing clubs at which amateur photographers could show their pictures to each other. Thus, in order to "use" the research, a new institutional role had to be invented. (The case has a frustrating ending. The plan was never tried out because the imminent war diverted the company's energies to other problems.[7])

A recommendation made by Marvin Taves and other sociologists at the Office of Aging (now the Administration of Aging) also illustrates the invention of a new role. Retired American workers, it was found, are restless and dissatisfied because they no longer have a distinct role in our industrial society. At the other end of the age spectrum, research has demonstrated that young children in institutions need sustained relationships with adults in order to develop healthy personalities. This being the case, Taves asked whether retired individuals could not work closely with institutionalized children for several hours a day. Many older people might see this type of child-care as an important and useful contribution; to be responsible for young people who look to them for counsel and companionship might even given them a feeling of status. This idea reportedly proved successful, both for the older persons and the children.[8]

New Services for Newly Discovered Needs

New types of services are usually built upon the identification of unmet needs. These needs may not always be deemed important by the target population, but the client can still capitalize upon them. The discovery of needs which can be served or exploited is of course the main purpose of advertising research. The existence of the need really must be inferred. McPhee and Brown report a very simple instance. A survey of newspaper reading habits before World War II found that while most columns in those days were directed at the female audience, the few male-oriented columns had a devoted readership. It was concluded that an increase in male-oriented columns might result in an increase in total readership, and although McPhee and Brown suggest that this is exactly what happened in the postwar period, the study findings themselves did not guarantee the outcome.

A rather complex example is found in a programming decision made by NBC some 25 years ago. At that time, about 20 percent of American women already listened to the daytime radio serials of CBS. There seemed little chance of luring them away to other programs of that type. The problem was to develop a program that would attract another 20 percent who listened to the radio but not to daytime serials. A detailed study of their listening habits helped the broadcasters determine their preferences. One group liked programs which were not as emotionally involving as the serials; others preferred features with more factual content. The task was to combine these elements into one new type of program which would keep the audience listening to NBC during the morning. The resulting program, the "Today" show, is still on the air, evidence that the creative guesses of the decision-makers were correct.[9] (Incidentally, the fact that the invention was made by the client rather than the researcher is irrelevant at this point, since we want to stress only the cognitive aspect by which a recommendation is reached.)

In both of the above cases, the need or desire was suggested by research, and the invention consisted of thinking up services to meet the new need. Now let us look at cases in which the leap from need to action is especially large and the inventions are built upon inconsistencies or tensions between presumed needs. Thus, in attempting to devise psychological-warfare strategy against the Japanese in 1944, researchers in the Foreign Morale Analysis Division of the Office of War Information began a study of Japanese morale, using data from prisoner interrogation reports, captured diaries, official documents, and broadcasts. They found the Japanese continued to have great faith in their emperor and in the objective of the war, although they were beginning to grow war-weary and were no longer as fanatically determined to resist as had been assumed. In particular, dissension over military strategy was developing. The researchers concluded that psychological warfare directed against the emperor might only serve to strengthen resistance, whereas propaganda against the military leaders would be effective if these leaders were accused of not serving the emperor well.[10]

Sometimes the invention is derived from the principle that a negative attitude toward an activity can be gradually modified by reinforcing the "exceptions" to that activity. When the first steam laundry was introduced in Vienna around 1930, it found little response among Austrian housewives. A study revealed the main source of this resistance.[11] At that time, the cultural role of most women as keeper of the home was still such that doing the laundry oneself was a source of status and self-esteem. But the study also analyzed the deviant cases, women who sent their laundry out in situations of stress: sick children, an invasion of houseguests, holiday entertaining. Quite often such exceptions became the rule and housewives remained customers of the steam laundry. Once this was pointed out to its manager, he decided to concentrate his promotional material on the theme of stress. He obtained lists of recently deceased persons and wrote to the bereaved families; in newspaper advertising, he alluded to the periodic physiologic stress women are subject to. Thus, in addition to applying a psychological model, the tactic requires the invention of ways to locate stressful situations. (This particular invention may strike some as a bit sinister, but the normative issue is not our immediate concern. Incidentally, the laundry registered a marked increase in clients.)

Cantril reports an attitude study done prior to the Allied invasion of North Africa in World War II. Interviews in strategic African areas indicated that sentiment against a British invasionary force was strong because of the fear of permanent occupation by the British. The military leaders therefore decided that it was better to use American rather than British soldiers. In addition, the population was reassured about the temporary purpose of the landing; President Roosevelt, a trusted public figure, spoke repeatedly on the radio about it.

SOME POTENTIAL EFFECTS THAT MUST BE TAKEN INTO ACCOUNT

We have mentioned before that counterarguments against all these inventions can be raised in terms of possible consequences not covered by research. They must be assessed, even in the absence of pertinent data from the original study. (The relation of this problem to the original design of the study will be touched on and discussed in more detail later.) A piece of research cannot possibly cover every possible ramification. We have identified four types of consequences that the research might not have dealt with, but that are crucial to policy inventions. We call them potential effects.

It is important at this point not to confuse our concern with a closely related but still distinct conceptual idea. Sociologists and historians have been impressed by the fact that many actions have unanticipated consequences which the actors overlooked at the beginning of the undertaking. This is, of course, perfectly true. As a matter of fact, a whole school of management theory has been dubbed "incrementalism": it says that one should proceed in small steps so that one can always make corrections when the execution of a plan begins to deviate from the original intention. Our approach takes advantage of such wisdom by admonishing the applied sociologist to try to anticipate the nature of these consequences and to consider them in making his recommendations, even if he has only a vague notion of their probability. We talk of potential effects. Obviously no definite rules can be given as to how to deal with them. The purpose of the classification and descriptions contained in the following pages is essentially a didactic one. The hope is that retrospection will sharpen sensitivity to future contingencies.

Side Effects

Effects of a policy invention on goals other than those for which it was designed are usually called side effects. Though these often are crucial in using social science data, they can only be estimated after the research. For example, many criminologists agree that the recent increase in muggings is caused at least in part by a corresponding increase in the number of heroin addicts who turn to crime to support their expensive habit. Yet, many oppose making heroin or addictive substitute drugs legally available at low cost, since they fear doing so would have a possible undesirable side effect, namely, an increase in addiction itself (and no one can be sure it would not).

In the example of the study which led to the recruitment of older people in child-care programs, the following argument might be made: The old people could become sick or possibly even die while their young charges were still at a very tender age. This could intensify the children's feeling of rejection. Presumably these possibilities were discounted in policy deliberations, but one cannot really be sure.

It would be interesting to know the extent to which a given objection was given detailed consideration. Published reports are rarely that explicit. In the absence of detailed candid interviews with policy-makers or the notes of observers at policy conferences, we can only hazard a guess. Perhaps future case studies will be specific enough to permit the identification of patterns.

Feedback Effects

Another type of potential result is known as the feedback effect. A policy invention might successfully change a troubling condition, yet this change may set in motion other factors which neutralize the effects of the initial step. This possibility frequently arises when a problem is not confined to one locale. For example, suppose a study shows that violence on TV programs has disturbing effects on children with aggressive personalities. Eliminating TV violence might simply lead these children to seek out alternative sources of stimulation, such as violent sports, comic books, novels, or movies with the same deleterious effects as television. (In fact, a study by Feshbach[12] showed that children who did not view TV were more likely to have violent dreams.)

Possible feedback effects were considered in D. Caplovitz' book *The Poor Pay More.*[13] The study shows why poor people pay more than middle-class people for durable goods such as furniture and appliances. Being poor credit risks, they have little access to middle-class credit facilities and are forced to deal with merchants who are willing to offer credit but charge a higher rate to cover possible losses. In addition, these merchants typically are neighborhood store owners or peddlers who have personal contacts with their clients. In their dealings with these merchants, poor people also seem to be less sophisticated than middle-class people, and frequently report being tricked into purchases costing much more than they had planned to spend.

Caplovitz recommends a program of consumer education aimed especially at poor people who have just moved and are thus likely to purchase furniture on credit. He suggests that they be taught how to shop around and how to utilize such community agencies as legal-aid societies and the small-claims court. Toward this end, neighborhood consumer clinics and even door-to-door counseling services could be established. Such a program might be more effective than protective legislation, because low-income consumers often do not know when their rights have been violated, nor what to do if they have.

According to Caplovitz, other possible tactics might have undesirable feedback effects. Efforts to prevent the widespread use of credit, perhaps by withdrawing legal protection for merchants who offer credit to those who do not meet minimum requirements, or by regulating prices, should not be relied upon, because they might "stimulate deviant patterns other than those now in effect," such as increased dealings with loan sharks or with peddlers, either of which are practically uncontrollable.

Consumer education thus emerges as the most promising remedy. Still, we could raise the possibility of a new feedback effect. If the poor become more sophisticated credit consumers, what would prevent merchants from simply raising prices to maintain profits? Poor people, still denied access to middle-class credit facilities, would be forced to pay the higher prices, and thus would not benefit in terms of purchasing power. A minority report by a Canadian Senate Special Committee on Poverty reviewed Caplovitz' book and concludes: "Consumer education, which seeks to help the poor shop wisely and stretch a dollar, is then, largely irrelevant; the solution lies not in advising the robbed, but in catching the robbers."[14]

Caplovitz probably recognized this, since in his final paragraph he explicitly hedges his recommendations. Until poverty itself is eradicated, he says, the consumer problems of the poor may remain unsolved. But it is important to point out that Caplovitz is merely acknowledging the existence of the gap between knowledge and decision, that he does not advise abandonment of the program ideas. (Today, as a matter of fact, Caplovitz would no longer stress consumer education so much as the imposition of legal constraints on merchants.)

Interaction Effects

A third type of potential complication might be called the "interaction" effect, where there are interlocking factors related to the policy-maker's problems. The invention of a solution requires speculation about these joint relationships. For example, Project Head Start was initiated partly in response to recommendations of educators who emphasized the importance of preschool experiences in determining long-range educational potential. Yet, as the evaluation studies have shown, there was always the possibility that preschool programs, while effective in themselves, would fail to produce long-term benefits. As ghetto children moved into the traditional public schools, they would not be motivated to develop the advantages derived from Head Start.

The relevant literature reflects a considerable difference of opinion on what to do about the possibility of interaction effects. E. Rosenfeld[15] argues that in the case of juvenile delinquency, it is futile to try to decide which one of many interacting factors should be attacked. Thus, J. H. Noble's evaluation of intensive resocialization camps for juvenile delinquents shows only a very small likelihood of having any effect at all, and in any case, they are temporary. Everyone would probably agree that the reason for the failure is an interaction effect. The effects of even successful resocialization camps are neutralized when children return to conditions at home.[16] Rosenfeld proposes a multipronged effort involving psychological counseling for delinquents, family support, community organization, and so on. The argument is that success in dealing with only one of these aspects would be ineffective without parallel success in the others.

Other authors argue that some of the relatively simple one-pronged strategies may work after all, without becoming too involved in the complexities of the total situation. For example, Etzioni and Remp have reviewed several examples of what they call "technological 'short cuts' to social change."[17] These include the drugs methadone and antabuse, educational television, the breath analyzer, the intrauterine device, and gun control. Each of these technologies (or, in the case of gun control, the removal of a technology) is judged to be at least potentially effective in solving some complex social problem at relatively low cost. The distinctive feature of such inventions may be that they do not require personality changes, extensive resocialization, or exceptional moral qualities.

In the case of complicated and chronic social problems, many interaction effects have to be ignored. The philosophy underlying the various Presidential Commission reports was to list programs dealing with a myriad of interdependent causes. Often, when there are many interdependent causes, a policy-maker will nevertheless cling to the hope that if one of them can be manipulated, some positive results can be produced and perhaps the other factors will, at least in part, take care of themselves.

A typical example is to be found in the policy discussions about poverty. Poverty has often been analyzed as resulting from two interdependent causes: lack of opportunity and lack of motivation. What should a poverty program focus on? Gans pointed to the difficulty of dealing with low motivation. He argues that opportunity should receive attention as a temporary measure to be used while effective ways to raise motivation are being sought. This can be justified partly by pointing to the effects of opportunities on motivation, which indicates that perhaps part of the motivational problem would take care of itself.[18]

In the field of applied organizational analysis, the question of what to do about possible interactions among interlocking factors related to a problem arises in nearly identical form. Whyte and Hamilton have discussed this matter, beginning with a concrete example taken from their Tremont Hotel Project. One episode focused on the hotel's coffee shop, where waitresses, displeased with working conditions, had a high absenteeism rate. Interviews with the waitresses revealed that the location of the water spigot had come to symbolize management's seeming insensitivity to their situation. The girls had to walk outside the coffee shop to fill water glasses for their customers. They had been told that the hotel was going to be renovated, and therefore they should stop bothering the management with complaints about the water spigots. To the employees, this meant that if "They won't give us a water spigot, what do they care about us?" These facts were presented to management, and the condition was corrected. Moreover, a new system of upward communication was established in the hotel, so that employee concerns could be more effectively handled in the future.[19]

Whyte and Hamilton contrast their approach to that of Argyris. In his work for industrial and business firms, Argyris seeks to increase free, informed choices by members of the organization. He believes that one way of increasing organizational effectiveness is to provide top management with some kind of T-group training. This training, intended to help members accept responsibility for their own ideas and feelings, to be receptive to the feelings of others, and to be open to new ideas and feelings, is seen as a prerequisite to a wide range of organizational improvements. Once the emotional problems of the members are treated, the organization can move ahead with the development of rational plans to deal with technical difficulties.

In short, Argyris tries to improve the attitudes of top management to pave the way for organizational change, while Whyte and Hamilton try to show top management what organizational changes are needed and why. The latter two explain that they are in agreement with Argyris about the relevance of organizational structure and individual attitudes to organizational problems, but that they differ from him in the assessment of which should be given immediate attention in a practical effort at change. Argyris does not ignore the organizational environment, but thinks that since management must approve all changes, attempts at change should start with them. Whyte and Hamilton still feel that not all organizational problems will be solved by attitude change, because attempts to change attitudes alone may prove futile in the long run. In the end, however, they recommend a combined approach. In their own experience at the Tremont Hotel, resistance to change by one key executive was a main obstacle with which they could not adequately cope. They wondered if they might try to involve him in some kind of human-relations training experience (p. 215). In general, they mention the need for "balance," but leave it to future work to determine how this balance can be achieved in concrete cases.

We conclude with two cases where the participants in a decision were aware of alternative possibilities based on research findings. But in both cases there were reasons not to follow the most obvious line suggested by the studies.

Glock[20] describes the experience of a private welfare organization that wanted to enforce its antidiscrimination policy. The national headquarters asked for a study to determine rank-and-file opinion, and the study showed near unanimity in support of the principle of nondiscrimination. Nevertheless, the headquarters feared that regardless of their public stance, church-sponsored local groups might disband if they were actually forced to admit members of other faiths.

As our other example, we take one of a series of Treasury Department studies aimed at raising more money through the sale of war bonds during World War II.[21] One proposal was to reduce the time-span between purchase and maturity. A survey found that purchasers usually cashed their bonds because of some unforeseen emergency such as medical expenses or tax bills rather than on some capricious impulse. Many prospective bond buyers indicated they would buy more bonds if the redemption period were shorter, and if they did, perhaps they would not cash them prematurely. Of course, it is possible that those who intended to buy more bonds might not actually do so; moreover, once people owned a substantial number of bonds, they might be more likely to cash them on impulse. These potential effects may have been discounted by the policy-makers because of the practicality of the proposed policy change, and also because a policy failure in this case would cost little. The decision could easily be reversed.

Future Uncertainties

A final type of residual effect should be mentioned because it is perhaps the most problematic of all. Unforeseen changes in a situation rendering a proposed policy ineffective can occur for reasons completely beyond the policy-maker's control. A classic example is Ford Motors' decision to produce the Edsel. It was designed to appeal to Ford owners who were "trading up" to competing makes of medium-priced cars. As Wilensky suggests, a major reason for the failure of the Edsel was the rising interest in small foreign and economy cars, brought on in part by the recession of the late fifties.[22]

While occurences such as recessions may not be predictable, certain future changes or shifts in technology, population patterns, and population values can be inferred from developing events. This is the business of the futurists, and one of their contributions has been the development of new methods of speculation about the future, e.g. the well-known Delphi technique.[23]

There is, of course, no absolute distinction between the invention gap and our second gap, the choice between alternative strategies. But the distinction seems to us to be useful as an analytic technique.

THE CHOICE BETWEEN ALTERNATIVE STRATEGIES

The second "gap situation" we identified earlier was that of empirical research carving out alternatives which then have to be weighed. We can distinguish a number of typical sets of alternatives.

Changing People or Changing Organizations

The choice between two alternatives occurs most frequently when studies show a poor fit between an organizational arrangement and the people who are supposed to make use of it. The problem then arises whether the organization should be modified (assuming the decision-maker has control over it) or whether one should try to reeducate the target population directly.

Consider the example of poor families who do not make use of free health centers available to them. The sociologist called in for help has, on the one hand, turned to studies of lower-class culture, and on the other, to the relevant sociology of bureaucracies. R. Elling[24] combined these two elements and concluded that a lower-class cultural bias prevents poor people from utilizing services administered in the bureaucratic way with which middle-class people are familiar. Within the poverty culture, it has been found, life is concentrated on local interests and face-to-face relationships. Elling maintains that the formal impersonality of the average clinic or hospital effectively removes it from the very clients it should serve. He suggests that a new health-service organization is necessary, one run on an intimate, neighborhood basis, able to direct local residents to the traditional health center in which the full armamentarium of medical care and preventive services is available. The storefront operation would provide general health service and counsel; it would not be speciality-oriented.

Elling's proposal sounds convincing. But the sociological analysis could have led to a different prescription, in which the policy-maker would try to change the people's attitude of apathy and powerlessness rather than adapt the bureaucracy to the prevalent attitude. The implicit assumption is that this might prove too difficult. It could be that the best solution would combine experimental institutional modification with an attempt at attitude-restructuring. However, the limitations of most budgets would probably require an explicit decision about the proportion of funds to be allocated to each alternative.

Another example of a gap involving a choice between changing people or organizations is reported by C. and Z. Loomis.[25] The Agricultural Extension Service (AES) had set up a program to make information on new construction available to farmers. A study showed, among other things, that farmers in need of such advice were likely to rely on the suggestions of contractors and lumber dealers rather than on the AES. This finding made the option of adapting to the farmer more clear-cut—the service could diffuse its information through the channels farmers already used. (This example parallels the Suchman research discussed in Chapter 4.)

Deciding Between Alternative Target Groups

We have already referred to target groups in our discussion of the translation phase; now they reappear. Suppose the population can be divided into two groups that differ in their receptivity to a message. Both the nature of the attitudes as well as the approximate size of the two groups must be ascertained. One group may be unaware of the message; another actively resistant to it. A proposed strategy may affect different groups in different ways. The policy-maker faces the choice of targets, a choice that must be intertwined with the feasibility of the various options for hitting the targets.

Sometimes, all of the target groups display resistance, and a choice must be made toward which group to direct efforts. McPhee and Brown's example[26] of research on "deviant behavior" among Army recruits in basic-training camps illustrates this. The research showed that such behavior among younger single men was "due to simple 'animal spirits' of such young people in general." Among older married men, it occurred as a reaction against rigid discipline. The recommendation here was to focus the effort on the older married men, since the Army could affect them positively by changing its leadership style.

But the problem does not end here. Sometimes a decision to concentrate on one subgroup may have indirect effects on the other. In another example, this from business, we find that manufacturers of breakfast cereals concentrate on the children's market, putting toys and games into their boxed cereals to compete with those of other firms. As a result, when young people grow up, they tend to consider cereals children's food. Indeed, statistics show that after roughly age fifteen, per capita cereal consumption declines rapidly. The manufacturer's neglect of the adult market may be detrimental for the industry as a whole. As far as is known, no manufacturer puts Whitman poems instead of whistles into his boxes. Presumably this reflects a policy decision to concentrate only on one target group.

Interestingly enough, the same issue arises in a culturally higher context. H. Zetterberg[27] found that a museum he was studying had developed close contact with the local schools. It was an efficient way to get the children of the community to visit the museum. But as a result, the museum came to be considered "kid stuff," which could cripple efforts to attract other segments of the population. Here, there was an expressed interest in expanding the market to include other audiences.

A more complex effort to identify and choose target groups can be seen in efforts to control overpopulation in developing countries. It appears that this is not an impossible task. For example, one study shows that in urban Ghana, five children is the desired average family size, while the actual average is seven.[28] This discrepancy makes it possible, at least in principle, to divide the population into two groups: those who have more children than they want because they do not know enough about birth control, and those who want more children to insure a sufficient number to support certain cultural and religious traditions.[29] Obviously the first group would be hospitable to birth-control propaganda, while the latter would be more resistant. To make a policy decision, it would first be necessary to know something about the relative size of the two groups. The literature suggests that the basically resistant sector is much larger; one would, therefore, have to know how difficult it is to influence this larger group if, as a matter of fact, it can be done at all.

The Choice Between Similar Inventions

Here, in contrast to the choice of targets, the dilemma is that a series of inventions have been designed to attain the same basic goal. The goal itself is not in question. How does one weigh the future effectiveness of the various techniques?

Let us first consider the area of delinquency. In the thirties, Clifford Shaw organized the Chicago Area Projects.[30] His theoretical rationale was uncomplicated: Juvenile delinquency was seen as a result of inadequate community control mechanisms to instill proper respect in the young for established law. In line with this idea, Shaw proceeded to design social devices which would provide such control in high-delinquency areas. The local involvement of parents was seen as indispensable to the establishment of moral authority among the potential delinquents; no other group could supply even a minimal working basis of legitimacy. Parents were recruited to participate in the operation of the project programs; when possible, they were organized through local churches and schools. The promise of community recognition tied to the participation of parents in activities sanctioned by these established institutions was acknowledged as a stimulus. Today, Shaw's analysis would probably be couched in terms of "role models." While Shaw considered parents the obvious role models, today one can find policy-makers experimenting with the recruitment of rehabilitated criminals, ex-addicts, and sports stars. It would be interesting to know the rationale for choosing one role model rather than another.

Some data on this matter can be found in the Coleman study commissioned by Congress to help deal with inequalities in educational opportunity. One widely cited finding was that, other things being equal, the performance of black students on specially administered academic achievement tests was better if their classrooms contained a higher proportion of white (middle-class) students. The most obvious policy implication was the need for school desegregation. But it could be anticipated that some white parents would strongly resist such an effort and the movement would not meet with quick success. What were some alternative strategies for achieving the same goal, better education for blacks? Coleman[31] himself suggested some alternative implications of his studies, which in effect attempt (without racial mixing) to reproduce the benefits of integrated classrooms by seeking the dynamics that account for their effectiveness. He focuses on two elements. First he attributes some of the differences between mixed and unmixed classrooms to the role of the teacher. In classrooms containing more white (and, therefore, on the whole, more advanced) students, teachers may set the curriculum at a more advanced level than they would for black students alone. Coleman proposed that the use of programmed teaching machines and new incentives for teachers, based on the academic improvement of black students in unmixed classes, might lead to some of the same results as racial mixing. Furthermore, higher performance among black students could also be achieved if students in unmixed classes could be brought into contact with more advanced students during the school day (without formal reassignment) through intramural academic competition.

Of course, technical considerations are not the only factor here. Coleman and many legislators would in the end opt for desegregation as the best means of improving educational achievement because they consider it a worthwhile social goal in itself.

It seems to us that what occurs in the choice between alternative strategies is a kind of implicit cost-benefit analysis. The parameters of such an analysis cannot be precisely measured. Figuratively speaking, filling the gap between knowledge and recommendation of a solution would amount to expressing the feelings one has about the difficulties implicit in the implementation of each of the alternatives, and what returns might be expected. Many times, there is the additional complication of the need for value choices.

Choosing a Preferred Value

Values play a role in all decision-making, but in some cases an applied study raises additional value questions. A study may show that two different goals are really incompatible in the sense that emphasizing one would tend to undermine the other. To make a decision, one is forced to rank these goals in order of importance. In the examples we have already discussed, this has not been necessary.

A good illustration of this new type of perplexing situation is the way in which research was utilized in the 1954 Supreme Court decision on public-school desegregation. The NAACP drew upon past findings of the Society for the Psychological Study of Social Issues. These studies concluded that in cases in which blacks were consistently subject to segregation, feelings of inferiority and exclusion hampered their educational and economic aspirations. Thus, separate schools were ipso facto unequal. This directly challenged the Court's earlier "separate but equal" doctrine. A choice between holding the right of localities to choose their own systems of education or that of blacks to equal educational opportunity was inescapable. This choice (which was made in favor of equal opportunity) had not been intellectually or legally necessary before segregation per se was linked to deprivation.[32]

Research forced new value judgments also in the case of the decision to extend food rationing late in World War II.[33] Because the war was lasting longer than anticipated, existing food supplies had to be more stringently rationed. A study was done to determine whether the existing ration-coupon system would serve the purpose, or whether the coupons in use would have to be invalidated and new ones issued. The answer depended on how many coupons were still in circulation. The study showed, in the policy-maker's view, that resources would be depleted if the then current coupons were honored. What could be done to persuade the American people not to use their coupons? No answer was found. To invalidate the coupons would be patently unfair to those who had saved them, placing their trust in the government's assurance that they would not be invalidated overnight. A great deal of opposition to invalidation was anticipated, but the study indicated that the conservation of resources depended upon the introduction of a new rationing system. The unfairness was disregarded, and a new system instituted.

The opposite decision was made in the case of the Columbia River Basin development project,[34] where human considerations were given priority. According to economic planners, locating farmhouses near the geographic center of the tilled land would be economically the most rational plan. But other studies showed that, left to their own devices, farmers tended to build their homes near those of other farmers, apparently out of desire for companionship. In the absence of reasonable substitutes for companionship based on geographic proximity, the planners were forced to choose between economic rationality, simply defined, and farmer morale. They decided in favor of the latter.

After this detour into the question of values, let us return to the notion that rational decision-making may be seen as an attempt to determine which possible course of action has the highest benefit-to-cost ratio. But if filling the gap between knowledge and recommendations means supplying assumptions needed for such an analysis, it is a kind of shadowy version.

Potential effects must be estimated because they may affect the empirical costs of a particular alternative. Generally, this conjuring up of potential consequences is a highly qualitative process. However, in recent years, there are those who have begun to emphasize the value of systematically explicating and even quantifying the cost-benefit analysis in decision-making. The trend surfaced first in the U.S. Department of Defense under the label of "Planning, Programming, and Budgeting System" (PPBS), and in 1965 was mandated for other government agencies. There is a growing literature* which formally describes the elements necessary for a comprehensive cost-benefit analysis and provides some illustrations.[35]

Kahn conveys the style of the cost-benefit analyst with the following quotation from E. C. Banfield:

> . . . consider how a school superintendent might act if his budget were raised to permit him to improve the education of his pupils. If he adopted the requirements approach, he would (let us say) hire more teachers because he knows that a higher ratio of teachers to children improves teaching. On the other hand, if he adopted the economizing or systems analysis approach, he would break the end "to improve education" into component ends (e.g., to improve the reading ability of handicapped children, to improve the math of college-bound ones, etc.) and then decide the terms on which he would trade off a marginal unit of benefit in terms of one and for a marginal unit of benefit in terms of another. In other words, the analyst first lists all of his objectives in detail and decides their relative priority. Then he is ready to consider the cost-effectiveness problem. At the same time he would be examining all the plausible ways of achieving the various ends that he seeks. He would carry on research to find out the marginal rate of return (in terms of his various ends) of

---

*There appear to be two quite different but related reasons why so much attention is given to such a simple proposal. One is that the use of cost-benefit criteria involves a radical departure from traditional budgeting practices in the federal government. The tradition is to justify each year's budget in terms of required increments of change from the previous year rather than in terms of over-all cost effectiveness. The second reason is that identification and precise assessment of all costs and effects of a given course of action is usually quite problematic, and thus in need of further clarification. This, of course, is the main theme developed here.

> investment in (say): 1. additional teachers; 2. raising teacher's salaries; 3. employing television and "teaching machines"; and 4. buying additional laboratory equipment. He would take into account as benefits and costs any side-effects that could be anticipated (e.g., the influence this or that action might have on the morale of the parents of the handicapped children). In the end he might well conclude that no course of action was best by all relevant criteria. . . . This in itself would have prevented him from making the most serious errors.[36]

Kahn is not completely beguiled by such an approach; he realizes its complexity, but thinks that in the social-planning field, such analyses do help to sharpen judgments.

Economists in the field of education have been particularly attracted to the cost-benefit technique. One analysis by Gary S. Becker[37] focused on the economic benefits of college education both for the individual recipient and the nation as a whole. The difference between the personal incomes of college and high-school graduates was measured, and it was found that this difference could be attributed largely to the college education itself (rather than to academic ability or to other differences between college and high-school graduates). The income difference was then weighed against educational costs. These were estimated with the help of college budgets, and they also include "opportunity costs," such as income sacrificed while a student attended college. A major conclusion was that while the rate of return for investment in college education was substantial, it was highest for white males, even when adjusted for differential ability. One might then compare the various rates of return with those from alternative commitments of funds, such as capital investments in business.

Our own perspective on the use of research would lead us to ask how various effects not included in the research itself were (or could be) estimated for the purpose of the cost-benefit analysis. For the above example, these might include possible intrinsic rewards of education, its effects on consumption behavior or on political ideology (side effects); and also the effects that increased investment in education might have on the economic value of education (feedback effects). Such effects were not dealt with quantitatively, but they obviously bear on decision-making.

A second example shows how a focus on quantifiable effects permits very sophisticated exploration of cost-benefit relationships. Research by G. G. Somers and E. W. Stromsdorfer was done to measure the effect of a training program on employment success and earnings.[38] The cost-benefit analysis relates these effects to direct and indirect costs of the program, but then the study goes further by calculating the time it takes to "repay" these costs. (It is relatively brief for males, longer for females).

A complex formula relates gains in monthly earnings and post-training total income to costs of training, according to a chosen rate of discount. Kahn notes that certain human gains have also to be considered in any such decision, e.g., "changes in self-image, status, family response, satisfaction." A controversy has developed over whether it will ultimately prove possible to incorporate these social values into a quantitative analysis which takes all such effects into account.

One of the dangers of decision formulas is that their simplicity may be overly seductive. Further inquiry into the uses of formal cost-benefit analysis is needed to determine in what way it clarifies (and whether it may sometimes obscure) the gap between knowledge and recommendation.

IMPLICATIONS FOR TRANSLATION

The emphasis in this chapter has been on the ideas and assumptions needed to bridge the inevitable gap between knowledge and recommendation. A focus on this problem may ultimately lead to an improvement in the design of applied studies which minimize this gap. Contributions to the design of applied studies might even evolve from situations in which these studies lead only to demands for further research. One should always ask whether the need for the additional research could have been anticipated. In general, it is hoped that more experience of both a positive and negative kind will be analyzed to find implications for translation.

Of course, it is very difficult to make reliable generalizations about how to minimize the gap. At the moment we have little to add to what we have said in Chapter 4. But our examples do reinforce some of the points made there. For example, the reader will note that the estimation of potential effects frequently implicates groups other than what in Chapter 4 we called the "primary target group." When should such collateral groups be included in the original research plans?

Our focus on typical gaps between knowledge and recommendation also underlines our discussion of the choice of variables. We noted in Chapter 4 how frequently the advice to study "manipulable variables" is given. We also suggested that this advice really oversimplifies the problem of translation of policy problems into research procedures. There are several reasons. First, whether a variable is manipulable or not is often uncertain. This is not only a matter of the policy-maker's resources. We have stressed the uncertainties surrounding policy inventions. For example, in the study done for the Kodak Company, it was discovered that film sales lagged because people stopped taking pictures when their friends tired of viewing them. Is this a manipulable condition or not? The answer could only come from experimenting with various solutions. The idea of film clubs might have worked, but since it was never tried, we still do not know whether the situation was manipulable or not.

Second, the fact that some causes of a problem are "manipulable" does not in itself ensure the utility of manipulating them. This follows from our discussion of "potential effects." Consider again one of the examples cited earlier. Caplovitz concluded from his study that two of the reasons that "the poor pay more" are (a) a strong culturally reinforced desire for expensive goods, and (b) lack of consumer sophistication. He regarded (a) as nonmanipulable, but he was more hopeful about (b). But as we pointed out, greater consumer sophistication among the poor might not solve the problem, because of a possible "feedback effect." The local merchants' monopoly on credit for high-risk customers could give them the power to charge them high prices, however alert the consumer might have become.

Third, information can be useful even when it does not directly concern manipulable variables. Not all strategy inventions are guided by formulations of the "causes" of a problem. As a matter of fact, many studies are useful because they identify conditions which can be used to help the policy-maker achieve his goals; he does not feel it necessary to search for underlying causes.

We have mentioned several examples which illustrate this. In the study of Japanese morale during World War II, there was no effort to discover the manipulable causes of high morale. Instead, there was a search for an understanding of the way the Japanese thought about their country and the war, and probing for potentially exploitable weaknesses or vulnerabilities. A similar example is to be found in Abrams' account of the use of surveys by the British Conservative party in the 1959 general elections. The surveys found that many young, well-paid manual workers identified with the middle class rather than the working class. The party leaders found this kind of information very useful in developing a campaign theme which would appeal to these potential Conservative supporters. It did not seem necessary to conduct research on the causes of their shift in allegiance. Slogans such as "Don't Let Labour Ruin It," and "You Never Had It So Good" were invoked.[39]

Of course it may be useful to look for "manipulable" causes of problems, but it should be borne in mind that the manipulability of any specific cause can always be in doubt, and that identifying manipulable causes may be neither necessary nor sufficient to finding a solution to the problem.

RECOMMENDATION AND IMPLEMENTATION

One final distinction must be made. We have stressed the intellectual aspect of the gap between knowledge and recommendation. But it might very well happen that external factors forestall the application of a reasonable recommendation. The necessary funds or personnel might not be available; internal power struggles might interfere; the situation may have changed from the time of the original study. This chapter has dealt only with the gap between knowledge and recommendation, paying little attention to the external factors which might affect implementation. The distinction between "external" and "internal" is of course somewhat vague. Some external features will have to be anticipated in the recommendations themselves; thus, for instance, a recommendation which assumes unlimited funds would be absurd. Other factors, such as the secret political ambitions of the client, might be unknown to the sociologist. In the next chapter the division of labor between client and sociologist is discussed and the relation between recommendation and implementation covered in greater detail.

NOTES

1 P. F. Lazarsfeld *et al.* (eds.), *The Uses of Sociology* (New York: Basic Books, 1967), p. xxvii.

2 M. Tumin, "Some Social Consequences of Research on Race Relations," *American Sociologist,* III, 2 (1968), p. 119.

3 D. P. Moynihan, *Maximum Feasible Misunderstanding* (New York: The Free Press, 1969 [1970 ed.]), p. 193.

4 P. Rossi, "No Good Idea Goes Unpunished: Moynihan's Misunderstanding and the Proper Role of Social Science in Policy Making," in L. A. Zurcher, Jr. and G. M. Bonjean (eds.), *Planned Social Intervention* (Scranton, Pa.: Chandler, 1970), p. 79.

5 R. K. Merton and E. Devereux, *Use of Social Research in the Solution of Business Problems* (New York: Bureau of Applied Social Research), 1956.

6 R. Likert and R. Lippett, "The Utilization of Social Science," in L. Festinger and D. Katz (eds.), *Research Methods in Behavioral Science* (New York, Holt, Rinehart and Winston, 1966).

7 P. F. Lazarsfeld, "Evaluating the Effectiveness of Advertising by Direct Interviews," *Journal of Consulting Psychology,* V (1941), 170–78.

8 G. Steib and H. Orbach, "Aging," in Lazarsfeld *et al.* (eds.), *op. cit.*, p. 628.

9 P. F. Lazarsfeld and F. Stanton, *Communications Research, 1948–1949* (New York: Harper, 1949), pp. 73 ff.

10 Cf. A. H. Leighton, *Human Relations in a Changing World* (New York, 1949); Ruth Benedict, *The Chrysanthemum and the Sword* (Boston: Houghton-Mifflin, 1946); Gene Lyons, *The Uneasy Partnership* (New York: Russell Sage Foundation, 1969), pp. 118–19; and L. W. Doob, "The Utilization of Social Scientists in the Overseas Branch of the Office of War Information," *American Political Science Review* (1947), 649–67.

11 Personal communication by the senior author.
12 Seymour Feshbach and Robert Singer, *Television and Aggression* (San Francisco: Jossey Bass, 1971).
13 D. Caplovitz, *The Poor Pay More* (New York: The Free Press, 1963, 1967).
14 I. Adams *et al.*, *The Real Poverty Report* (Edmonton, Alberta.: M. G. Hurtig, 1971, pp 77–78.
15 E. Rosenfeld, "Social Research and Social Action in Prevention of Juvenile Delinquency," in A. Gouldner and S. M. Miller (eds.), *Applied Sociology* (New York: The Free Press 1965), pp. 367–89.
16 J. H. Noble, "The Uncertainty of Evaluative Research as a Guide to Social Policy," in Louis A. Zurcher and Charles M. Bonjean (eds.), *Planned Social Intervention* (New York: Chandler Publishing, 1967).
17 A. Etzioni and R. Remp, "Technological 'Shortcuts' to Social Change," *Science*, CLXXV (1972), 31–38.
18 H. Gans, "Urban Poverty and Social Planning," in Lazarsfeld *et al.* (eds.), *op. cit.*, pp. 445–48.
19 W. F. Whyte and E. L. Hamilton, *Action Research for Management* (Homewood, Ill.: Irwin-Dorsey, 1964), p. 211.
20 C. Glock, "Applied Social Research: Some Conditions Affecting its Utilization," in *Case Studiesin Bringing Behavioral Science into Use* (Stanford, Calif.: Institute for Communications Research, 1961).
21 A. Campbell, "The Uses of Interview Surveys in Federal Administration," *Journal of Social Issues*, May, 1946, pp. 15–18.
22 H. Wilensky, *Organizational Intelligence* (New York, Basic Books, 1967), p. 23.
23 A. Oxenfeldt, *Futurism* (New York: Bureau of Applied Social Research, ONR Technical Report No. 5, 1973).
24 R. Elling, "The Design and Evaluation of Planned Change in Health Organizations," in A. Shostak (ed.), *Sociology in Action* (Homewood, Ill.: Dorsey Press, 1965), pp. 292–302.
25 C. Loomis and Z. Loomis, "Rural Sociology," in Lazarsfeld *et al.*, *op. cit.*, p. 667.
26 W. McPhee and L. Brown, *Some Useful Roles of Social Research* (New York: Bureau of Applied Social Research, 1960), p. 56.
27 H. Zetterberg, *Social Theory and Social Practice* (Totowa, N.J.: Bedminster Press, 1962).
28 R. Hill, "Research on Human Fertility," *International Journal of Social Science*, XXII, 2 (1968), 233.
29 Cf. e.g., K. Davis, "The World's Population Crisis," in R. K. Merton and R. Nisbet (eds.), *Contemporary Social Problems* (2nd ed., New York: Harcourt, Brace & World, 1966).
30 S. Kodrin, "The Chicago Area Projects—A 25-year Assessment," in D. Valdes and D. Dean (eds.), *Sociology in Action* (New York: Macmillan, 1965), pp. 462–74.
31 J. S. Coleman, "Toward Open Schools," *The Public Interest*, IX (Fall, 1967), 20–27.
32 K. B. Clark, "Desegregation Background: The Role of Social Scientists," in Valdes and Dean (eds.), *op. cit.*, pp. 295–305.
33 J. Kershaw and H. Alpert, "The Invalidation of Food Ration Currency, December 1944," *Journal of Social Issues*, III, 4 (July, 1947), 40–48.
34 Loomis and Loomis, *op. cit.*, p. 660.
35 A. J. Kahn, *Theory and Practice of Social Planning* (New York: Russell Sage Foundation 1969); pp. 40, 240n; see also Alice M. Rivlin, *Systematic Thinking for Social Action* (Washington, D.C.: The Brookings Institution, 1971).
36 Kahn, *op. cit.*, p. 243, quoted from E. C. Banfield, "Three Concepts for Planners," in E. C. Banfield (ed.), *Urban Government* (rev. ed.; New York: The Free Press, 1969), pp. 613–14.

37 G. S. Becker, *Human Capital* (New York: National Bureau of Economic Research, 1964).

38 G. G. Somers and E. W. Stromsdorfer, "A Benefit-Cost Analysis of Manpower Training," in Somers (ed.), *Proceedings of the Seventeenth Annual Meeting of the Industrial Relations Research Association* (Madison, Wisc.: Industrial Relations Research Association, 1965).

39 M. Abrams, "Public Opinion and Political Parties," *Public Opinion Quarterly*, XXVII, 1 (1963), 9–18.

SIX

The Relation between Policy-Makers and Social Scientists

In the analysis of research utilization, we have employed a conceptual framework which emphasizes two levels of interaction between policy-makers and social scientists: the cognitive and the social. In the previous three chapters, we concentrated on the cognitive level and emphasized that sociology can indeed be useful in policy-making, but that its utilization is far from a trivial intellectual exercise. This is by no means intended to deflect attention from the fact that intellectual transactions are greatly influenced by the social framework in which they take place. On the contrary, the social and intellectual aspects of utilization constantly influence each other, and neither can be completely understood in isolation from the other. These mutual influences are in fact one of the main topics explored in the growing literature on applied sociology.

The topic of social interaction can be organized with reference to the phases of the cognitive cycle discussed earlier. We can ask what social conditions determine the intellectual decisions made at a particular stage, and how the social and intellectual circumstances existing at one stage affect what happens in the next.

We begin by considering the initiation of applied social-science studies. What factors determine which particular policy problems are converted into applied studies, and who initiates the effort? Next, how are the work and control divided between researcher and policy-maker in the stages of the cognitive cycle? In particular, who translates policy problems into relevant research designs and who fills the gap between research knowledge and policy recommendations? This is one of the most controversial aspects of the organization of applied studies.

Finally, consider the outcome of utilization efforts. At this point, two major issues can be distinguished. First, how does the policy-maker react to the recommendations that grow out of applied studies? More generally, what is the relationship between recommendation and implementation? To what extent do political or ideological commitments of policy-makers interfere with an appraisal of the scientific merits of a policy recommendation? Under what conditions can policy-makers be influenced by applied studies, and what is the relevance of the way in which the cognitive cycle has been completed?

Second, how does the nature of communication affect the outcome? Many authors have pointed to various communication problems as a major barrier to the use of applied studies. The policy-maker may be unaware of a particular study relevant to his needs, or study results may be presented to him in a way he cannot easily understand. On the other hand, the researcher faces a number of difficulties in deciding how to present his findings.

There is not yet systematic evidence to test every hypothesis which can be projected about the interaction between policy-makers and social scientists. Therefore, we will attempt to map out various problems, using as illustrations the brief case studies already available in the literature. This can be viewed as a logical first step toward a more comprehensive empirical analysis of the social process of utilization.

WHO INITIATES AND USES RESEARCH, AND WHY?

Only a small proportion of decisions, big or small, involve the use of social research. But some policy-makers and sociologists are more predisposed toward utilization of research than others. Corporations and government agencies use sociology far more than, let us say, unions or churches. Likewise, survey research and concepts of social stratification are used more often than the sociology of art. It would be difficult to provide a detailed accounting of research utilization for all policy-makers and social-science specialties. Some idea of the general distribution of utilization can be obtained from various statistical studies, such as those by M. W. Riley[1] and Ellis,[2] and from books treating individual instances.[3] Rather than attempt to describe and account for these distributions, we shall only outline the elements which may affect the initation of a new effort in research/policy collaboration, or a shift in focus of an existing effort.

Sociologists as Initiators of Applied Research

Historically, the policy concerns of sociologists have greatly influenced their choice of problems for study, though this fact is rarely emphasized.

Almost every classical writer in the sociological tradition worked with policy implications in his mind—Comte, de Tocqueville, Marx, Weber, Durkheim, Spencer, Ward, and many others.

Today, the policy interests of sociologists are reflected in their choice of research in a variety of ways. Sometimes work is done to prove some ideologically or politically controversial point, or to expose some social condition that needs amelioration. For example, O. Klineberg's research[4] showing that the I.Q. of black children went up after their parents moved to the North was probably motivated as much by the desire to show why social conditions need to be changed as to develop social theory. Michael Harrington's well-known book *The Other America*[5] is also of sociological value, but the underlying motivation for his study was clearly social criticism. Incidentally, in both of these cases there is evidence that policy was ultimately affected. Klineberg's research proved useful in developing the NACCP case for the 1954 Supreme Court ruling on school segregation,[6] and Harrington's study is often given credit for stimulating major government action to eradicate poverty.[7]

Sometimes a social scientist initiates research intended to pretest a particular social program he thinks is important, as for example the major research study testing the impact of a guaranteed annual income on the motivation to work initiated by the University of Wisconsin's Institute for Poverty Research.[8] An example in which the purpose is to challenge an existing program is the recent research by Rosenhan,[9] which purports to show that one consequence of the vagueness of current criteria of mental health is the relative ease with which healthy people can be admitted to mental institutions and be treated as though they were suffering from serious mental disorders. To prove this, Rosenhan simply sent a number of normal people to various California mental hospitals with instructions to claim they had been hearing voices, without misrepresenting themselves in any other way. Each of these pseudopatients was admitted as a schizophrenic. The pretense went undetected, and each "patient" was finally released weeks or months later as a "schizophrenic in remission." Both the above cases illustrate again how the policy interests and theoretical interests of social scientists can quite easily converge on a single research site.

In recent years, some sociologists have become committed to the idea of policy-relevant research. They have attempted to mobilize other researchers toward this end through such new periodicals as the *Journal of Applied Behavioral Science*, *Transaction*, and *Social Policy*, or by organizing special conferences on policy research. The "policy sciences" movement is really an effort on the part of social scientists to spell out how the social sciences can best be mobilized for policy purposes and to indicate the potential benefits of interdisciplinary cooperation toward this end.

The policy interests of sociologists are also reflected in the writing of policy manuals which are intended as sources of general advice to practitioners in various fields. Books on urban administration, leadership, and political negotiation can be cited as examples.[10]

Actually, it is rather rare for outside researchers to convince the actual decision-makers to support new applied-research ideas. Instead, sociologists usually appeal to a third party—a government or foundation sponsor in the business of taking risks on such research. A typical strategy is illustrated by a group of University of Michigan researchers who conducted a series of studies relating the characteristics of work-group leaders to industrial productivity and job satisfaction. They secured initial support for research from a sympathetic government sponsor (Office of Naval Research) and then gradually persuaded the ultimate clients (corporations) of the potential benefits of the work. As D. Katz *et. al.* described their strategy in 1951,

> Industrial concerns are recognizing the value of this research and are giving it increasing support. As this support grows, the research will be extended, in accordance with the original plan, into a wide variety of business organizations, into other governmental agencies, the armed forces, additional labor unions, and social welfare and voluntary organizations.[11]

The social scientists Cloward and Ohlin proceeded along somewhat similar lines. Their academic work on the causes of juvenile delinquency led them to develop policy ideas which they themselves incorporated into antidelinquency program (Mobilization for Youth) accepted by the Federal government.[12] Research by Deutch and Collins on racial prejudice in segregated and unsegregated housing projects involved the local housing authorities from a very early stage. These officials were under pressure to resolve the conflict between their obligations to current tenants and their obligations to outside groups. Yet even there, the research was sponsored by an interested foundation.[13]

Rather than "robinhooding the client," to use Rossi's phrase,[14] it appears that researchers must usually rely on some sponsor who has no direct decision-making responsibility in the area. Clearly, this may create problems limiting the utilization of sociologist-initiated research in respect both to the formulation of the research design and the communication of the results.

In the United States, the foundations have long taken an active part in involving sociologists in applied research. The Carnegie Foundation played a major role in encouraging Gunner Myrdal to write his famous analysis of racism in American society, *An American Dilemma.*[15] Research on mass media was largely initiated by the Rockefeller Foundation in the thirties. The purpose of the research was to explore the basis for many of the predictions then being made about the likely effects of the commercial use of the radio on industrial society.

The Russell Sage Foundation, an important sponsor of social research in the United States, states as a major objective the desire "to improve the utilization of social science knowledge." According to its formal statement of operating policies, "The interest of the Foundation in a particular subject does not ordinarily end with the preparation and publication of a report, but usually continues into at least the early stages of practical utilization of the findings."[16] It would, of course, be interesting to see a detailed analysis of the extent to which the Russell Sage succeeded in achieving utilization; in point of fact, a major assessment has recently been undertaken.[17]

The ability of social scientists and other outside agencies to spot instances in which social-science resources may prove useful depends in part on their awareness of the context in which decisions are made. Conventional education and training in the social sciences ordinarily do not involve the development of a special skill to perceive potentials for relevance to policy. Working from positions in varying degrees removed from decision-making, the researcher may fail to acquire this facility. By himself, then, he must work with a knowledge of policy problems which is at best that of a more or less well-informed layman. For some, and perhaps for many types of policy problems, this layman's knowledge is more than adequate, and may even be an advantage. Social criticism by sociologists, initiated independently, may not be well timed for use by policy-makers, but it can have the virtue of identifying and addressing problems with which no policy-maker is dealing. But the initiation of direct relations between the sociologist and the policy-maker most often occurs at the request of the policy-maker, rather than of the sociologist. It is, therefore, important to ask about the conditions under which policy-makers commission research.

Policy-makers as Initiators of Applied Research

Variations in the predisposition of policy-makers to utilize research for particular policy problems might be analyzed in much the same way as the predisposition to use any service or product. An appropriate model might be Kadushin's study *Why People Go to Psychiatrists.*[18] The parallel, here, is that the service is used by only a small proportion of the eligible population; the major question is the way in which people come to define themselves as being in need of that relatively exotic service.

In the present discussion we will focus on four subtopics: conditions precipitating the use of social research; the retention and diffusion of existing research programs; the effects of interested third parties on the initiation of research; and ideological resistance to the use of expert advisers in the area of social policy.

Precipitating conditions. The first impression one gets from the literature is how often research is requested because of some major change in the policy-maker's situation, rather than because of a new awareness of the relevance of research to chronic problems. We have described the following examples elsewhere.

A museum faced a decline in attendance and called on researchers to determine the reasons for the decline and for ideas on how to attract more support for its program.[19] The establishment of social research in the Navy was attributed to the fact that rapid technological change brought new and more complicated forms of social organization which were more difficult to manage.[20] Research in the trading-stamp industry developed during the sixties, when trading stamps came under increased attack from consumers, whereas the preceding decades had seen business expansion but little research.[21] A change of circumstances may or may not mean that research is suddenly relevant to the decision-maker's problems; the change simply makes him aware of how little he really knows about the situation he faces and how much he needs outside help.

Frequently research is precipitated by a crisis of some kind. At such a point of heightened uncertainty a great deal of research may be initiated by policy-makers. A volunteer welfare agency, forced to adopt a completely new program, initiated research to find ways to retain the support of its workers.[22] With the advent of a new type of warfare, the Army Air Force confronted the need for a dramatic increase in trained air crews and research was carried out.[23] Settlers in a national forest in Louisiana set fires to areas containing new seedlings, and the Forest Service undertook research.[24]

A common complaint of social scientists about doing research in an applied setting is that a cumulative research program cannot be developed in many such situations because one is always "putting out fires" (in the last example this is almost literally true). The fact that research tends to be commissioned in response to rapid change or crisis is obviously a potential obstacle to its effective utilization. Researchers must either risk a hastily designed project based on the most readily available data or conduct more careful and painstaking studies, which may be completed too late to enter into decision-making.

Obviously neither option is completely satisfactory; Lipsky shows how the Kerner Commission research illustrates both pitfalls. The first option was pursued by the staff researchers. A team of six social scientists headed by Robert Shellow was charged with responding to the President's request for an investigation of the riots of 1967 and an analysis of their causes. Data were collected on 23 cities by teams of interviewers armed with a loose, open-ended questionnaire, and a preliminary report entitled "The Harvest of American Racism" was presented in less than three months. This report was controversial but, as social science, everyone agreed it was inadequate.

> This effort of the social scientists was abortive. The social scientists were informed that the draft of their report had been rejected by staff directors. They were told that it was not authoritative enough to win the support of the Commissioners. The staff directors did not conceal their distress at the "looseness" of the social scientists' major effort or the difficulties that would be experienced over some of the more controversial findings.[25]

Outside contract research for the Commission followed the second path of more deliberate, systematic (and tardy) inquiry.

> With one exception, these studies, however valuable, did not substantially contribute to the immediate development of the Commission's inquiry. Social scientists, by and large, proved unable or unwilling to conduct sophisticated research on short notice and with abbreviated procedures. Thus, the Commission had to be content with contract research which would not be available to influence commission deliberations, but only later would add to an understanding of civil disorders [p. 77].

The dilemma can only be forestalled by anticipating which problems are likely to become most serious, so that researchers can be given sufficient lead time. Some writers are not optimistic on this point. For example, P. Green blames social scientists themselves, citing "the failure of mainstream social science to foresee any of the major crises that now threaten the United States."[26] According to this view, "crisis research" is likely to be with us for some time. Efforts to eliminate the problem by employing social scientists full time over a period of years have never been systematically evaluated from this perspective. Y. Dror reports an instance in which a team of sociologists in a Dutch planning agency "developed a strategy of stockpiling answers by trying to anticipate the probable questions and doing necessary studies in advance." His only comment was "this did not always work."[27] As a matter of fact, it would be interesting to know if it ever worked!

Sometimes the policy-maker may utilize research after he becomes aware of a specific insight or piece of information which speaks directly to a recognized problem. Consider the special case of "pick-up" utilization, in which an already published finding can be immediately used by the policy-maker for a specific practical purpose. The following example has a number of revealing ramifications. In a study of the 1940 election carried out by Columbia's Bureau of Applied Social Research, the notion of "horizontal opinion leadership" was developed.[28] The point was that contrary to conventional notions, opinions did not trickle down from the top to the lower strata of the community. In fact, each social level had its own "influentials." After publication of *The People's Choice*, this finding came to the attention of a company which published magazines for low-income groups. The company had developed the public-relations device of talking about the "wage-earner market." The objective, of course, was to convince advertisers not to restrict their advertising to middle-class magazines. The finding about horizontal opinion leadership provided unexpected support for this policy. The publishing company underwrote a second study by Columbia's Bureau to explore the whole complex of "personal influence" further.[29] Since then, in the competition for advertising revenues, magazines have used the argument that they attract readers who are influential in some specific segment of the population.

The example is not a classic case of utilization, to be sure, but this exploitation of the existing research preceded any other type of commercial application. There were also some less pleasing side effects. To identify "influentials," the Columbia studies used a technique whose validity has been repeatedly corroborated since: by a series of interconnected questions, people described the issues on what and how often they were asked advice. From their replies, an index of opinion leadership was constructed. This technique came to the attention of another magazine, a news weekly which took pride in the fact that it had a large readership in upper-level occupations. The publishers wanted to substantiate their contention by using a more direct sociological index of influence, so they also commissioned a pilot study. The results were disappointing to them, although in retrospect not surprising. True, the index characterized the high-status people as concretely influential. However, many other real influentials were of lesser status. More disappointing from the client's point of view was the fact that this latter influential group hardly ever read their news magazine. They were not concerned with national and international affairs and were properly tagged as local, in contrast to the cosmopolitan opinion leaders. The study was duly published in an academic collection,[30] but was definitely not picked up for utilization by the client. "Pick-up" utilization is probably still rare.

There is one other situation in which the policy-maker initiates the utilization of a study in a way unintended by the researcher. This involves studies in which the researcher wants access to a research site controlled by the policy-maker, and the policy-maker asks that in return, the researcher include the study of certain policy-relevant problems. J. Kramer provides an example in which the policy-maker was the leader of a local Jewish community organization.

> The sociologist entering the minority community to get information is also asked to give it. In the reciprocity of the field, the community grants the observer an inside view of its social life in exchange for an outside view of its social structure. . . . One agency . . . [asked] us to find out what we could about local interest in Jewish organizations as an unpaid postscript to the interview.[31]

The example makes clear that negotiations of this kind may involve several potential "clients" representing diverse interests. Even the researcher who wants to do an autonomous study may find that he must agree to provide specific information to a variety of clients.

Retention and diffusion of existing research programs. Once a policy-maker does have positive experiences with social science, the likelihood that he will call upon its advice in the future is of course increased. In the milk-shortage example cited in Chapter 5, the fact that the Department of Agriculture had its own research division in part explains its willingness to consult researchers in the emergency, whereas the local Agricultural War Boards did not do so as readily. Sometimes, long-term relationships exist between policy-makers and outside research groups; as for example, the Treasury Department's commissioning of successive projects by the Survey Research Center. When a sociologist has provided useful information or recommendations in the past, it might be assumed the ground is laid for a continuing relationship.

However, there are contrary examples which suggest that being useful and creating good will are not identical. Dror describes the experiences of a researcher who worked for an Israeli tax-collection agency. He made useful contributions to policy but, in the end, the agency officials were antagonized and the position of researcher was abolished. In one unpopular study, a sociologist investigating reasons why tax payments were so often late found that collection agents were reluctant to charge mandated fines. They preferred to maintain amicable public relations. The sociologist's advice that the agency require more strict enforcement was finally implemented. But still there were difficulties, and Dror's diagnosis summarized the situation:

> The sociological adviser entered an agency which had no experience with such positions; therefore, the situation was nonstructured and his role definition very loose. He did not succeed in building up a realistic image of his position, either for himself or for the organization. Perhaps he engaged prematurely in hostility-generating specific studies without adequate prior educational activities. He apparently did not show sufficient initiative and salesmanship. There are some indications, however, that had he stayed on, many of the difficulties would have resolved themselves [p. 421].

That is, antagonisms may arise not only from inadequate work (or from personality conflicts), but also from the fact that sociological advice can be painful even when useful. Probably the converse is also true: intellectually inadequate work may be tolerated if it serves other purposes of the policy-maker (a point we return to below in connection with "third parties").

Spread of the predisposition to use social science is facilitated by the *exchange of elites*. Probably the failure of groups such as churches and unions to avail themselves of social science advice results in part from the fact that few of their leaders move between business and government. The relevance of social science research to the case brought before the Supreme Court by the NAACP in 1954 was recognized mainly because the staff overlapped significantly with the Society for the Psychological Study of Social Issues, which, in previous inquires, had devoted special attention to the effects of segregation on personality development.[32]

A detailed report of a parallel case comes from the history of the Bureau of Indian Affairs (BIA).[33] John Collier had been the Commissioner for a long time; anthropological research had been commissioned under his administration and a certain tradition had been established. During World War II, BIA was put in charge of one of the War Relocation Centers (the concentration camps housing Japanese-American civilians during the war). Collier immediately hired a number of experienced field researchers to play advisory roles in the camp's administration. As it happened, that particular camp was more successful than one which resorted to armed suppression of its inmates. The War Relocation Administration in Washington, which had responsibility for the camps, was persuaded by anthropologists that the successes were related to the use of advice from the anthropologists, and it extended their research to other camps in the system.

In the absence of existing staff interchanges, an intermediary sometimes helps to initiate research. H. Zeisel[34] reports that a court wanted to carry out an experiment aimed at speeding up insurance trials: one part of the trial would decide the question of liability; then, only if liability was found to exist, would the court go on to consider evidence to determine the award. The court asked the University of Chicago Law School to conduct the experiment, which in turn called on a sociologist for assistance. In this case, the law school was a natural middleman, although not explicitly set up for the purpose. Important, here, is the fact that the policy-maker does not himself need to know what sort of social science expertise might be relevant for the problem he poses.

Schools of business probably play a parallel intermediary role. Government agencies certainly play a middleman role for high-level policy-makers. No sociologist was directly commissioned by Congress to study financial aid for students. Instead, Congress asked for a study and delegated responsibility for it to the Office of Education; it was that agency that decided on the experts to be consulted.[35]

Response of Third Parties to Research Initiation

Initiating a research project is not only an intellectual decision; it is also a political act, since it envisages the likelihood that policy-makers will become involved in utilization of the research. Unless a project is kept secret, it affects outside groups while it is under way, by usually alerting people that new decisions on a topic are being contemplated.

Whether this represents a plus or minus from the decison-maker's standpoint depends on the expectations created. At one extreme, we have the notorious Project Camelot.[36] This Defense Department–sponsored study of revolutionary potential in South America generated such an intensely negative reaction in Chile that, in addition to the research itself being canceled, the very relation of social science to government was called into question. New guidelines were established to prevent the initiation of any further major research projects in foreign areas without the consent of the State Department. At the other extreme, we may place many of the recent Presidential commissions, such as the Kerner Commission on Civil Disorders.[37] Whatever the actual motives of the President in establishing the commission, the initial appointment of relatively liberal public figures to head studies of the causes of the 1967 wave of ghetto riots seemed to generate favorable expectations during the crisis period (at least among liberal intellectuals and journalists), while avoiding any immediate action save the restoration of order.

Appropriate advance consultation with third parties probably reduces the likelihood of opposition, as C. Sellitz *et. al.*[38] have suggested. They give the example of a school system which planned research on the effect of education on the "character" of students. Teachers objected to this research on the grounds that no problem existed and that the benefit to education would be greater if the money were spent on teachers' salaries rather than on researchers. In this case, the objections were overcome in a series of meetings at which the research was explained to the teachers' satisfaction. Students—the subjects of the research—were not consulted in this instance. It is well known that subjects who are fully aware of the research purpose may be "contaminated" and behave differently than they otherwise would. In a study for the Supreme Court of potential resistance to various means of school desegregation in the South, L.M. Killian[39] suggested that the only way to get reliable answers from respondents was to keep the research operation as secret as possible. But the situation is complicated by obvious ethical considerations. R. C. Angell[40] regards it an unethical to proceed with applied research without at least taking the interests of affected groups into account. One can do this without direct consultation, of course, but not everyone is happy with such a procedure.

Nonuse of Expert Advice

The willingness to consult experts may be increasing, as J. K. Galbraith[41] suggests, but there is still widespread resistance. Experts may not be called in because of a belief that their advice is obtuse or just plain wrong or because they themselves are arrogant or unresponsive. An example of such attitudes can be found in Michael Royko's anecdotal portrait of Chicago Mayor Richard J. Daley. Actually, the use of social scientists never came up explicitly, but Daley's attitude toward experts is nowhere more clearly expressed than in Royko's summary of Daley's characterization of newspaper reporters: "Reporters are like experts. What do they know?"[42]

Certainly the question is not entirely one of close-mindedness, at least not always. Many experienced and sophisticated decision-makers tend to feel that excessive reliance on scientific inquiry can become a real handicap. Particularly in cases in which the policy-maker is most genuinely eager to solve a problem, strong pressures against a scientific attitude may be likely to develop. The editors of *The Uses of Sociology* put it this way:

> Administrative leaders owe their success partly to their ability to make quick decisions involving great risk or uncertainty. Such decisions are typically based

on the intuitive assessments of somewhat opaque situations. It might well be that executives do not necessarily distrust or misunderstand the social scientist; rather, they fear that an important property of theirs, a natural gift for decision-making, might be impaired by too much concern with its rational aspect. The aversion of poets and other creative groups to literary and artistic criticism is often based on this kind of fear [pp. xxii–xxiii].

The question is to what extent is nonuse of experts prudent and rational, and at what point does it become risky and irrational.

Debate over the utility of the social scientist's perspectives takes somewhat different forms in different applied settings. In medicine, for example, Martin Hyman describes the controversy between statistical and clinical approaches to problems of health-care delivery. "Clinical medicine aims at the understanding of individual patient-cases . . . sociology is traditionally concerned with generalization to reasonably large populations." Hyman suggests that clinically oriented people may find it difficult to appreciate the relevance of the statistical approach. His concrete example is a disagreement between a sociologist and a medical social worker on how to present information on the concept of social class to medical students.

The sociologist wanted to review the empirical literature and base the lecture on generalizations abstracted from this literature. The social worker preferred that the lecture consist of a detailed description and analysis of individual cases. She reasoned that in this manner the relationship between social class and response to frustration would be viewed by the students in a manner appropriate to future practitioners: as only one part of the total and unique picture of factors to be taken into account in dealing with an individual patient.[43]

According to Hyman, the statistical orientation of many sociologists in medicine means that compared to psychologists and anthropologists, relatively few of them are involved in clinical discussions.

In the area of foreign-policy planning, the parallel controversy concerns the competing claims of specialists and generalists. W. P. Davison traces the generalist position to an underlying occupational ideology:

A part of the prejudice against students of human behavior stems from the belief that foreign policy is an area that should be dealt with by generalists. The Foreign Service, somewhat like the military establishment, has traditionally insisted that any officer should be able to perform any job. He should not be a geographical or functional specialist, but should have a well-rounded appreciation of all the major factors entering into international relations.[44]

But again, the resistance to social-science expertise among diplomats may not be based entirely on convictions on the nature of effective decision-making. Davison remarks on a negative opinion of the work of social scientists:

> There is still a deep suspicion of social science among many foreign affairs practitioners, especially those of the older generation. There are also strong prejudices against the use of the word "science" in connection with behavioral studies, and the objection is frequently heard that the results of social research are trivial, incomprehensible, or obvious to anyone who cares to use common sense [p. 407].

Attitudes such as these may help to explain why the State Department funded only the preparation of bibliographies on relevant foreign policy and a few studies "drawing mainly on work originally performed with other ends in view" (p. 409).

The Defense Department has a much larger social research operation, and one might expect that its prevailing attitudes would be more favorable to social research. Yet D. C. McDonald reports continuing resistance in the military to the conduct of research. Military officers, like foreign-service officers, pride themselves on being generalists. According to McDonald, this is reinforced by the types of tasks officers perform.

> The combat situation does not always conform to the preordained plans; fighting units may become unexpectedly separated from each other, whole segments of the military machine might become knocked out or partially impaired, and so forth. This means that the commanders must be capable of improvising autonomous action. . . . Officers must, therefore, be trained to be self-reliant in circumstances which require it. Self-reliance also means self-sufficiency; the commander must not be so dependent on specialists that he is paralyzed in their absence.[45]

In the case of military technology, the officer is forced to rely on experts. But he has not given up the claim to expertise in such areas as personnel management and leadership. "The consequence of all this is that many officers tend to perceive the social science researchers as something of a threat to administrative authority rather than as a valuable resource" (Chapt. 5, p. 23). McDonald suggests that this attitude varies directly with the need for self-sufficiency in military roles. Thus, the officer in charge of a nuclear-submarine fleet which stays at sea for two months at a time without contact with shore stations denounced social researchers to Congress and prevented their connection with his fleet.

What degree of self-reliance is really essential to effective leadership? When is research really needed? An illustration of policy-makers closest to a problem who were most vulnerable to a false sense of certainty has already been given in Chapter 5. In confronting a scarcity of milk production during World War II, the local Agricultural War Boards (being in constant contact with many farmers) felt reasonably sure they knew what the problem was. They were convinced the farmers lacked facilities for increased production. Given their closeness to their constituents, they were certain that whatever understanding they might lack could not be furnished by outsiders. However, the Federal Department of Agriculture suggested independent research on the problem. The Boards thought it a waste of time, but they finally consented, and as it turned out, their original diagnosis actually proved incorrect. Farmers *did* have facilities and an adequate labor supply, but they failed to increase milk production because they feared a price drop once the war ended and wanted to avoid being caught with an excess supply. Many of them had little understanding of government price guarantees. The study results also revealed the cause of the Boards' misinformation: They had had contact mainly with an elite, very well-informed group of farmers who were in fact producing at capacity. In short, proximity of the Boards to the problem prevented them from seeing how little they really understood it.[46]

DIVISION OF LABOR AND CONTROL

In the cognitive utilization cycle, the researcher often provides more than merely the research. There is a great degree of variability in this respect, however. At one extreme, there is the case in which the policy-maker himself identifies the problem, decides what information he needs for a particular decision, and then asks the researcher for this specific information. Instances like this have been reported in the literature, and in those cases it is doubtful whether we can talk of utilization at all. At the opposite extreme, there is the general sociologist who sends messages to the policy-maker after he has done his own independent study and drawn his own conclusions. Here, the major uncertainty is whether the recommendations will ever be used.

The dilemma as to division of labor and control is central to much of the debate over the vast bulk of applied sociology which falls between these two extremes. There are at least two views of how the over-all administrative coordination should occur. One seems to assign the task to a new kind of professional. Y. Dror describes him in a way which hardly leaves any place for the old decision-maker. The man is able

> to deal in a broad innovative, and open-minded way with problems, a kind of "expert generalist"—a contradiction only in traditional terms, but not in emerging reality. Policy analysts well illustrate such a new type of professional, who is a specialist in a general problem-solving approach and method.[47]

K. Archibald is less radical. Based on 15 detailed interviews with academicians in defense research, she distinguished three types of orientations to social science utilization; the academic, the clinical, and the strategist.[48] The men in the first group do their work and leave it to the practitioners to make use of it or not. Archibald's main interest is in comparing the clinical and strategic approaches, and she clearly favors the latter. The clinical type treats the "client" like a patient who needs help either because of personal deficiencies or because he is under social pressures he cannot cope with. The strategist thinks of the client as a colleague who wants to merge his own practical knowledge with the more systematic approach of his adviser. Interchange is frank and the decisions are likely to be made jointly. Archibald actually speaks of the sponsor not as a client but as an "alter," because "what is a client system . . . from one point of view (or at one point in time) may be resources or environment from another."

In our discussion of this whole problem, we will separate the division of labor in formulating the research design from the division of labor in formulating recommendations and facilitating their implementation.

The Division of Labor in "Translation"

One of the great dangers at the translation phase of the cognitive cycle is that of following too closely the prescriptions of the client. To as great a degree as possible, the sociologist should take the position of first critically examining the definition of the problem as presented and only then deciding on the nature of the research. A negative example, *The Academic Mind study,* was presented at the end of Chapter 4.

Much of commissioned applied research can be criticized in hindsight as not sufficiently responsive to the real interests of the client. Take the poverty problem, on which so much research has been done. Most of this research focuses on the impoverished groups themselves. Yet, policy discussions often focus on the nonpoor: Will they support expensive programs to aid poor people; what kinds of programs are likely to receive support; what are the main centers of resistance; how can they best be won over?

It is obvious, however, that the policy-maker may have information and ideas relevant to the design of useful research whose significance might be overlooked by the sociologist. A number of authors have stressed the need for more extensive contribution from the policy-maker in the research-design stage. Sellitz *et al.* as well as Likert and Lippitt[49] argue that the participation of the policy-maker in research design helps strengthen the relation between the proposed research and the policy problem, reducing the possibility of irrelevant results. They believe that client participation in this phase also makes utilization more likely because of the greater likelihood that the policy-maker will understand the implications of the research results when they come in.

Coleman has argued recently that the lack of such input for most government policy research is a major reason for nonutilization:

> Much research on applied problems in the United States is really not policy research because it is formulated by the investigator, in the absence of policy problems. This is because research funds for policy research are placed in the hands of agencies that have little control over policy.[50]

H. Orlans also stressed that one way in which social research could be made more useful would be for policy-makers to specify in much more detail exactly what information is needed.

> Before research can be relevant to national needs, it is necessary to specify what knowledge *is* needed that can realistically be obtained by research. In short, some sort of practical and specific, and not illusory and general, objectives must be agreed upon between those who sponsor and those who conduct research.

Orlans provides no general instructions on how to achieve this sort of cooperative participation. Input from policy-makers could take a variety of forms. But he clearly thinks policy-makers as well as social scientists have a role to play.

> This [specification of research objectives] is by no means as easy as it sounds . . . . In general, executive agencies—and particularly those with the largest programs of applied social research, such as the Office of Education, the Public Health Service, and the Office of Economic Opportunity—can be faulted for not enunciating sufficiently clear and limited [research] goals; the social science community, for not hewing closely enough to these goals (sometimes because they were not adequately consulted before the goals were set); and the politi-

cal, budgetary, and appropriations process, for rendering the goals inherently unstable.[51]

Case studies in applied sociology could make a significant contribution by indicating as clearly as possible those contributions of the policy-maker which were incorporated in the formulation of a research design.

Probably the major reason researchers would give for avoiding the participation of policy-makers in research design is the fear that their own independence in the conduct of the research would be limited and truly critical investigation hampered by the interference of laymen untrained in social science. The value of increased contributions to research designs by policy-makers and the cost in terms of interference with the independence of the research enterprise could be weighed against each other. However, a recent study by E. M. Glaser and S. H. Taylor[52] provides evidence that applied research is most likely to succeed when there is at least some kind of intensive interaction, even discord, between researchers and policy-maker. Glaser and Taylor analyzed ten selected research projects sponsored by the Applied Research Branch (ARB) of the National Institute of Mental Health. ARB had rated five as very successful in terms of the quality of the research, its relevance to original objectives, and the extent of dissemination. The other five had received low ratings. An examination of all relevant NIMH documents and interviews with researchers, administrators, and potential users showed that the successful researchers had interacted more intensively with all nonresearch parties, and that the research began with greater disagreement and tension.

> The successful projects evidenced a more dynamic, issue-laden interaction which frequently led to conflict and the need for revisions and compromise [p. 142] . . . . The projects' own team members were encouraged to question and challenge all issues and procedures during the course of the research [p. 143]. In contrast, the less successful projects were calm and uneventful [p. 142] . . . . Less successful projects tended to discount, avoid, and discourage the suggestions and critical reactions of other persons [p. 143].

Conflict had not produced "disabling" revisions of the research: rather, it had stimulated it. It was the less successful projects which proceeded without "interference."

In our own review of the literature, we have found few concrete cases in which the participation of policy-makers has tended to limit the freedom of the researcher critically to analyze field-induced problems, although it undoubtedly limits his freedom to investigate autonomous research problems of strictly professional concern at the policy-maker's expense. Complaints from researchers suggest that their major disagreements with policy-makers about applied research designs rarely concern scientific issues. F. Ruderman did report one such complaint in the social-work field, and it concerned methodology rather than theory. The social-work sponsors reportedly regarded systematic interviewing as an inappropriate means for getting information from respondents.[53] But this type of problem seems to be encountered only infrequently.

More common are restrictions which can be traced to some political or normative consideration of the policy-maker. For example, objections are sometimes raised to the use of controlled experiments in which differential treatment of subjects is involved. R. A. Brymer and B. Farris[54] report that a study on the effects of social-work service on delinquency rates was limited by social workers themselves who felt that the use of "controls" would discriminate against certain groups and could not be justified by the research goals (see also H. Bynder[55]). There is substantial difference of opinion about the real need for this type of restriction. Zeisel makes a case for experimentation even in the relatively sensitive field of law.

> Several circumstances . . . argue in favor of the experiment, even in legally sensitive areas. First, it is by no means certain that the experimental treatment makes any difference; the uncertainty is in fact the reason for the experiment. Second, discrimination in an experiment is by definition only temporary; after it is concluded and the best solution is found, the solution will be applied to all. Finally, there are areas at the fringe of the law where random assignment is more tolerable because the right involved is not sufficiently important to merit special attention.[56]

Still, experiments may be opposed because of the legal entanglements that could arise, even if the experiments can be justified morally. Only special legislation can forestall such objection.

Perhaps the most common complaints arise when policy-makers impose restrictions on the type of question which can be included in interview schedules and questionnaires because of a concern about political repercussions. For example, it is rumored that social researchers studying problems facing the South Vietnamese government during the late sixties were prevented from conducting a survey which included direct questions about popular attitudes toward the government. Military officials were said to have been worried that such questions might in themselves encourage dissatisfaction. Perhaps another worry was that results showing widespread dissatisfaction could leak out and cause political damage to the government and its war effort. Such restrictions obviously limit the cognitive value of the research. Social researchers may disagree with the policy-maker about the necessity of restrictions in particular areas, but the question is one of political judgment and not of scientific priorities.

From the point of view of the client, the primary consideration is what the researchers will do with whatever independence is granted them. A researcher with complete freedom to be imaginative and constructive also has the freedom to be irrelevant. A. Pasanella[57] reports that when the College Entrance Examination Board began giving the Educational Testing Service lump sums for research without strings, "the plan disintegrated into support for studies in which E.T.S. was interested but the C.E.E.B. was not." In the end, a proposal system was reinstituted.

It is probably rare for sociologists unilaterally to alter the terms of an arrangement once it has been made, although they may often feel the need to do so. An exception reported by Clairmont and Magill[58] illustrates what may happen. The Nova Scotia provincial government commissioned researchers to evaluate the success of an urban-renewal project which had relocated residents of a Negro ghetto in Halifax and leveled the ghetto dwellings. Interviews with former ghetto residents were planned to measure their satisfaction with the relocation experience. The researchers discovered what they regarded as significant hostility in former residents toward the treatment they had received, and concluded that further economic assistance should be provided by the city. When the city's response was deemed inadequate, the research strategy underwent a drastic change. In order to provide former residents with ammunition needed to press demands for assistance, the researchers quietly undertook investigations of the decision-making process leading up to the relocation program. Public documents from city files were examined and city officials interviewed. A report was prepared for public distribution. The provincial government was informed of the change in the researchers' plans, but, not too surprising, its reaction was unenthusiastic. In effect, the researchers had changed clients mid-way. Instead of doing research as initially planned, they had become self-appointed consultants to those who had previously been the objects of the project.

Sociologists are aware that some policy-makers are quite distrustful of research and researchers. Even when sociologists are hired for staff positions in nonacademic agencies, mutual expectations are not always clear. J. Riley[59] has analyzed this situation in some detail. He suggests that to alleviate their anxieties, researchers be given higher status positions in such agencies; but policy-makers will not create more secure positions for researchers until their own uncertainties are resolved. F. Goldner says his own experiences suggest that fears about the sociologist's lack of commitment to organizational needs can be reduced if the sociologist explicitly evinces such concern. "I had to lean over backwards to show concern for the needs of the organization as my superiors saw them, although these might be different from the needs as I saw them."[60]

The completion date for the research is usually set by the policy-maker. As Miller[61] and others have noted, a researcher may have to be prodded into committing himself to a time schedule and forgoing the time needed to elaborate every qualification as is the practice in academic circles. But it is acknowledged that the policy-maker does have the right to limit the time available for research, if, in his judgment, a decision must be made soon. On reflection, however, this appears to be something that a researcher might legitimately question. Though desirable, a quick decision might be inadvisable until more information is in.

The Division of Labor in Recommendation

The question of division of labor arises again in the formulation of recommendations. Sometimes the researcher simply presents facts, sometimes he makes recommendations; sometimes he participates in discussion. Interestingly, the literature seems less concerned with the independence of social scientists in this regard. The main consideration is the kinds of competence required to fill the gap between knowledge and decision in different cases.

What is the appropriate division of labor in various circumstances? Clearly we can find cases in which the experience and ideas of the two (and indeed of third and fourth) parties enter, sometimes at different points in the process of formulating recommendations. Policy-makers are most likely to consider which risks should be taken and which side effects are most critical. For example, a trading-stamp study assessed the relative market value of the offering of trading stamps versus discounting merchandise. The study found that women *preferred* discounts to stamps, but it also showed that they are much less likely to notice whether prices are lower in stores without stamps, since their second preference, the stamp, is much more visible.[62] Only a very subtle and probably inconclusive experiment could show what finally determines action: a prime preference which is difficult to realize or a secondary choice which is easily made because the path to it is well "lighted." The store manager has to make the decision himself, without the prompting of social science.

In determining recommendations, it is sometimes useful to talk with the people who are actually slated to carry out the details of a proposed plan. E. Rosenfeld called special attention to this possibility as she discussed the use of certain research on juvenile delinquency.[63] This research had indicated that certain types of gangs helped their members gain access to drugs. The policy recommendation was to try to transform these gangs by involving them in local recreation centers and settlement houses. What was overlooked was the possibility that, instead of reforming the gangs, this strategy would corrupt the "squares." Rosenfeld feels that discussions with people in the field might have prevented this mistake because "people who for many years continue in one type of work as a rule accumulate a wealth of intimate knowledge of the great variety of forces, pressures, interests, and conditions that play a role in the situation in which they work." Those who want to draw on this information in planning strategies, she says, must "dodge or get around the heads of the various agencies, who often are far removed from the work experience of field workers."

The physicist Alvin Weinberg uses the term "trans-scientific" for questions that "can be stated in scientific terms but are beyond the proficiency of science to answer."[64] This is essentially what we have in mind when we refer to the "gap between knowledge and decision," and Weinberg wants the public to debate such questions. However, the sociological profession should not abdicate its responsibility. Some members will work on field-induced studies, and those who do should be trained to go beyond their research and help in spelling out its implications up to the final stage of practical decision. A theory of utilization (yet to be worked out) should provide the appropriate foundation.

The whole problem of division of labor in the cognitive cycle was raised some time ago in an insightful essay by Max Millikan.[65] His arguments focused on the point that often too much division of labor is maintained. "An effective marriage of knowledge and action is seriously inhibited by an exaggerated emphasis on the virtues of the division of labor." A strict division of labor really implies, according to Millikan, a misunderstanding of how each party's competence relates to the joint enterprise. The general misunderstanding is summarized this way:

> Decision-making and the pursuit of systematic knowledge have come to be regarded as separable activities, and it is supposed to be inefficient for the researcher to concern himself with policy decisions or for the policy-maker to probe too deeply into research techniques. The policy-maker is supposed to recognize what it is he needs to know and to be able to levy a clear requirement on the researcher to supply the missing knowledge. The researcher, using techniques which it is his business and nobody else's to understand, is in turn supposed to answer the questions put to him.

We strongly agree that "the relations between knowledge and action are infinitely more complex and reciprocal than this image would suggest." But the form of the appropriate division of labor is still to be worked out. We hope to show through examples that further clarification will come from a detailed scrutiny of concrete experience with various possible ways of dividing the cognitive tasks.

The material which follows tries at least to sensitize students to additional aspects of the problems and situations involved.

THE IMPLEMENTATION OF RECOMMENDATIONS: A CONTINUING DISPUTE

Most social scientists feel that their recommendations on topics ranging from poverty and race relations to war and peace to personnel policies are more often rejected than accepted. The mood at recent sociological meetings reflects this complaint. The American Sociological Association convention in 1968 was devoted to the theme of the uses of sociology, and at the 1972 convention, the President of the Association, W. J. Goode, asserted that the American government has persistently ignored sociologists' recommendations in the areas of race relations, crime, housing, and political protest.

The client's resistance to social science recommendations is sometimes ascribed to prior political or ideological commitments.[66] That is, the client may not really want to pursue the goals in question (whatever he may say publicly), or may have ideological "blinders" which prevent him from accepting the social scientists' research findings. H. Wilensky[67] and M. Janowitz[68] both cite persistent Pentagon belief in the military efficacy of bombing in Vietnam as illustration of this pattern. In Janowitz' view, the persistence of a commitment to bombing required a "monumental lapse of collective memory" which ignored past research.

> Future historians will be able to point out that research during and after World War II in Europe and Japan, including the massive United States Strategic Bombing Survey and the documentation of the Korean conflict, should have supplied a basis for the intellectuals of the sixties to recognize the limited impact air warfare would have on the political and social structure of North Vietnam. American policy in South Vietnam has never been based on realistically understanding that the social and political impact of strategic air warfare would be negligible and most likely counterproductive [pp. 24–25].

Such resistance is not limited to military officials or government bureaucrats, as T. Pettigrew's summary of response to research on race relations makes clear:

> The "unqualified integrationists" will question any study that does not find racial desegregation of all types to have significant and lasting value to all the children involved. Members of the "educational establishment" in good standing will not easily accept findings that suggest that "compensatory education" programs in ghetto schools are not the answer to the typically low academic achievement of impoverished black children. Garden-variety "white segregationists," North and South, will reject any research data that indicate that white children are not academically harmed by interracial classrooms. And "black power advocates" will brand as "racist" any results that reveal below-grade-level performance of children in all black schools. Yet all four of these ideology-violating findings are commonly uncovered by competent investigations.[69]

The literature on applied sociology is full of complaints about the persistence of policy views in the face of contrary social science–based recommendations. No one was surprised when the then President Richard Nixon came out for the reimposition of capital punishment as a crime deterrent, and that he singled out "social theorists" for criticism, rejecting research such as Sellin's[70] showing that the death penalty has no measurable deterrent effect.

Ambiguity Because of the Gap

A very important caveat must be entered here. When a policy-maker rejects the social scientists' recommendations, it is not necessarily true that he either disagrees with his goals or challenges his competence. There is also a third possibility. He may agree with the social scientist's goals and defer to his knowledge, yet still object to the gap assumptions used to reach his recommendations. Such objections may be reasonable or unreasonable. The use of the term "resistance" in such cases really implies that the objections are thought to be unreasonable, in rational terms, and that political or ideological motives are probably involved. It does not necessarily meant that the policy-maker is blind to the findings of science.

Difference of opinion on the plausibility of specific gap-assumptions, rather than value conflicts or nonutilization, may be involved in many of the policy disagreements between social scientists and policy-makers. For example, many social scientists have advocated the large-scale busing of school children to achieve racial balance as a means of promoting equality of educational opportunity and other social goals. Research indicating the probable benefits of busing is available and cited. Obviously, the decision to make this a top priority in the racial field may depend in part on assessment of several "potential effects": the anticipated reactions of white parents, teachers, and students to such a program; whether a viable educational program can be maintained; how many whites will remain in the integrated schools; and so on. Contrasting assessments of these consequences are possible. No social scientist can claim that his own assessments are supported by precise scientific evidence in each instance. At least some of the policy-makers who oppose busing may nonetheless desire racial equality. They may feel that too many unknowns are involved in busing. It is important to examine such instances of rejection of recommendations to determine whether they involve disagreement on gap-assumptions, because this analysis opens up the possibility that further studies which attempt to "close the gap" may change policy-thinking at a later time.

If "potential effects" are ever really decisive in the rejection of recommendations by policy-makers with strong ideological predispositions, then it should be possible to find cases in which research has dealt so thoroughly with possible objections to a recommendation that the policy-maker does finally accept it, despite his initial predispositions. Such cases are admittedly difficult to find, but one candidate is the use of research in the desegregation of the U.S. Army. Here was a client who was inititally quite hostile to desegregation making a policy-decision making the Army one of the first American institutions to undertake wide-range desegreation. It is important to study such cases in detail, even though in the end one might disagree with those who give great weight to the role of research in bringing about desegregation. Whatever the judgment on this, such cases can suggest some conditions under which applied studies may affect policy even when the policy-maker has opposite leanings.

A Case Study: Desegregation in the U.S. Army

Between the Civil War and World War II, the U.S. Army maintained a rather rigid policy of racial segregation. Moreover, Negro units were rarely if ever assigned to combat duties. The official rationale for these policies was couched in terms of morale and military efficiency. It was maintained that any attempt to integrate Negroes into white units would undermine morale among the white troops, and might even lead to violence. In addition, Negroes were supposed to be inferior fighting men, better suited to service roles within the military (e.g., messmen, drivers, etc.). According to R. M. Dalfiume's[71] historical account, such ideas, well-established doctrine within the military hierarchy, were repeatedly offered up to justify the segregation policy.

The first studies of the problem by the Army's Research Branch during World War II were simple opinion surveys. These surveys showed that the majority of black soldiers were opposed to segregation on principle, yet about half of them accepted it as a "practical necessity." Almost 90 percent of the white soldiers approved of segregation. What did such findings imply for the Army's segregation policy? The social scientists argued that attitudes do not always predict behavior (an idea we discussed earlier), and that gradual desegregation would "not necessarily" be met with violent resistance from whites. However, Army officials reached different conclusions:

> If segregation was abandoned, the Army reasoned, it would certainly be a blow to the morale of 90 percent of its strength, and it might result in bloody conflict. Many high-ranking Army officers also argued that segregation suited most Negroes because they were accustomed to it in civilian life. On the surface, the opinion surveys tended to confirm the beliefs of Army officials about the necessity of maintaining segregation, and they in turn interpreted them this way. . . . Few questions of Army policy were decided on the basis of soldiers preference, but the War Department overlooked the social scientists' qualifications of their findings, preferring to see them as confirming their predilections about the necessity of segregation [pp. 78–79].

In short, the findings had little effect on anyone, because they could so easily be interpreted as consistent with the rationale for practically any policy position.

It would hardly seem appropriate to apply the term "resistance" to the Army response to the study. The gap between knowledge and decision was in fact quite large. This of course does not mean that the Army would have responded favorably to recommendations for integration based on research which more directly challenges their ideological assumptions—nor does it mean the opposite.

A very different type of research was made possible by a special circumstance later in the war. There was a shortage of white infantry replacements after the Battle of the Bulge. To help make up for the shortage, platoons of black soldiers volunteered to complement previously all-white companies in the European land war. This forced desegregation in effect set up an actual experiment which the Research Branch studied in detail. Some rather surprising findings emerged. The experience of desegregation produced a favorable rather than unfavorable change in the attitudes of whites toward blacks in the Army.

> White men of the integrated units had experienced a profound change of opinions towards Negroes. Whereas only a third of the white soldiers had expressed a favorable opinion of having Negroes in their companies before this experiment, afterward 77 percent said they had become more favorable, and none said they were less favorable.

A similar improvement was found in the attitudes of officers and sergeants in integrated units.

> Of the white officers 84 percent of the white sergeants said that the Negro soldiers in their companies performed well in combat. Only 1 percent of the sergeants and none of the officers said they did not do well [p. 100].

The attitudes of men in integrated units contrasted sharply with the attitudes of men in divisions not participating in the experiment, 62 percent of whom opposed the inclusion of Negroes in their units.

These findings directly address the official rationale for both segregation and noncombat assignments for blacks. Some kind of follow-up would normally be expected. However, many officials were opposed to it. Two reports on official reaction to the study indicate a tendency to discount the study itself and to cite what we call "potential effects." Dalfiume says that "those within the Army who held to the old ideas about black soldiers . . . looked upon this experience as only an experiment that proved little." He also mentions that "they feared publication of the survey results would lose support for the peacetime draft proposal among powerful Southern senators in Congress and would encourage agitation for further experiments by Negro organizations." Davenport also reports a twofold rejection of integration. A General Officer is quoted as criticizing the study itself as biased:

> The study is quite general in its treatment of fundamental concepts and basic facts. Some conclusions appear supported by information obtained specifically for preconceived results, or by opinion and impression of the researcher. Information from which the deductions are drawn is from anonymous sources, without authentication, on some important issues "volunteered."

The same officer also felt there was no transfer of findings between emergency and nonemergency situations. "The report is based upon opinions formed while the informants were in combat, and is admittedly limited to impressions received during such period."[72] Davenport, a social scientist with experience in government agencies, attributed these reactions to bias, ignorance of social science methods, or a combination of both. We tend to see them as components of the gap between finding and recommendation. But be that as it may, it makes little difference in the present case. The study had little immediate effect on Army policy. When the war ended, the Negro platoons were detached from their white units.

The story does not end here, however. A minority of War Department officials, concerned about the racial situation in the military for some time, were predisposed toward integration. Their reactions to the integration experiment were quite different from those of the majority. Dalfiume reports that "the few who believed that integration was the solution to efficient utilization of manpower continued to remember this experience [with research] as proof that they were right" (p. 101). Promoting this view required political steps. At the urging of relatively liberal aides, Secretary of War Patterson established a board of inquiry, the so-called Gillem Board, to review research on Negro manpower in the military and testimony of civilian and military witnesses. The Board concluded that "there was ample evidence to show that in certain instances, small composite units, Negro platoons in white companies, when ably led, were eminently successful even though relatively heavy casualties were suffered.[73] The Board chose not to see the experience as an isolated "experiment" without wider implications. In fact, it turned around and reinterpreted previous field reports which had impugned the performance of Negro soldiers in all-black units. "Previous official reports on Negro units do not reflect many factors which may have been contributing causes of the substandard performance in combat"[74] The "contributing causes" referred to here are poor leadership and excessively oppressive policies in the Negro units.

In its recommendations, however, the Gillem Board did not call for complete desegregation of the Armed Forces. Instead, it wanted continued experiments with "composite organizations" after the war, integration in certain kinds of assignments and in recreational facilities, and equal opportunities for advancement within the military hierarchy. Off-duty housing was to remain segregated. Full integration was seen as a long-term goal, to be achieved at some unspecified date in the future.

The Gillem Board thus struck a kind of compromise. Its composition suggests that its members may have been predisposed to accept the arguments about the military competence of blacks. In fact, the board had been established in response to representations made to the Secretary of War by Truman Gibson, a Negro civilian aide. On the other hand, one can ask why the Gillem Board did not go further in its recommendations. A. Rose, a prime contributor to the research effort, viewed even the Gillem Board compromise skeptically: "While the Gillem Board of the Army gave serious consideration to the report and paid lip service to its principles, it did not recommend the abolition of segregation."[75] But the Board may have had a legitimate fear that integration in a peacetime context would evoke different responses than on the frontlines. Its recommendation that Negro units in the United States "be stationed in localities where community attitudes are most favorable"[76] would indicate that it had reservations about the general applicability of the study findings. The studies themselves contained no data on civilian reactions. Whether the difference between the position of the Board and that of the social scientists was basically political or intellectual is hard to say.

Of course, in the end, further experiments with integration in the Korean War proved rather successful. Partly as a result of social science studies which examined this experience, a policy of complete integration was eventually adopted, with considerable success. Most of the fears of those who had opposed integration proved unfounded. But these facts should not prejudice the way in which the earlier deliberations are described. This case study indicates that even when the gap between knowledge and decision is reduced and initial objections to a recommendation are refuted in subsequent research, changing a policy-maker's initial predispositions may require political action. In this case it seems important that certain groups within the policy-maker's organization already were predisposed toward integration. But their political effectiveness may well have been enhanced by the availability of strategic information which forced top authorities to keep the door open for possible policy changes.

This whole story points up yet another difficulty. It turns out to be questionable whether the social science recommendation per se really had any impact in counteracting Army ideology. On the one hand, Davenport and Taylor both thought that the research was consequential. On the question of "composite organizations," Davenport says: "The study of attitudinal reactions to the use of Negro platoons in this type of organization was without doubt an important factor in shaping the Board's opinion on this point" (p. 36). Taylor puts it this way: "So clean-out were the results as the researchers were able to present them, that they proved convincing to a high Army Board (the Gillem Board) laying plans for the post-war Army."[77] On the other hand, racial tension in American society as a whole was increasing, with noticeable repercussions throughout government. Indeed, President Truman came out on the side of those who favored an integrated Army. This can hardly be irrelevant to an explanation of changing Army policy. Of course, Truman himself may have been influenced by the research, but the question of causality must remain in some doubt.

The Acceptance of Recommendations

As a matter of fact, the acceptance of recommendations raises precisely the same questions as those raised by their rejection: What is the role of political pressure and ideological bias? Pettigrew describes this parallel as "double bookkeeping":

> The technique is quite straightforward: If the findings fit the political necessities, fragile studies are accepted as rigorous; if the findings do not fit the political necessities, rigorous studies are disparaged as inconclusive. The United States Department of Health, Education, and Welfare provided an unfortunate prototype of this technique in 1967. To support the politically expedient programs of "compensatory education," the department issued an essentially anecdotal report and claimed it proved the success of Title I programs under the Elementary and Secondary Education Act of 1965. In truth, the department has yet to undertake a rigorous evaluation of this $1.5 billion annual national investment. In contrast, the department regarded the report of the United States Commission on Civil Rights, *Racial Isolation in the Public Schools*, as "not definitive" in its research indicating the benefits of the politically inexpedient process of racial integration of the schools [p. 45].

At the extreme, some authors warn that the social scientist should be wary if a policy-maker seems too receptive to his recommendations. There may be unexamined biases of which neither are aware and which may lead to difficulties later. One example is Moynihan's critique of the role of social scientists in New York's Mobilization for Youth program. Moynihan felt that the applicability of the Cloward-Ohlin "opportunity theory" to delinquency prevention was oversold and that much more caution should have been exercised in its application.[78] In the same vein, R. A. Peterson cites the example of the "human-relations" approach to industrial management, which he and others attribute to the influence of social theorists and researchers.

> The early studies in this ["human relations"] tradition found that when workers were given the *feeling* that they were participating in managerial decisions and were made to *feel* part of the larger work team, they responded with higher productivity and lower absenteeism. This seemed like a panacea for management; productivity could be increased with an expenditure of nothing more than charm.[79]

This strategy, according to Peterson, led to "disappointment." Interestingly enough, he traces the failure to two possible sources. One is methodological error in the early studies. The effects of participation may have resulted from "increased surveillance over workers during the study, and not a product of management's more human approach." The other possible source of error is an erroneous assumption used to bridge the gap between knowledge and decision. In some instances, "where management only *appears* to give workers decision-making power, the hypocrisy itself becomes the focus of added worker dissatisfaction."

THE COMMUNICATION OF RESEARCH RESULTS

Frequently, nonimplementation of recommendations is attributed to a simple lack of communication between the social scientist and the policy-maker. For example, O. Oranti reviewed three studies evaluating the Office of Economic Opportunity (OEO) Community Action Programs of the sixties, which he claims were ignored in policy-making. He offered the following explanation:

> Too few of the senior administrators are familiar with the studies; there is little systematic analysis of the reports and no routinized way for the findings to be distributed either to the community action agencies that administer the programs or to the regional offices of OEO that increasingly pass on fund applications.[80]

The explanation for such lack of communication may be quite simple: Sociologists may be more concerned with getting on with the next project than with alerting policy-makers to the implications of past studies. Researchers differ markedly in their sense of obligation to make results known to relevant decision-makers. Some do little or nothing. The opposite extreme is illustrated by the heroic efforts of Wolstetter, who, while at the Rand Corporation, gave a total of 92 briefings to bring his study of U.S. Air Force Base locations to the attention of top military officials.[81]

Even when research results are made available, policy-makers may be too busy to read long reports, particularly in cases where there has been a change in staff. Cantril describes a dramatic instance of this from the experience of the Institute for International Social Research at Princeton. Near the end of the Eisenhower Administration, Lloyd Free surveyed Cuban attitudes toward the Castro government and found that Cubans considered Castro a great improvement over Batista, were optimistic about the future, and felt that their best chance lay in political stability. The study was circulated widely in U.S. government circles and reported in the *New York Times*. During the transition to the Kennedy Administration, however, the report appears to have been shelved. Support for the disastrous Bay of Pigs invasion was one unfortunate consequence. Cantril relates that

> Shortly after the ill-fated invasion attempt, a copy of the report was sent to Arthur Schlesinger, Jr., who was then serving as a Special Assistant to President Kennedy. In his note of acknowledgment to Lloyd, Mr. Schlesinger wrote: "I read with interest your Cuban report—and only wish that a copy had come to my attention earlier."[82]

Information loss may be one of the most troublesome organizational aspects of administrative turnover, and this is underlined when it occurs despite the enormous informational resources available to the President's staff.

Negligence is not always involved when a study does not reach relevant policy-makers. Sometimes lack of communication really reflects a desire for self-protection. Staff members may not want to be the bearers of bad news; the study may reflect negatively on their own branch of operations. This point was demonstrated experimentally by J. Eaton.[83] He submitted research reports with various recommendations to a group of social-work officials and asked what they would do with the report. Reports which indicated successful operations were passed on to superiors, while those indicating failure were sent back to their source with methodological comments. This indicates how the communication problem is related to the hierarchical location of the participants.

The reception of applied studies by the policy-maker may depend as much on the style of communication as on their actual content. A policy-maker who asks a simple question may hope for a simple answer, but sociologists are trained to probe details and amplify subtleties. This problem has been noted frequently in the literature. Some think that reports are typically too theoretical,[84] that they lay excessive stress on qualifications and technicalities,[85] and that they use jargon with which nonsociologists are unfamiliar.[86] The art of writing a report for a non-technical audience is one that must be learned.

Recommendations have to be presented persuasively or they will not be adopted. The following two cases taken from two presidential commissions are especially good examples of such skillful presentation. In the Presidential commission on violence, Zimring argued for stringent gun laws. He collected a large amount of data showing that the mere existence of guns could lead to fatalities. While accumulated evidence was necessary to support his basic position, one of his examples was especially striking. After the Detroit race riots in 1968, the number of registered guns increased drastically because people were concerned with their own self-defense. Zimring was able to show that parallel to this increase of rather indiscriminate licensing of guns there was an increase in suicides and accidental fatalities involving guns. This one example alone perhaps carried more weight with the busy legislators than the more detailed report based on all available data.[87] The second example comes from the Population Commission, which was confronted with the task of presenting the consequences of population growth as concisely as possible. What were the relations between fairly involved demographic projections (with respect to population size as well as to age distributions) and the economic, environmental, and fiscal variables? The device chosen was to compare (graphically) the consequences of the two- versus the three-children family on resource and energy consumption. This ingenious simplification succeeded in conveying a sense of the range within which future developments could be expected to fall.[88]

Another type of communication problem concerns the formulation of the recommendations themselves. Here it seems that the difficulty is that recommendations may become identified with the study, so that if the client disagrees with the recommendation, he may reject the research in toto rather than search for more useful implications. On the other hand, if recommendations are not stated, no one may bother to examine the policy implications.

According to some experienced writers, such as Glock and Sellitz, these problems are aggravated when communication is written rather than face to face. The sociologist may consider a written report to be the main product of his work, but when the sociologist simply sends the report on to his sponsor, utilization is unlikely.

When a report reaches a wider audience than the specific sponsor, there can be troublesome consequences if the report was not conceived for a lay audience. A classic case to illustrate this point is the ill-starred Moynihan Report.[89] This document, which originated in early 1965 in the Office of Policy Planning and Research of the U.S. Department of Labor, discusses the relation between family structure in the black community and the "cycle of poverty," and proposes to fight poverty by "enhancing the stability and resources of the Negro American family." The Report was apparently intended for exclusive use by high-level officials of the Johnson Administration, but it was "leaked" and quickly received wide distribution. Many blacks became intensely hostile to the Report, which they perceived as an attempt to hold blacks morally responsible for their economic plight and to justify intervention in the private lives of black families. Rainwater and Yancey argue that this hostility resulted from a great deal of misunderstanding about the actual content of the report. According to their analysis, this misunderstanding was largely a result of the way in which the Report was presented in the press.

> The controversy, at least in its full public acrimony, was primarily a result of the nature of the press coverage of the report during the post-Watts time of poor communication and tenseness between the Administration and the civil rights movement [p. 155] . . . . A *revised report . . . probably would not have precipitated a public controversy such as did in fact develop, nor would it have destroyed Moynihan's thesis (as embodied in President Johnson's Howard University speech) as a platform from which the Administration could argue for concrete programs.* There would have instead been enthusiastic support from some parts of the civil rights movement, grumbling and indifference from others, or a grudging willingness to use such a revised report as authority for negotiation with the Administration about a variety of programs (much as Benjamin Payton, a black religious leader, sought to use the Howard Univesity speech before its close connection with the Moynihan Report made that impossible . . .) [p. 165].

It is interesting to look at Rainwater and Yancey's suggested "revisions" of the Moynihan Report. They address two aspects. In the first place, causal analysis is not clearly enough distinguished from moral responsibility. For example, the report speaks of the "failure" of Negroes to achieve certain goals. Here Rainwater and Yancey point out that "In this context failure has the unfortunate connotation of individual responsibility rather than being a simple descriptive adjective." A section on the "roots of the problem" should have emphasized more the contemporary sources of the problem rather than the historical background of slavery and reconstruction. The whole problem of illegitimacy should be treated more carefully. According to Rainwater and Yancey, Moynihan in no way wanted to absolve whites for the condition of blacks; he emphasized the family structure because it seemed to be an important but neglected aspect of the problem. That this emphasis was perceived as an effort to shift the blame was a plausible misunderstanding.

Another type of problem concerns the formulation of proposals. Here it is the vagueness of the Report to which Rainwater and Yancey attribute part of the confusion. The vagueness was intended to keep options open. Yet, emphasis on the family seemed to some to be an effort to derail the existing efforts in the area of jobs and discrimination. This, according to Rainwater and Yancey, was not intended by Moynihan, who merely wanted to add to the existing list of concerns. Some feared that increased "emphasis on psychiatric social work and family-life education approaches" were being planned, but Rainwater and Yancey believe this to be untrue.

Many social science reports will inevitably be summarized and passed along channels over which the sociologist has no control. Whatever the merits of Rainwater and Yancey's "revisions," it is probably inevitable that even politically sophisticated social science will be misread and misunderstood.

NOTES

1 M. W. Riley, "Membership of the American Sociological Association," *American Sociological Review,* XXV (1960), 914–25.

2 W. W. Ellis, "The Federal Government in Behavioral Science: Fields, Methods, and Funds," *American Behavioral Science,* VII (1964), 3–24.

3 E.g., P. F. Lazarsfeld *et. al.* (eds.), *The Uses of Sociology* (New York: Basic Books, 1967); A. B. Shostak (ed.), *Sociology in Action* (Homewood, Ill.: Dorsey, 1965); A. Gouldner and S. M. Miller (eds.), *Applied Sociology* (New York: The Free Press, 1965).

4 O. Klineberg (ed.), *Characteristics of the American Negro,* (New York: Harper, 1943).

5 Michael Harrington, *The Other America* (Baltimore: Penguin, 1963).

6 Cf. K. B. Clark, "Desegregation Background: The Role of Social Scientists," in D. Valdes and D. Dean (eds.), *Sociology in Use* (New York: Macmillan, 1965;, p. 300.

7 Cf. U.S. House of Representatives, Committee on Government Operations, *The Use of Social Research in Federal Domestic Programs* (Washington, D.C.: U.S. Government Printing Office, 1967).

8 U.S. Office of Economic Opportunity, "Further Preliminary Results: The New Jersey Graduated Work Incentive Experiment," May, 1971, mineo.

9 D. L. Rosenhan, "On Being Sane in Insane Places," *Science,* January 19, 1973, pp.250–258.

10 E.g., F. C. Ikle, *How Nations Negotiate* (New York: Harper & Row, 1964).

11 D. Katz *et. al., Productivity Supervision and Morale Among Railroad Workers,* (Ann Arbor, Mich.: Institute for Social Research, 1951), p. vii.

12 Herbert J. Gans, "Urban Poverty and Social Planning," in P. F. Lazarsfeld *et. al.* (eds.), *The Uses of Sociology* (New York: Basic Books, 1967), p. 452.

13 C. Sellitz *et. al.*, "The Applications of Social Research," *in Research Methods in Social Relations,* rev. ed. (New York: Henry Holt and Company, 1964), chapt. 13.

14 P. Rossi, "Researchers, Scholars, and Policy-makers: The Politics of Large Scale Research," *Daedalus,* January, 1964, p. 93.

15 Gunnar Myrdal, *An American Dilemma* (New York: Harper, 1944).

16 Russell Sage Foundation, *Annual Report 64–65* (New York: Russell Sage Foundation, 1965), p. 3.

17 Personal communication from Lindzey Churchill, Russell Sage Foundation.

18 New York: Atherton Press, 1969.

19 H. Zetterberg, *Social Theory and Social Practice* (Totowa, N.J.: Bedminster Press, 1962), chapt. 4.

20 D. McDonald, *Some Problems in the Organization and Use of Social Research in the U.S. Navy* (New York: Bureau of Applied Social Research, 1971).

21 A. K. Pasanella, with J. Weinman, *The Road to Recommendations* (New York: Bureau of Applied Social Research, 1973).

22 C. Y. Glock, "Applied Social Research: Some Conditions Affecting Its Utilization," in C. Y. Glock, *et. al.*, *Case Studies in Bringing Behavioral Science into Use* (Stanford, Calif.: Institute for Communication Research, 1969), pp. 17–18.
23 Stuart Chase, *The Proper Study of Mankind*, rev. ed. (New York: Harper Colophon Books, 1963), pp. 50–57.
24 R. Likert, "Behavioral Research: A Guide for Effective Action," in R. Likert and S. P. Hayes, Jr. (eds.), *Some Applications of Behavioral Research* (Paris: UNESCO, 1967), pp. 20–22.
25 M. Lipsky, "Social Scientists and the Riot Commission," *The Annals*, 394 (March, 1971), 75–76.
26 P. Green, "The Obligations of American Social Scientists," *The Annals*, CCCXCIV (March, 1971), p. 15.
27 Y. Dror, "Public Administration: Four Cases from Israel and the Netherlands," in Lazarsfeld *et. al.* (eds.), *op. cit.*, p. 423.
28 Lazarsfeld *et. al.*, *The People's Choice* (New York: Columbia University Press, 1968).
29 E. Katz and P. F. Lazarsfeld, *Personal Influence* (Glencoe, Ill.: The Freee Press, 1955).
30 R. K. Merton, "Patterns of Influence," in P. F. Lazarsfeld and F. Stanton (eds.), *Communications Research 1948–1949* (New York: Harper & Bros., 1949).
31 J. Kramer, "Resistance to Sociological Data: A Case Study," in Lazarsfeld, *et. al.* (eds.), *The Uses of Sociology*, pp. 783–84.
32 Clark, *op. cit.*
33 A. Leighton and E. H. Spicer, "Applied Anthropology in a Dislocated Community," Appendix to A. Leighton, *The Governing of Men*, (Princeton, N.J.: Princeton University Press, 1945); G. Lyons, *The Uneasy Partnership*, New York: Russell Sage Foundation, 1969, p.53.
34 H. Zeisel, "The Law," in Lazarsfeld *et. al.* (eds.), *The Uses of Sociology*, pp. 81–99.
35 C. Weiss, *The Consequences of the Study of Federal Student Loan Programs* (New York: Bureau of Applied Social Research, 1970).
36 I. L. Horowitz (ed.), *The Rise and Fall of Project Camelot* (Cambridge, Mass.: MIT Press, 1967).
37 Otto Kerner, *Report of the National Advisory Commission on Civil Disorders* (New York: Bantam Books, 1968).
38 *Op. cit.*, pp. 461 ff.
39 L. M. Killian, "The Social Scientist's Role in the Preparation of the Florida Desegregation Brief," in Shostak (ed.), *op. cit.*, pp. 129–34.
40 R. C. Angell, "The Ethical Problems of Applied Sociology," in Lazarsfeld *et. al.* (eds.), *The Uses of Sociology*, pp. 725–40.
41 J. K. Galbraith, *The New Industrial State* (Boston: Houghton Mifflin, 1967).
42 Michael Royko, *Boss: Richard J. Daley of Chicago* (New York: Signet Press, 1971), p. 18.
43 Martin Hyman, "Medicine," in Lazarsfeld (eds.), *The Uses of Sociology*, p. 124.
44 W. P. Davison, "Foreign Policy," in *ibid.*, p. 408.
45 D. C. McDonald, *op. cit.*, p. 21.
46 R. Likert and R. Lippitt, "The Utilization of Social Science," in L. Festinger and D. Katz (eds.), *Research Methods in Behavioral Science* (New York: Holt, Rinehart and Winston, 1953), pp. 630–38.
47 Y. Dror, *Ventures in Policy Sciences* (New York: American Elsevier, 1971).
48 K. Archibald, "Alternative Orientations to Social Science Utilization," *Social Science Information*, IX (April, 1970).
49 Sellitz *et. al.*, pp. 457–58. Likert and Lipitt, *op. cit.*, p. 612.
50 "Ten Principles Governing Policy Research," *Footnotes*, I, No. 3 (March, 1973), 1.
51 H. Orlans, "Making Social Research More Useful to Government," *Social Science Information*, VII (1968), 152–53.

52 E. M. Glaser and S. H. Taylor, "Factors Influencing the Success of Applied Research," *American Psychologist,* February, 1973, pp. 140–46.
53 F. Ruderman, "Sociological Research in the Field of Social Work" (mimeo.).
54 R. A. Brymer and B. Farris, "Ethical and Political Dilemmas in the Investigation o Deviance: A Study of Juvenile Delinquency," in Gideon Sjoberg (ed.), *Ethics, Politics, and Social Research* (Cambridge, Mass.: Schenkman Publishing, 1967), pp. 297–318.
55 H. Bynder, "Sociology in a Hospital: A Case Study in Frustration," in Shostak (ed.), *op. cit.*, pp. 61–70.
56 H. Zeisel, "Reflections on Experimental Techniques in the Law," *Journal of Legal Studies,* II, No. 1 (1973), 108.
57 A. Pasanella, *ETS Research and the College Board* (New York: College Entrance Examination Board, 1968, (mimeo.).
58 D. H. Clairmont and D. W. Magill, *Nova Scotian Blacks* (Toronto: McCelland Stewart, 1974).
59 J. Riley, "The Sociologist in the Non-academic Setting," in Lazarsfeld *et. al.* (eds.), *The Uses of Sociology,* pp. 789–805.
60 F. Goldner, "Role Emergence and the Ethics of Ambiguity," in Sjoberg (ed.), *op. cit.*, 1967, p. 255.
61 S. M. Miller, "Prospects: The Applied Sociology of the Center-City," in Gouldner and Miller (eds.), *op. cit.*, p. 965.
62 Personal communication from A. Pasanella.
63 E. Rosenfeld, "Social Research and Social Action in Prevention of Juvenile Delinquency," in A. Gouldner and S. M. Miller (eds.), *op. cit.*, pp. 367–80.
64 Alvin Weinberg, "Science and Trans-Science" (editorial), *Science,* 177 (1972), 211.
65 Max Millikan, "Inquiry and Policy: The Relation of Knowledge to Action," in E. Crawford and A. Biderman (eds.), *Social Scientists and International Affairs* (New York: Wiley, 1969), p. 280.
66 P. Rossi, "Testing for Success and Failure in Social Action," in P. Rossi and W. Williams (eds.), *Evaluating Social Programs* (New York: Seminar Press, 1972), p. 32.
67 H. Wilensky, *Organizational Intelligence* (New York: Basic Books, 1967), pp. 24–34.
68 M. Janowitz, "Arms Control Research," *American Sociologist,* 1971, pp. 24–25.
69 T. Pettigrew, "Race Relation Research," *American Sociologist,* 1971, p. 46.
70 T. Sellin, in Royal Commission on Capital Punishment, *Minutes of Evidence* (London: Her Majesty's Statoinery Off., 1951), p. 647; quoted in Zeisel, *op. cit.*, p. 93; cf. also Daniel Glaser, *Adult Crime and Social Policy* (Englewood Cliffs, N. J.: Prentice-Hall, 1972), p. 35, who cites Sellin (ed.), *Capital Punishment* (New York: Harper & Row, 1967), pp. 135–60.
71 R. M. Dalfiume, *Desegregation of the U.S. Armed Forces* (Columbia, Mo.: University of Missouri Press, 1969).
72 R. Davenport, "The Negro in the Army—A Subject of Research," *Journal of Social Issues,* III, No. 4 (1947), 36.
73 *Ibid.*
74 Quoted in Dalfiume, *op. cit.*, p. 150.
75 A. Rose, "Army Policies Toward Negroes—A Report on a Success and a Failure," *Journal of Social Issues,* III, No. 4 (1947), 31.
76 Davenport, *op. cit.*, p. 98.
77 P. S. Taylor, "The Relation of Research to Legislative and Administrative Decision," *Journal of Social Issues,* III, No. 4 (1947), 52.
78 D. P. Moynihan, *Maximum Feasible Misunderstanding* (New York: Free Press, 1970).
79 R. A. Peterson, *The Industrial Order and Social Policy* Englewood Cliffs, N.J.: Prentice-Hall, 1973), p. 91.
80 O. Oranti, "Program Evaluations and the Definition of Poverty," in U.S. House of Representatives, *op. cit.*, vol. 2, p. 310.

81 B. Smith, *The Rand Corporation* (Cambridge, Mass.: Harvard University Press, 1966), Chapt. 6.

82 H. Cantril, *The Human Dimension* (New Brunswick, N.J.: Rutgers University Press, 1967), chapt. 1.

83 J. Eaton, "Symbolic and Substantive Evaluative Research," *Administrative Science Quarterly*, XXI (1956).

84 W. P. Davison, "Foreign Policy" in Lazarsfeld *et. al.* (eds.), *The Uses of Sociology*, pp. 406–7.

85 Gans, *op. cit.*, p. 465; Luchterhand, *op. cit.;* Dror, *op. cit.*, pp. 422, 425.

86 N. Gross and J. A. Fishman, "The Management of Educational Establishments," in Lazarsfeld *et. al.* (eds.), *The Uses of Sociology*, pp. 340, 342; Riley, *op. cit.*, p. 794.

87 Franklin E. Zimring, "More Firearms—More Firearms Violence," in *Firearms as Violence in American Life*, Part II, chapt. 2 (Washington, D.C.: Government Printing Office, 1969).

88 C. Westoff, Report to the American Sociological Association, 1973.

89 L. Rainwater and W. Yancey, *The Moynihan Report and the Politics of Controversy* (Cambridge, Mass.: MIT Press, 1965).

SEVEN

Some Problems in the Organization of Applied Social Research

We mentioned in Chapter 3 that the whole phenomenon of utilization could be looked upon as a cognitive process taking place in an organizational setting. Originally our intention was to give both these approaches equal space and weight. Finally, we decided to give the cognitive side precedence, because it was more in need of clarification. In this final chapter we shall restrict ourselves to a small group of organizational problems and end with mapping out a general set of problem areas.

1. We shall begin with a discussion of the difficulties North American universities encounter in trying to integrate applied social research with their traditional framework. The arrangements, variously called institutes or bureaus or centers, will be reviewed and a new role, that of the managerial scholar, will be discussed.
2. We shall then turn to the research and development centers sponsored by the government and generally attached to universities.
3. From there we will move to research institutes not connected with universities. They are usually divided into profit-making and nonprofit units. But this difference will turn out to be of little importance. The real issue, as we see it, is university affiliation.
4. We then shift from the research side to the "client," the organization which uses social research and is expected to provide general support; at the latter point we meet the somewhat paradoxical term "mission-oriented basic research."
5. We also want to treat the question of research departments in large organizations, whether government or business. What is the proper position of a research department in a multidivisional organization, and what are the foreseeable relationships, the interplay between administration and research department? At this point we will have

reached the limits of our present knowledge and will have to be satisfied with a few examples which we have studied.

6. Finally, the question has to be faced as to where the sociologist will come from who will work in organized research settings, academic or otherwise. Our final section is devoted to the education of applied sociologists.

UNIVERSITY INSTITUTES

When American colleges first began to teach the natural sciences, laboratories were small and inexpensive. When the natural sciences won acceptance as part of the curriculum, larger laboratories were seen as a necessary part of the basic budget. When finally extremely costly equipment was needed, Federal support and "consortia" had become a legitimate feature of the educational establishment. The path from small beginnings to large budgets was fairly smooth. By contrast, sociology spun more quickly to empirical work, and even the initial budget requirements were relatively large. From the outset, funds for interviewers, calculators, and tabulators had to be obtained from outside sources, from contracts which included money for supporting services. Thus, the introduction of empirical social research into American universities was intimately tied in with its appeal to potential users. Institutional improvisations were needed to handle this new situation: centers, bureaus, laboratories, were created to cope with the financial and technical problems of collecting relevant information. But relevant for what? Obviously, "applied research" was only justified if it contributed to the teaching functions of the academic institutions. But expositional lectures in sociology were organized around theoretical developments, with examples taken from anthropology, from history, or from commentaries on contemporary life. How was one to integrate the work of the new "institutes" with the traditional academic departments?

By 1960, this problem had received international attention. The West European universities were accustomed to the term "institutes"; they did not have departments in the American sense. Each discipline had a top professor—somewhat similar to the American medical schools—and the other faculty members were hierarchically organized around him, with funds available for studies inaugurated by the "chief." History and philosophy provided the pattern.[1] What was the situation in the United States? UNESCO asked Paul Lazarsfeld to review the new developments there. Helped by a generous grant from the College Entrance Examination

Board (which had funded studies at various American institutes), he rendered a report which was published in 1961 in *Information*, the journal of the International Social Science Council.[2] Because it is not easily accessible in this country, a brief summary might be helpful.

The 35-page review begins by discussing "the driving forces behind the creation of these institutes." Three sources are distinguished, described here in condensed form:

> a. *Individual social scientists* who want to do large-scale studies and who need staff, technical facilities, and money to carry on, because they become intrigued by the new challenge of the empirical social sciences without caring what the subject matter on which they try out the new tools; they hope that institutes will permit them to remain scholars and still participate in the decisions of public administration, politics, and economic affairs; and who also want to add an increment to a meager university salary by doing consulting work without "going into business of their own."
>
> b. *University administrators* who want to serve the local community and the state legislature in order to improve the public image of their institution; who see that organized research institutions in other universities confer prestige and attract superior graduate students, and who want to bring order into a confusing set of contractual relations assumed by an increasing number of individual professors or departments.
>
> c. *Various philanthropic groups and government agencies* who look for data of a kind not provided by the conventional sources of social bookkeeping.

The review then turns to some distinctions made as a result of a questionnaire sent to 94 universities which had awarded ten or more doctoral degrees in the year 1957–58. The "institutes" involved were found to be either specialized or general purpose with respect to research topics. Specialized units outnumbered broad-range units by more than two to one. Further, the general-purpose units divided rather evenly into those which were autonomous in the sense that they developed their own programs, and those which claimed that they were mainly facilitating the research activities of individual faculty members. The distinction was somewhat difficult to make, however, because the academic tradition favors the rhetoric of facilitation, while the inner dynamics of such institutes press towards increasing autonomy and self-direction.

In states which are fairly prosperous, the legislatures are quite willing to authorize steady increases in university budgets. If the administration or some influential group in these universities favors the creation of special social research units, budgetary approval is not difficult to obtain. The private universities, on the other hand, have a rather limited endowment, and it is much more difficult to get them to finance a new type of endeavor. In addition, there is the battle of prestige between these two types of institutions. Until recently, private universities were the most respected, but now some of the public universities are moving rapidly into the front rank. For some cf these upstarts, the research institute is one way of adding status. Thus, sometimes established prestige makes for resistance to the very innovations which newly affluent universities accept to acquire respectability. Two indicators support this general observation: in state universities the initiating role of the administration is stronger than that of the faculty; in private universities, the prime mover is more likely to be the faculty. There is also a difference in the financial structure: the relative contribution from the university to the support of the units is twice as large among public universities as among private institutions (pp. 18–20).

A considerable part of this early study is given to the problems created by relations between institutes and teaching departments. A major "project" needs a hierarchical work structure, which has great advantages for postdoctoral training but is not congenial to an academic tradition. The senior members of the institute are competent and would like to do some teaching, but this might fractionate the curriculum. At the time of the study, the Ford Foundation had commissioned a number of "self-studies" by social science departments. The UNESCO report notes that each of these studies mentions the institute-department problem in terms of organizational climate—"style of life" at Stanford, "community of distinguished scholars" at Harvard. It would not be a bad idea, the authors say, to have a kind of "super-institute which makes the nature and future of applied social research its principle object of study" (p. 27). At a later occasion, Lazarsfeld discussed the institutional consequences of research institutes;[3] they necessarily train men who are able and not embarrassed to combine intellectual and administrative leadership. Even if his unit only facilitates faculty research, an institute director must train a staff able to advise on important research functions. It is not impossible that on specific topics, the collective experience of the institute staff is greater than the skills of the individual faculty member. In an autonomous unit, all this is even more pronounced. Here the staff carries out a self-contained work schedule. A hierarchy is needed, proceeding often from assistants to project supervisors to program director and, finally, to the director himself. The last is not only responsible for reports and publications, he is also concerned with maintaining what is sometimes called the image of his operation. Its prestige, its attraction for staff and students, and its appeal to clients are self-generated, not derived only from the reputation of the teaching departments. The professional staff sees its future careers as closely bound up with the destiny of the unit, a fact which sometimes makes for challenging problems in human organization.

To put it in different terms: the institutes create a new type of role—the managerial scholar, and this has implications for a general problem in higher education. Nowadays, our universities have a serious problem which can be characterized as an "academic power vacuum." When graduate education in this country began, no one doubted that the university president was an important figure. Today, however, we witness a dangerous divergence: academic freedom is more and more interpreted in such a way as to keep the administration out of any truly academic affairs; and the faculty, in turn, has come to consider administration beneath its dignity. But educational innovations are, by definition, intellectual as well as administrative tasks. And, so, they have fallen into a no-man's land: the president and his staff wait for the faculty to take the initiative; the professors on their side consider that such matters would take time away from their true scholarly pursuits. As a result, many of our universities have a dangerously low level of institutional development. The inability to incoroporate applied social research into the university structure is one symptom of this retardation. Maybe the somewhat chaotic appearance of institutes will create the type of person who remains a scholar and still can exercise the leadership necessary to find appropriate organizational solutions.

It seems that the problems raised in 1960 have not really been resolved, they have only acquired more general importance. In the UNESCO report it was mentioned that the land-grant colleges were least likely to have institutes (p. 19); the explanation—that they were basically devoted to utilization anyway, and therefore not affected by the department-institute problems—seemed plausible. But it now turns out that a similar problem has developed within the land-grant institutions, too. In 1972, two members of Pennsylvania State University published a book called *Beyond Academic Departments*, with the subtitle *The Story of Institutes and Centers.*[4] Their main concern was with the Institutes for Research on Land and Water Development, which had proliferated in the land-grant colleges. But they also include social science centers in their review, and their analysis completely bears out that of the 1960 UNESCO Survey. Even their chapter headings underscore the parallel: "Origins," "Structure," "Institutes and the University," etc. They end with 20 pages of "Conclusion and Recommendations." We fully agree with them and urge their careful study to the attention of our readers. The two authors were able to devote much more space then we can to what is their main topic, while for us it is only one of a larger list.*

RESEARCH AND DEVELOPMENT CENTERS

Since World War II, universities have been drawn into applied research is still another way, with various government agencies located on campuses which would do research in broadly assigned substantive areas but with considerable freedom to choose specific topics and to experiment with new ideas. Harold Orlans has traced the origin of these R&Ds in considerable detail.[5] They are transformations of intramural research done within government agencies by expert civil servants. They evolved when atomic research, astrophysics, oceanography, etc., became so complex that most of the work had to be done at places where more scientific personnel and more sophisticated equipment was available. In the natural sciences, they were mostly the outgrowth of activities developed during World War II; some of them, however, started earlier. Finally, the Cooperative Research Act of 1963 created a Research and Development Centers Branch within the Office of Education which sponsored nine university-based educational research and development centers. These centers

> grew out of concern that project research efforts had tended to be fragmentary and non-cumulative, that they had not succeeded in bridging the gap between research and practice, and that educational research has not succeeded in involving a broad enough array of disciplines outside of education. The Research and Development Center was conceived to remedy these concerns by permitting the gathering of a critical mass of interdisciplinary talent and other resources in a university setting to hear on a significant educational problem.[6]

Except for the newly created poverty institute at the University of Wisconsin, the educational R&Ds are the only ones which use social scientists on a large scale. In a way, the educational R&Ds are somewhat similar to the institutes proposed by the Brim Report. But their work is not directed toward the solution of basic social problems, rather, they are supposed to advance knowledge which can be used anywhere in the highly decentralized network of American education. They do not have a specific client but a vaguely designed problem area, such as teacher education, early learning problems, educational administration, etc.

---

*The parallel between the Ikenberry-Friedman book and the Columbia concern is the more impressive as their bibliography shows that they were not aware of that earlier effort.

Whatever their topic, the R&Ds have raised an interesting organizational issue. Originally they were conceived as following a linear procedure which would start with some basic research, followed by exploratory investigation of where the insights could be used. Then some specific development would follow, which would adapt the new idea to daily use. In practice, however, the relation between research and developmet turns out to be more complex.

The modification of the "linear model" was done in three directions. For one, the question was raised at what point the *initiation* of a utilization process actually occurs. That it often showed *discontinuities* was the second observation. Finally, the *feedback* between its various phases was increasingly stressed.

Initiation. A research director/manager in the Office of Education has written:

> Those of us who have worked intensely on problems of research policy in education see shortcomings. The model does not emphasize sufficiently that initiative for different kinds of actions *can take place at any point in the continuum* and that those initiatives may come from locations other than where the action itself is to be performed. The model unwittingly implies that innovations begin with the findings generated by fundamental research.[7]

Whether the utilization process starts with "fundamental research" or is originated by the agencies needing help has also been addressed by students of industrial research. One such study was for the Materials Advisory Board of the National Research Council. Ten case histories were chosen because the participants believed them to be good examples of scientific research and engineering collaboration, and these cases were analyzed intensively. The point which stood out most clearly was that "Basic research by itself rarely produced a technological opportunity which was quickly recognized and developed. Far more frequently, an urgent need initiated a search for a solution from prior basic knowledge. An individual with a well-defined concept of a technological need started the successful research-engineering interaction."[8]

These findings are supported by a similar study carried out by the Material Advisory Board of the Department of Defense called "Project Hindsight." This study showed that innovations used by the military typically begin in the development rather than in the fundamental research stage. Of the innovations studied, 91 percent had their origin in technology and only 9 percent in science. And 95 percent of these innovations were stimulated by a recognized defense need rather than by following up the technological implications of a newly generated research finding.[9] The linear model is therefore clearly inaccurate in its implication that technological innovations typically have their birth in the generation of new knowledge in the "fundamental" or "basic" research stage.

Discontinuities. If a problem is raised somewhere within the purposive organization or acting community, it is not necessary that it be referred to the research department or the "research community" for the creation of the necessary knowledge. After all, research has been going on anyhow and the task might just be to retrieve pertinent information. This modification of the linear model might be called the "storehouse" variation. But how is this connection made? One way is through personal interaction.[10] According to the Material Advisory Board's study: "Very frequent interaction with persons engaged in scientific research is essential. . . . In most cases, the science that led to the technological solution was available before the dialogue began." If research findings accumulate in a "storehouse" of sorts, then the "storehousekeepers" are those in the community of scientific researchers. These researchers are valuable to the development technicians, not necessarily because the work they are doing at the moment is directly relevant to the development effort, but because they are most likely to be familiar with past research which might be of use to the technician.

As the store of research results increases, special retrieval systems must be developed, and these in turn will evoke new organizational problems. The Office of Education has organized an Educational Research Information Center (ERIC). It is an electronic system which is supposed to help teachers and school administrators, but is, in fact, used mainly by students writing dissertations. The explanation is quite simple. A person in the firing line of daily activities is not trained to ask questions; the mere availability of information in a retrieval system is not enough. The Office of Education, together with Columbia's Bureau of Applied Social Research, has experimented with various ways of overcoming this difficulty with the help of intermediary agents.[11]

Feedback. Whereas the linear model implies a unidirectional flow of information, the reconceptualization emphasizes the continuous and multidirectional interaction between the various components of the research/consumer system. Robert Glaser, who originally thought of the Educational R&D Center as a mile-long transition belt from "basic" research to implementation, has since called for an "instructional psychology." This notion is important not only because he tries to improve the process of utilization, but because he sees in it a positive contribution to the general progress of knowledge.

> Many sciences have shown tremendous progress as a result of attempts at applications, and a stance for the application of psychology to education seems quite clear at this time. The behavioral and social sciences are at a point in their development where they absolutely require the direction and disciplining effects that come from contact with real world problems. . . . What knowledge and theory that has been accumulated now needs the elaboration and correction that result from such an engagement.[12]

The last quotation is interesting because it corroborates the position in the first chapter: work on concrete problems often makes major contributions to the stock of significant generalized knowledge in a discipline. But whether the R&Ds are a stable form of collaboration between government and universities is not at all clear. In an appendix to his book, Orlans has listed about 50 such agencies as they existed on campuses in 1969. But of the ten educational R&Ds included there, about half have disappeared since, and some in the hardware field have gone beyond their relation with the original governmental sponsors. They were permitted to take on contracts from other sources, and some servered their government connections altogether and became independent corporations. By taking this turn, they have followed a marked trend in applied sociology. More and more research centers have developed in recent years which are not affiliated with universities.* Though we do not yet know the specific consequences of this trend, we can describe the problems it implies.

THE PROBLEM OF UNIVERSITY AFFILIATION

As we mentioned earlier, the independent research centers are divided into two groups according to whether they are commercial or so-called nonprofit units. The distinction is rather vague, and for our purpose, quite irrelevant. But university affiliation makes a big difference to us. Two sharply contrasting views can be found in the literature. Robert Nisbet,[13] in an essay in *Commentary*, sharply opposed university affilia-

*The Rand Corporation, created by the Air Force in 1948, is the prototype of all R&D centers relevant to the social sciences. Because it was never based at a university, it is not included in our discussion. Its history, however, is very interesting and has been ably described by Bruce Smith. Rand is also well known for acquiring other contacts in addition to its original sponsor and for spawning a number of independent commercial research agencies.

tion: "On a rough guess I should think at least 75 percent of all existing institutes, centers and bureaus in the academic sphere of the university should be phased out." Barzun and Mills have expressed similar opinions. Lazarsfeld scolded the universities for not having been hospitable to the social science research bureau, and urged a better integration.[14] What are the arguments pro and con?

The university centers enrich the teaching of social sciences and give students the opportunity to learn empirical research by apprenticeship. The nonaffiliated institutes drain good people from the academic scene without contributing to the methodological or substantive core of knowledge in the various disciplines. Some of the major independent centers counter the lack of contribution to academia by proposing to develop their own doctoral programs. The Rand Corporation of Santa Monica has started to experiment with such a program. Even a commercial organization like A. D. Little has applied to the Massachusetts Board of Education for a degree charter.

The main argument against affiliation is that professors working in university institutes, overly busy trying to get contracts, neglect their teaching duties and are not easily controlled by the university administration. Those who favor applied research centers within universities argue that all the disadvantages would disappear if only universities were to provide funds to maintain the core of an administrational and professional staff so that the pursuit of contracts becomes less hectic and can be guided more by intellectual and educational interest. (It seems, incidentally, that this support is easier to obtain in public universities; there it is only necessary to persuade a subcommittee of the legislation.)

A long list of further arguments could be drawn up. Affiliated centers are more likely to innovate, unaffiliated ones work more expediently. The staff of the latter spend more time in getting acquainted with the details of a client's operation; faculty members keep better track of the relevant literature, etc., etc. But it seems worthwhile to assess the factors which would affect the probable future of the two trends.

Universities might feel forced to include applied research in their own structure because they have been criticized for their isolation from local and regional problems. On the one hand, health and other social services require research help, and on the other hand, the expansion of the university complex encroaches on residents and may do harm to the local tax structure. The Carnegie Commission on Higher Education felt obliged to publish a special monograph, *The Campus and the City,* which discusses all the problems involved in detail.[15] Requests for services would lead one to predict an increase in university-affiliated centers, but even so the development would be slow. The trend toward unaffiliated centers is in our opinion closely related to a problem of personnel. People who combine the needed organizational talent with substantive academic achievement are quite rare. The managerial scholar has an understandable tendency to strengthen his center, and he can do that through government contacts which allow 50 percent or more of the grants to be used for administrative overhead. In an unaffiliated center this overhead is at the disposal of the director. But if the center is university-affiliated, the administration often needs and keeps the overhead for the general purposes. If the university administration cannot leave to the institute its overhead for its own development, the number of unaffiliated centers will probably increase, because their greater financial flexibility is attractive to the managerial scholar.

If policy centers multiply and perhaps even obtain independent status in higher education we would witness a rather interesting reversal of a historical trend. Until recently, universities in Europe as well as in the United States had a tendency to absorb intellectual functions performed by private agencies; the abolition of commercial medical schools as a result of the Flexner report is the best-known example. Such an inverted trend away from the university would put the responsibility on the leaders in the movement to report in more detail about their organizational experiences and to spell out much more precisely their cognitive role in the utilization process.

MISSION-ORIENTED BASIC RESEARCH

Much of the literature holds that both government and business should not only do research of immediate utility for their own enterprises but should also support research of a general nature which might be useful in the long run. There is a certain ambiguity in this idea. It implies partly that supporting general research has an element of social responsibility. But since the government is responsible to its tax payers, and business to its shareholders, it is not clear how far the responsibility for general support of basic research should go—even leaving aside the eternal question as to what is meant by basic research.

At one point Robert Merton developed a formula in an effort to answer this complex question. An insurance company sponsored a symposium on research related to the general problem of life insurance. Merton contributed a paper in which the whole problem is stated in sociological terms. Science is an institution in its own right, parallel to, say, the family, the economy, religion, or education. While these institutions are interdependent in various ways, each maintains a measure of independence. The relation between business firms and basic scientific research can now be seen as a special case of the relations between two connected but independent types of social institutions.

The relations between the two institutions are analyzed in terms of a principle he calls "potential of relevance." The idea is roughly as follows: science is divided into a number of substantive sectors, as is business. It is in the interest of business to support basic research, but the corporations are free to choose what sector of the research world they want to support.

> . . . Different sectors of the spectrum of basic research have differing probabilities of being germane to current and future functions of various types of organizations. Applied to the case of business organizations, the concept gives rise to the policy of *supporting those lines of inquiry* in basic research *which*, so far as can be judged, *will have the greatest degree of relevance for the particular firm*. (This is removed from the policy of supporting applied and developmental research directed toward the solution of specific problems.)[16]

Merton is confident that his principle is able "so far as possible to maintain simultaneously the integrity of basic research and the integrity of the business firm." Whether or not trends in academic work are influenced by available sponsorship is of course debatable. But Merton is aware that at a given time some basic sciences have little potential of relevance for any organization. It is then the task of private and public foundations to support these interstitial areas. He also reminds the reader that he is talking about business, because that is the topic of the symposium in which he is participating. But clearly the principle applies to the relation between science and government, thus making sense of the somewhat paradoxical term "mission-oriented basic research." After developing his general idea, he applies it to the specific relation between basic social research and the life-insurance business. He sketches out a large number of relevant topics. In addition to the more obvious connection with population and family research, he mentions such ideas as the time perspectives of various classes of people and attitudes toward death.

In principle this seems like a good answer, but it does not solve all the problems. An organization consists of many parts. Management either can delegate the support of basic research to one officer or it can establish a mission-oriented basic research unit within its own frame. In both cases, a typical role conflict is likely to develop. Persons in charge of supporting general research activities will have to defend their decisions to the top administration, which is likely to be more conservative on this point.

We can give an example from the very organization which supported the work of which the present text is a major product. For a variety of reasons, the U.S. Navy's Office of Naval Research has a branch which is in charge of maintaining contact with the academic community and has a budget for the purpose of financing unsolicited social research proposals. The division has to report periodically to a chief officer, a Navy man without any special interest in social science work. Our colleague Joel I. Brooke was given the opportunity of examining a folder of notes and outlines evidently designed as a compendium of ideas intended as source material for presentations to high-echelon officers. Many of these papers were not dated, but the content of the file indicates that they went back about ten years. They clearly emphasize both basic research as a long-range speculative venture and the specific contributions of basic research to current Navy activities. For example, one report on past work quotes a statement made by the chief of Naval researchers as supporting evidence:

> The Navy's present position and leadership in the field, and careful analysis of the definite role which basic research plays in all development activities at all times leads to the conclusion that basic research must continue at a well-considered high level.[17]

Here we see a neat blend of two themes. One is basic research as a competitive status symbol. "We don't want to lose leadership in the field." The second is the utility of basic research; it plays a "definite role in development activities."

Interviews with Navy personnel conducted by Brooke have the same character. The basic aspect of the program has its appeal; as one research manager explains it, "We should show that the Navy was not exclusively involved in small application research." But basic research also has its problems. In one case an originally critical admiral seems to have been assuaged because his own church sent members for T-group training to the National Training Laboratory at Bethel, New York, an activity based on research supported by Group Psychology Branch funds. The church's use served to legitimize the Navy's sponsorship.

Most presentations to management stress the mission of basic research without any expectation of immediate payoff. But this is usually accompanied by suggestions of possible or actual utilization, a recognition that the goal of basic research was not sufficient unto itself in this Navy context.

Thus, in an undated presentation by the Branch director: "Although all the funds in our branch are for basic research and are so utilized, there is often a payoff to the Navy of applied results and of benefits."

The draft goes on to note that outside research personnel brought into contact with the Navy through Group Psychology contracts had offered advice on a wide variety of problems to operational sectors of the Navy.

Another paper from the files, undated, but which interior evidence would place in the latter half of the fifties states: "Although the Group Psychology program is not aimed at the immediate production of practical end items, it has during its life produced some." The report then goes on to list improved sociometric measures, measures of morale, leadership, and delinquency. It mentions that some of these had been tried on Navy groups.

The ambivalence of the academic community toward utilization has been described in our first chapter. Now we see the same ambivalence on the part of the utilizing organization. There it is a conflict not within the same role, but between different roles which an organization assigns to different people in the hope that the end result will be balanced. To what extent this actually happens, and under what circumstances, will have to be answered by future inquiry.

LOCATION OF SOCIAL RESEARCH IN LARGE ORGANIZATIONS

The role of research departments in large organizations has interested many sociologists, but the discussions are based mainly on research in the physical sciences. Thus, there is some information that large organizations with semi-monopolistic powers are more likely to set up in-house research departments; they have more opportunities for utilizing unexpected findings. Many studies have been devoted to the organization of technical research departments, often using sophisticated indexes of their degree of bureaucratization as compared to, say, production or sales departments. Invariably, the latter had stricter hierarchies, because their goals were more clearly defined than was research. The successful directors of research outfits within organizations look very much like our "managerial scholars," although the balance between administrative and substantive competence is more tilted toward the former. Studies of the career lines of researchers in large organizations have identified the danger of talented social scientists being seduced by top management positions; higher rewards within a research career have been suggested.

But despite these investigations, we really do not know if the findings apply to *social research* divisions embedded in large organizations.

Because our study of the utilization process was supported by a generous grant from the Office of Naval Research, we had the opportunity of becoming acquainted with the social research activities of the Navy. This enabled us to raise a question not treated in the literature: What happens to in-house behavioral research within a larger organization structured around the execution of a complicated technology?

Our colleague Douglas McDonald visited the various human-research agencies of the Navy, studied their tables of organization, and inquired into their contact with each other and with the operating centers of the Navy.[19] Now most of their research is concerned with "hardware": ships, airplanes, weapons. This is successfully organized in a linear system similar to the one described above for the early Research and Development Centers. As a matter of fact, they even have their budget assigned to a number of accounting divisions which go along the following list: Category 6.1 (Research), 6.2 (Exploratory Development), 6.3 (Advanced Development, 6.4 (Engineering Development), 6.5 (Management and Support), and 6.6 (Operational Systems Development).

But McDonald also found that the human problems research of the Navy could by itself be classified according to how closely it was related to "hardware" development. He arranged their various "laboratories and "branches" into four groups along this line. Hardware research and development itself (I) was by far the central concern, and it absorbed the most attention. At a step removed were personnel research and development programs (II), which addressed the problems of designing the manpower complement to the hardware systems. Research and development con-

A Continuum of Navy Research and Development
According to the Proximity of Its Subject Matter to
Materiel R&D

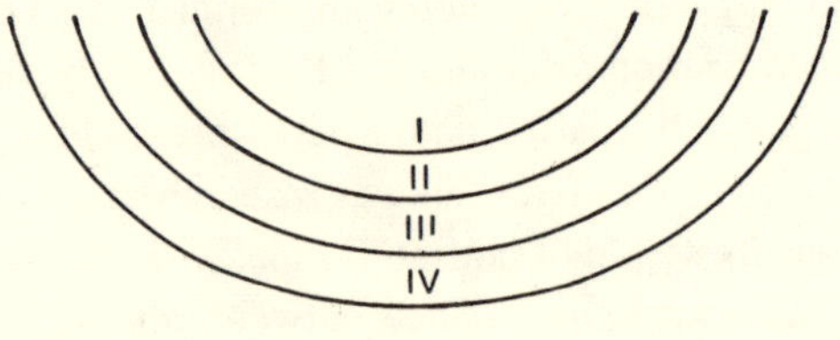

I. Materiel R&D
II. Personnel/Manpower R&D
III. Bio-Medical R&D
IV. Psychiatric R&D

cerned with providing biomedical support to this manpower (III) were somewhat further removed from the Navy's central concerns. And even more peripheral were the psychiatric research and development efforts (IV).

One effort of McDonald's study was to see what modifications in the rigid unilinear organization became necessary the more remote a research group was from exclusive concern with hardware. What were the correlates of this "distance"? Obviously Group I has by far the largest budget, and the 6.1–6.5 system adopted to begin with for its purposes seems to work well; but this group was not included in our inquiry. Social research closely related to hardware Group II development is alloted a large budget, is carried out in a more bureaucratized organization, is typically initiated by the client rather than by the researcher, and the utilization of research findings generally follows an institutionalized course. Research in the more peripheral areas, in contrast, is less routinized, is carried out in less bureaucratized organizations, is often researcher-initiated, and the implementation process is often a more fortuitous affair.

The general pattern also can be observed within the broad research areas. For example, the Navy's behavioral research in the manpower/personnel area (II) is split into two principal categories. One is the man-machine systems R&D, which is closely tied to the development of *new* hardware systems. The second includes R&D on personnel training, which covers a broader range of activities. Not limited to the personnel requirements of new hardware systems, it also deals with the evaluation and improvement of existing training programs and manpower structures. The impetus for this lies in the fact that manpower and training are absorbing an increasingly large proportion of the cost of a new weapons system.

In the man-machine systems department, behavioral researchers are called in to participate in the early planning stages of a hardware R&D project. The researchers familiarize themselves with the hardware system, determine what kinds of behavioral operations it requires, and design a personnel structure to operate it. Routine investigations are made: Is it best to have one man or two perform this task? Shall the Navy establish a new occupational category or should it upgrade existing ones? In a routine fashion, a set of recommendations are submitted to a planning manager with a cost-benefit analysis of the various options, and the research findings are thereby incorporated into the ongoing hardware R&D process.

The training research component of Navy personnel/manpower R&D is somewhat less routinized than man-machine systems research, because it is not so closely tied to the creation of a new weapons system. Freed from weapons-system development schedules and their close supervision by engineering-oriented managers, the training research group encounters a wide range of less predictable research problems. Unlike man-machine research, which addresses itself to a blueprint on the drawing boards of the hardware designers, training research can address itself to all of the Navy's existing programs. For example, some researchers went to sea and discovered that the task required of an electronics technician required far less training that the Navy was investing in him. The training researchers therefore designed a 27-week program to replace the existing 45-week one, creating a closer fit between training and task requirements.

Because findings from researcher-initiated studies are frequently more difficult to implement than findings from client-initiated studies, the implementation of this kind of work is generally a less routinized affair than is the case in the man-machine departments. One of the potential clients in an upper-level policy-making office complained that the training research laboratories did a lot of "useless basic research," even though the budgets of all the laboratories were for "applied" research. This was attributed to the "excessive" autonomy of the researcher. Given the absence of a routine passage from study to implementation, the researcher often has to become a salesman, hawking his research and persuading potential users to act on his findings. Often this sales effort is aided by agents in a middle-management office standing between the personnel research laboratories and the client organizations, and is even less susceptible to routinization. Like the work in the training research laboratories, most research programs in the psychiatric research laboratories (IV) in this area are not tied to the development of *new* hardware systems but are begun in response to problems perceived in the ongoing Navy activities. But the psychiatric researchers are allowed even more autonomy in their choice of work for several reasons. One is that the regular Navy officer often does not know what kinds of behavioral phenomena are of interest to psychologists in the research laboratories, and therefore does not call upon the research laboratory for advice. For example, one admiral in a submarine fleet declared that there were no psychological problems in his unit, but admitted that the number of petitions for transfer out of his unit was three to four times the Navy average. Having been trained in engineering, he was hard pressed to understand the behavioral dynamics underlying the low morale in his fleet. Many officers are also hesitant to admit behavioral problems in their units because some see it as an admission of poor leadership. Because these officers do not readily bring problems to the attention of the research laboratory, the researchers are given much latitude in mapping out their own work.

The relative autonomy of the psychiatric researchers is also reinforced by the fact that the psychiatric research laboratories are not in the command hierarchy of the regular Navy officer, but under the charge of the specialized Medical Corps. These laboratories are therefore more institutionally isolated from many of their potential clients in the other sectors of the Naval hierarchy. The over-all effect of these various influences is that the social organization of these units resembles that of the academic "think tanks" rather than the organization of the physical science research departments. The members of this group are also likely to publish in scientific journals.

We have described this case in some detail because it exemplifies the type of organizational studies which are sadly lacking. Of course the crucial variables will differ in different cases. But the patient reader will have recognized that some themes will certainly recur elsewhere.

a. It makes a difference where a problem occurs. The researcher is in principle more sensitive to recognize one when he meets it, but he might not always have a chance to observe the organization in all its details. The operating side might not be aware that problem-solving help is available and at times might feel inhibited about asking for help.
b. Once a study is done, its utilization might depend upon where it originated. If it was requested by a high-ranking officer, its chances are better, provided that the originating officer has not meanwhile been transferred. In some large organizations it might be advisable to appoint an implementation officer whose task would be to mediate between research and operation.
c. It seems to make a difference at what point in planning the social scientist is called in. Even if he is only permitted to watch, his future utility will certainly be enhanced if he enters early in the process.
d. If a large organization has several research units, the contact they have with management will probably vary according to the nature of the problem on hand. But there are likely to be some units, like Group IV described in the preceding case, which at least temporarily do work commonly associated with the term "mission-oriented basic research."

On the initiative and under the leadership of Harold Lasswell, an increasing number of authors have begun to use the term "policy science." A journal by this title has existed since 1970, and an increasing number of university institutes as well as independent agencies call themselves "policy science centers." The senior author has elsewhere reviewed the strategy and research style of this movement. It probably comes close to the "enlightenment model" described in Chapter 1—as a matter of fact, Janowitz says so as he quotes from Lasswell's programmatic papers. "The Basic emphasis of the policy approach is upon the fundamental problems of man in society rather than upon the topical issues of the moment."[20]

For our purposes, the term seems to us too broad, and the literature of the group does not distinguish clearly enough the various steps of the utilization process. Thus, they properly stress that one should not uncritically accept the problem formulation of a client, but they say little about what we call the translation problem. They correctly state that the feasibility of a recommendation is an important feature, but they do not analyze any of the other essential cognitive steps on the road to such a recommendation. Policy scientists think of themselves as "generalists" and do not find it necessary to contribute to any specific academic discipline. They seldom publish their own studies; as a matter of fact, one of them has written that often all that is needed is a telephone call to the client; the report itself may be no more than a gesture. One can hardly imagine a textbook in policy research. The specificity of our goal and the broad vistas of policy science seem too dissimilar. Still, in the long run, this might be more a difference in rhetoric than a fundamental one.

We certainly agree with the emphasis on the specific training needed for one whose concern is the utilization of social research. And on this point, the journal *Policy Science* has done an unusually fine job. Two of its early issues are devoted to educational problems (Vol. I, No. 4 and Vol. II, No. 1, 1971–72). The issues are not easily available, and we, therefore, shall summarize here the main topics discussed by the eleven contributors. In sum they represent a prototype of the task to be performed; the authors disagree in details, but this too serves to clarify the choices which a specific institution will have to make. (A more recent program instituted by the University of Pittsburgh is described in another volume of this series.) The themes discussed in the two issues—designated hereafter as I and II—essentially fall into three groups: (1) What would be an appropriate curriculum for a degree in policy science? (2) What would be its position in an existing university setting? (3) What would be the long-range function of such an academic innovation?

At first sight, the curriculum ideas appear conventional enough. Anyone concerned with training in applied social research has made the distinction between formal lectures, seminars built around case studies, and internships in action organizations. The trilogy appears in a report from the University of Konstanz, Germany (I, 467), as well as in an experiment reported by the Rand Corporation of Santa Monica (II, 5). But a more detailed inspection seems warranted.

The Curriculum: Four Components

The *formal courses* proposed are of two kinds: Those of more or less conventional substantive character which are most likely to be taken at existing departments of universities, and those which are to be organized as a new venture by the policy science department. The list of the first type, usually called something like subject-matter courses, shows interesting differences; they permit a guess as to the background of the proponents or first leaders of the new venture. Thus, the program reported by the New York University Business School stresses courses in economics and emphasizes mathematical decision analysis (II, 62). A program proposed by Lepawsky of Berkeley, California, thinks of "graduate education in public policy" as an improved and much enlarged department of political science (I, 44). The policy science program of the State Univeristy of New York at Buffalo is seen as applied social science. Characteristically, one of the substantive areas of the curriculum is cognitive psychology (II, 35f). Scharf, in a note on Germany, sees the new development mainly as an extension of traditional legal training (I, 459ff.). (Incidentally, his historical remarks are in themselves very interesting, because the training of civil servants is such an old German concern.) It is an interesting question whether a conventional course in, say, criminology or urban planning would have to be adapted to be suitable for policy science students; but no reference to this point is found in the two issues.

The more specific policy courses have such titles as "Social Policy Foundation Analysis" and "Methods and Models of Policy Analysis" (e.g., I, 450). The general vagueness noted before in the publications of the policy science group is also reflected in the way they talk about their specialized courses. Only two places in the two issues give a somewhat more vivid picture; one is a report by Benka, a student who has participated in the public policy program of the Harvard Kennedy School of Government (II,

67ff.). He describes some of the courses and his own and his fellow students' reactions. The Buffalo report by Bunker contains a rather detailed description of what he calls the "circular process of formalization, decision, implementation and evaluation" (II, 36f.). Its discussion can be taken as a good guide for anyone who wants to describe a concrete case of a policy-maker acting on the basis of knowledge provided by a social scientist.

In addition to formal courses, practically every one of the programs mentions the central role of *case-study seminars*. But here again, concreteness is lacking, except for one paper which gives two specific examples. The New York University Business School has courses stressing what they call "situational normativism."

Two cases summarized for exemplification are a labor-management conflict at General Electric and a zoning problem in a New Jersey suburban community (II, 165f.).

The most detailed discussion of the case-study approach is given by Lasswell in a paper on "The Continuing Decision Seminar" (II, 43ff.). He describes it as a "nucleus of persons who are determined to work together over a number of years." They would follow a concrete project from inception to evaluation, using audiovisual techniques to keep abreast of details, and would form subgroups to study specific aspects. While the author does not give concrete examples, his ideas might well be kept in mind even if one plans only a more modest seminar.[21]

Actually, there is a considerable literature on the use of case studies in various professional schools, especially a comparative review by Barber. Two outstanding examples of policy discussions emanating from a concrete study are Lee Rainwater's book on the Moynihan Report[22] and the collection of Harvard essays on the Coleman Report.[23] What is the relation between formal, mathematically based decision theory and the detailed descriptive analysis of the role of social research in a situation where a concrete problem has to be solved? A conference sponsored jointly by two concerned groups at Columbia University and the University of Pittsburgh was devoted to this topic.

Finally there is the idea that any student in a policy science education program should spend some *internship* time in an action agency—the time varying from a few months to a whole year. There is as yet too little experience available to expect specific reports. Occasionally it is mentioned that these interns would be valuable sources for two kinds of documents: case studies on decisions of the sponsor they might at least peripherally have been involved in; and reports on the interns' own experiences which would help to answer questions as to how to organize such internships more systematically. How can business or public agencies be induced to accept internships and to make them productive for themselves and the intern? What should be the amount and sources of remuneration for the intern? How can the supervision be divided between the host agency and the academic department, especially if the internship takes place far away from the home base? As far as we can tell, the only careful study of these situations comes from outside the United States and outside the social sciences: Professor Jahoda's book on *The Training of Engineers*.

Policy Science and Other Departments

So much for the curriculum aspect of a policy science department within a university. How would it be *related to the other parts of the institution*? Not surprisingly, this problem is most systematically described by Crecine, an author who himself directs such a center, the Institute of Public Policy Studies, at the University of Michigan, Ann Arbor. According to him, three main problems have to be solved: whether such a center can make its own appointments or is dependent on consent from traditional departments; whether its curriculum is completely developed by the center or whether other liberal arts departments have influence on it; and finally, whether the center is financed solely by contracts or has a substantial core of "hard money." The two sides of these three problems lead to eight types which the author displays and comments upon (II, 35ff.). There is, of course, no doubt that complete reliance on soft money cannot make for organizational viability: this rules out four types. The remaining four are all possible, but the author seems to feel that an independent appointment policy is much preferable. That leaves two types, which are distinguished essentially by an independent or a shared curriculum. The author seems to have a preference for complete curriculum independence for three reasons. He feels that traditional arts and science departments have a derogatory attitude toward application work, and therefore their substantive courses would not be completely suitable for a policy science department; secondly, the latter would want to provide positions for practitioners without academic credentials, a point discussed before (II, 19).

Probably the most complicated issue is the question of hard money, which is always connected with the academic reward system. The promotion and the general recognition of a scholar is still very much tied to the specific audiences created by traditional departments. There is a danger that the members of a policy center will, after a while, become restless because they do not yet have a recognized reference group. Crecine seems to feel that the larger the number of policy departments and the more autonomous they are in their curriculum, the more likely it will be that talented people will look at policy science as a promising academic career. (The whole article contains more ideas on the organization of policy research training than we have space to mention. It deserves careful reading.)

One other contribution, less systematic but very thoughtful, comes, oddly enough, from a physicist at the Rockefeller University in New York. He obviously got interested in the development of new departments because so many new combinations become necessary in the natural sciences. He decided to interview a large number of social scientists (I, 470) and then to put down ideas in a paper entitled "Ph.D. Programs in Policy Sciences, How, When, Where, What and Why." Sunderland's interesting essay might serve well as a general introduction, because he touches on almost every point mentioned by the other authors. One new topic to which he comes back repeatedly is the distinction between two types of candidates in such a program: Those who come from the "soft" social sciences who need special training in mathematics and other formal topics, and those who have a more formal scientific background and should be made aware that "the over-all bias of the policy sciences field toward the more mathematical areas has led to an underestimate of the magnitude and importance of the task of achieving literacy in the softer areas" (I, 478).

We finally come to two contributors who turn the whole problem around. They raise the question whether the need for policy sciences should not lead to a radical reform of the whole university system. This change appears to them necessary for two reasons: society at large needs more guidance to solve its problems, and the desire of students for greater relevance makes a new "university orientation" necessary. One of the two authors, Ericson, a professor of management at George Washington University, refers vaguely to some experiments done in his institution (I, 439). But mainly this contribution is a strong plea backed by many quotations from other sources for a radically new role of the university at the time when man "now has a possibility of creating his own future as never before" (I, 431).

Even more radical is the other writer, Jantsch, a German who has periodically taught in the United States. He sketches a detailed reorganization of the new university which is in a graphic schema (I, 423). Space prevents us from going into detail. Jantsch wants a broadening of the old double function of the university into a trinity: education, research, and service. It is hard to say to what extent Ericson and Jantsch represent a sizable sector of the policy science movement. But it is certainly worthwhile to quote a characteristic passage by Jantsch (I, 408).

> The university ought to become society's strategic center for investigating the boundaries and elements of the recognized as well as of the emerging "joint systems" of society and technology, and for working out alternative propositions for planning aimed at the healthy and dynamically stable design of such systems. The major changes which this new purpose will bring to the universities include the following one:
>
> —principal orientation toward sociotechnological systems design and engineering at a high level, leading to emphasis on general organization principles and methods rather than specialized knowledge both in education and research.
>
> —emphasis on purposeful work by the students rather than on training.
>
> —organization by outcome-oriented categories rather than by inputs of science and technology, and emphasis on long-range outcomes.

Few authors would carry the idea of social science utilization that far. But it is the exception which probes the limits of the rule.

We have in this review used the policy science terminology of the original authors. Wherever they talk of "policy scientists" the reader could at every point have substituted "social engineers," and we have finally decided to talk of "applied sociologists." The content of this last section would not have changed. This is a peaceful note on which to close.

NOTES

1 L. Brauer, Mendelsohn-Bartholdy, A. and A. Meyer (eds.), *Forschungsinstitute—Ihre Geschichte, Organisation und Ziele* (Hamburg: Haltung, 1930).

2 Paul F. Lazarsfeld, "Observations on the Organization of Empirical Social Research in the United States," *Information*, Bulletin of the International Social Science Council, No. 39, December, 1961.

3 Lazarsfeld, "The Sociology of Empirical Social Research," *American Sociological Reivew*, XXVII, No. 6 (December, 1962).

4 Stanley C. Ikenberry and Renee C. Friedman, *Beyond Academic Departments: The Story of Institutes and Centers* (San Francisco: Jossey-Bass, 1972).

5 Harold Orlans, *The Nonprofit Research Institute* (Berkeley, Calif.: The Carnegie Foundation, 1972.)

6 *See* Gustave Rath, "People, Models and R. and D. Organizations," in Evelyn Glatt and Maynard Shelly (eds.), *The Research Society* (New York: Gordon and Breach, 1968), pp. 103–37, for an interesting discussion of different kinds of R&D models.

7 Thomas Gilbert, "A Structure for a Coordinated Research and Development Laboratory," in Robert Glaser (ed.), *Training Research and Education*, (Pittsburgh: University of Pittsburgh Press, 1962), pp. 567–78.

8 C. E. Kenneth Mees and John Leermakers, *The Organization of Industrial Scientific Research* (New York: McGraw-Hill, 1950).
9 Chalmers W. Sherwin and Raymon S. Isenson, "Project Hindsight," *Science*, CLVI (June 23, 1967), p. 1577.
10 The importance of personal contacts has also been stressed in Herbert Menzel, *et. al.*, *The Flow of Information among Scientists: Problems, Opportunities, and Research Questions* (New York: Bureau of Applied Social Research, 1958).
11 Sam D. Sieber, *et. al.*, *The Use of Educational Knowledge*, 2 vols., BASAR and U.S. Office of Education.
12 Robert Glaser, "Implementation of Training Research for Education," in E. R. Hilgard and H. G. Richey, *Theories of Learning and Instruction* (Chicago: University of Chicago Press, 1964), p. 181.
13 Robert Nisbet, "The Future of the University," *Commentary*, LI, No. 2 (February, 1971).
14 Lazarsfeld, "The Sociology of Empirical Social Research," *American Sociological Review*, XXVII, No. 6 (December, 1962).
15 Kerr Clark (ed.), *The Campus and the City: A Report by the Carnegie Commission on Higher Education* (Hightstown, N.J.: McGraw-Hill, 1972).
16 Robert K. Merton, "Basic Research and Potential Relevance," *The American Behavioral Scientist*, VI, No. 9 (May, 1963), pp. 86–90.
17 Joel I. Brooke, *The Office of Naval Research*, BASR report, 1972; (mimeo.).
18 Melville Dalton, *Men Who Manage* (New York: John Wiley & Sons, 1959).
19 Douglas McDonald, *The Behavioral Research in the Navy*, mimeographed BASR report, 1972.
20 Janowitz, *op. cit.*, p. 51.
21 Harold D. Lasswell, "The Policy Orientation," in Daniel Lerner and Harold D. Lasswell (eds.), *The Policy Sciences: Recent Developments in Scope and Method* (Calif.: Stanford University Press, 1951).
22 L. Rainwater and W. Yancey, *The Moynihan Report and the Politics of Controversy* (Cambridge, Mass.: MIT Press, 1965).
23 Frederick Mosteller and Daniel P. Moynihan (eds.), *On Equality of Educational Opportunity* (New York: Vintage Books, 1972).

Name Index

Subject Index